Study Guide

Life-Span Human Development

SEVENTH EDITION

Carol K. Sigelman
The George Washington University

Elizabeth A. Rider
Elizabethtown College

Prepared by

Elizabeth A. Rider
Elizabethtown College

WADSWORTH
CENGAGE Learning™

Australia • Brazil • Japan • Korea • Mexico • Singapore • Spain • United Kingdom • United States

For product information and technology assistance, contact us at **Cengage Learning Customer & Sales Support, 1-800-354-9706**

For permission to use material from this text or product, submit all requests online at **www.cengage.com/permissions** Further permissions questions can be emailed to **permissionrequest@cengage.com**

ISBN-13: 978-1-111-35137-3
ISBN-10: 1-111-35137-6

Wadsworth
20 Davis Drive
Belmont, CA 94002-3098
USA

Cengage Learning is a leading provider of customized learning solutions with office locations around the globe, including Singapore, the United Kingdom, Australia, Mexico, Brazil, and Japan. Locate your local office at: **www.cengage.com/global**

Cengage Learning products are represented in Canada by Nelson Education, Ltd.

To learn more about Wadsworth, visit **www.cengage.com/wadsworth**

Purchase any of our products at your local college store or at our preferred online store **www.cengagebrain.com**

Printed in the United States of America
1 2 3 4 5 6 7 15 14 13 12 11

Table of Contents

CHAPTER ONE

UNDERSTANDING LIFE-SPAN HUMAN DEVELOPMENT

OVERVIEW

This chapter introduces the field of life-span human development and the nature-nurture issue that is so central to understanding development. The chapter begins by defining life-span development and noting historical changes and cultural differences in conceptions of the lifespan. The chapter uses Bronfenbrenner's bioecological model to consider how individuals are affected by their ever-changing environments as well as how they can alter those environments.

A large portion of the chapter is devoted to discussion of how developmental scientists study lifespan changes. The goals of study include description, explanation, and optimization. Developmental study has progressed from the study of specific age groups to the study of the entire lifespan. There are seven assumptions of a lifespan perspective; these are described in this chapter and then echoed throughout the book.

Developmental research is guided by the scientific method and its emphasis on systematic observations. Researchers collect data using self-report measures, behavioral observations, and physiological measures. They use various methods: case studies to provide in-depth examination of one or a few individuals; experiments to establish cause and effect connections between variables; and correlational studies to show relationships or suggest connections among variables. An important part of this chapter is the description of three developmental designs—cross-sectional, longitudinal, and sequential—and their strengths and weaknesses.

LEARNING OBJECTIVES

After reading and studying the material in this chapter, you should be able to answer the following questions.

1.1   HOW SHOULD WE THINK ABOUT DEVELOPMENT?
1.   How do developmental scientists define development? What does the typical path of development look like across the lifespan?

2.   How has our understanding of different periods of the lifespan changed historically? What cultural and subcultural differences exist in perspectives of the lifespan?

3.   What are the main components of each side of the nature-nurture issue?

4.   What are the features of the bioecological model, and why is this perspective important to our understanding of development?

1.2   WHAT IS THE SCIENCE OF LIFE-SPAN DEVELOPMENT?
5.   What are the three goals of developmental psychology and the seven assumptions of the modern life-span perspective on human development?

1.3   HOW IS DEVELOPMENT STUDIED?
6.   What is the scientific method "mindset," and how is the scientific method used to study development?

7.   How should research samples be selected, and how might selection affect outcomes?

8.   What are the three main methods for collecting data, and what are the strengths and weaknesses of each?

9.   What are the essential features of the experimental method? What sorts of information can be gathered from an experimental study, and what are its strengths and weaknesses?

10.   What are the important features of the correlational method? What sorts of information can be gathered from this type of study, and what are its strengths and weaknesses?

11.   What are the advantages and disadvantages of the cross-sectional and longitudinal designs, and how does the sequential design resolve the weaknesses of these designs?

1.4   WHAT SPECIAL CHALLENGES DO DEVELOPMENTAL SCIENTISTS FACE?
12.   What challenges arise in studying development, and how can scientists address these issues?

13.   How can researchers ensure that they protect the rights of participants?

CHAPTER SUMMARY AND GUIDED REVIEW

The following summary provides an overview of the main points contained in this chapter of the text. Fill in the blanks with terms that appropriately complete the sentence. Scattered throughout the summary are questions in parentheses. These are meant to encourage you to think actively as you read and connect this summary to the more detailed information provided in the text.

1.1   HOW SHOULD WE THINK ABOUT DEVELOPMENT?
Defining Development

Development consists of systematic changes and continuities that occur in an individual between conception and death. Developmental scientists are concerned with three general areas of change and continuity, including physical, (1) _____, and (2) _____ changes. Biologists typically define (3)_____ as physical changes occurring from conception to maturity and refer to the deterioration of an individual as (4) _____. Developmentalists, however, argue that both positive and negative changes occur throughout the lifespan, and that (5) _____ includes both positive and negative changes in the mature individual.

Conceptualizing the Life Span

The lifespan is typically divided into several distinct periods. The age group, or (6) _____, to which a person belongs will in part determine the roles, privileges, and responsibilities that person will be granted. Some cultures recognize the transition from one period of life to another with special rituals called (7) _____. Societal expectations of how people should behave at different ages (age norms) set the stage for the sense of *when* life events should occur, called the (8) _____. The perception about the proper timing of life events is also influenced by subcultures, including group affiliation based on shared common heritage or (9) _____, as well as occupational/economic standing in society, referred to as (10) _____. Further, our understanding of the lifespan has been influenced by historical changes. For instance, it was not until the early 20th century that we recognized the transition from childhood to adulthood as special and designated this period of life (11) _____. More recently, we have begun to realize that there is an extended period of becoming a full-fledged adult that might warrant the label (12) _____. Life expectancy has increased significantly over the past century, from an average of 47 years to an average of 78 years, which has also changed how we must think about the entire lifespan.

Framing the Nature-Nurture Issue

The nature-nurture issue concerns the question of how environmental factors—the (13) _____ side of the issue—interact with biological factors to make us who we are. Those on the nature side of the issue note that development is largely the result of (14) _____ occurring from the genetically programmed biological unfolding of traits and behaviors contained in one's (15) _____. Those who emphasize nurture note how we change in response to the (16) _____. The relatively permanent change in behavior that occurs from environmental factors is called (17) _____.

Grasping the Ecology of Development

Urie Bronfenbrenner was concerned that researchers were not capturing *real* development because they were studying development out of its context. He developed a (18) _____ model that truly integrated nature and nurture. According to this theory, various environmental systems interact with a person. The system closest to the individual is the (19) _____ system. A person's immediate environments are interrelated through the (20) _____ so that events in one impact behavior and events in another. Children can also be influenced by the (21) _____, which includes social settings that are not directly experienced but still influential. The broadest context in which development occurs is the (22) _____ consisting of the shared understandings of how people in the group should live their lives, what we call (23) _____. (***Can you provide an example of each type of environmental system?***) In addition to these, Bronfenbrenner used the concept of (24) _____ to illustrate that changes in environmental systems occur throughout the lifespan in response to societal events.

1.2   WHAT IS THE SCIENCE OF LIFE-SPAN DEVELOPMENT?

Developmental psychology is the branch of psychology that studies the changes that occur between conception and death.

Goals of Study

One of the goals of life-span developmental psychology is to characterize or provide a (25) _____ of normal development and individual differences. In addition to this, developmentalists try to understand or (26)_____ why certain changes occur or do not occur. Finally, they try to (27) _____ development by enhancing capabilities and minimizing problems. (*Can you give an example of each goal?*) Professionals, rather than basing their practice and treatments on hunches or personal experience, should engage in (28) _____ by using research to guide their decisions.

Early Beginnings

The earliest studies of growth and development consisted of detailed observations of a single child that were published as (29) _____. These single-subject observations were not very scientific but paved the way for more in-depth examinations of individuals that comprise the (30) _____ method. Often considered the founder of developmental psychology, (31) _____ pioneered the use of questionnaires to collect more objective data from a larger number of individuals. Based on his observations, he characterized adolescence as a period of (32) _____.

The Modern Life-Span Perspective

For a number of years, researchers tended to focus on a specific age group, such as the study of infants or the study of old age, known as (33)_____. Today, the study of development assumes a life-span perspective with seven assumptions:

1. Development is a (34) _____ process: we change throughout our entire life.
2. Development does not follow a single universal path but is (35) _____.
3. Development includes both gains and losses at every age.
4. There is (36) _____ in human development, which means we can change in response to our experiences.
5. As Bronfenbrenner noted, development is shaped by the (37) _____ contexts in which it occurs.
6. Development is influenced by multiple factors.
7. Complete understanding of development requires input from multiple disciplines.

(*Can you give an example of each of these themes that illustrates the importance of the theme to the study of life-span development?*)

1.3 HOW IS DEVELOPMENT STUDIED?
The Scientific Method

Understanding development is best accomplished through the scientific method, which stresses that conclusions should be based on systematic, unbiased observations (data). To describe or explain a set of observations or facts, scientists develop a (38) _____, which consists of a set of concepts that might help us understand some experience. To test the validity of a theory, specific predictions or (39) _____, can be generated and should hold true if the theory is in fact valid. Some theories do a better job of explaining the observations about a particular phenomenon than others. The various elements of a good theory should fit together logically, or possess (40) _____. In addition, good theories can generate hypotheses that can be tested, either confirming or disconfirming the theory. This means the theory is (41) _____. Good theories also should be supported by the research conducted on them.

Sample Selection

Researchers cannot typically study all members of a population in which they are interested, so they select a (42) _____ from this population. Ideally, a (43) _____ sample is selected so that all members of the population have an equal chance of being selected. This allows the researcher to generalize to other members of the population.

Data Collection

There are three general ways to measure behavior. First, people can be asked to provide information about themselves using several types of (44) _____ such as interviews or questionnaires. (***What are several weaknesses of collecting data this way?***) Second, researchers might use a kind of behavioral observation called (45) _____ observation to directly measure people's behavior in their everyday surroundings. (***What are advantages and disadvantages of this measurement technique?***) Sometimes, researchers control some of the conditions under which they collect observations by using (46) _____ observations in hopes of eliciting the behavior of interest. Third, researchers may also use (47) _____ measures to assess internal variables such as heart rate and skin conductance. One such measure evaluates blood flow in the brain through use of (48) _____.

The Case Study, Experimental, and Correlational Methods

An in-depth examination of one or a few individuals is conducted as part of the (49) _____ method. To try to explain behavior or identify causes of developmental change, researchers often conduct an (50) _____. The researcher manipulates or changes some aspect of the environment, called the (51) _____ variable, and measures the effect that this has on the (52) _____ variable. In addition to manipulation of the variable of interest, participants in a true experiment must have an equal opportunity to end up in any of the groups, which is achieved through (53) _____. Finally, in a true experiment, all factors other than the independent variable must be held constant, a procedure called (54) _____. (***What are two major limitations of the experimental method?***) In some cases, when participants cannot be randomly assigned to groups, researchers might conduct a (55) _____.

Some developmental questions cannot be answered by experimentally manipulating the environment. In these cases, researchers may use the (56) _____ method, which involves determining whether two or more variables are related. (***Can you provide an example of a question studied with this method?***) The strength of the relationship between two variables is generally assessed with a (57) _____, which can range in value from –1.00 to +1.00. A major limitation of the correlational method is that it does not establish a (58) _____ relationship between the variables. (***Can you explain why the correlational method is not able to do this?***)

By combining multiple methods, we strengthen our understanding of development. A technique called (59) _____ allows the results from multiple studies on the same question to be synthesized into an overall conclusion.

Developmental Research Designs

There are three research designs frequently used to describe developmental change across the lifespan. By comparing the performances of people of different age groups in a (60) _____ design, researchers gain information about age (61) _____ In a (62) _____ design, the performance of the same group of people is measured repeatedly over time, yielding information about age (63)_____. The findings of developmental studies can be influenced by three factors. The effects of getting older are reflected in (64) _____. Effects of (65) _____ reflect the influences of being born in a particular historical context, and effects of (66) _____ reflect the influences of particular events that occur at the time data are collected. In a cross-sectional study, findings may reflect (67) _____ effects in addition to age effects because people of different ages are studied. Because people in a longitudinal design are repeatedly tested at different times, findings from this design may reflect changes due to (68) _____ effects in addition to age effects. The (69) _____ design combines the cross-sectional and longitudinal designs in a single study in order to disentangle effects due to age, cohort, and time of measurement. (*Can you describe situations where it would be appropriate to use each of these designs? What could you conclude about age effects from studies using each of these research designs?*)

1.4 WHAT SPECIAL CHALLENGES DO DEVELOPMENTAL SCIENTISTS FACE?

Conducting Culturally Sensitive Research

Because development is shaped by its cultural context, developmental scientists must be sensitive to the culture of their participants. For instance, researchers must be careful to avoid (70) _____ or the belief that their own group and culture are superior to whatever group or culture is being studied. (*What other factors should researchers consider in order to ensure that their research is ecologically valid?*)

Protecting the Rights of Research Participants

Researchers need to protect their subjects from physical or psychological harm by following certain standards of (71) _____. This involves informing participants of what the research will involve so that they can provide (72) _____. It also means that the researcher will (73) _____ participants after the study to inform them of its true purpose. Finally, participants must be protected from harm and guaranteed that their responses will be (74) _____.

Below is a list of terms and concepts from this chapter. Use these to complete the following sentence definitions. You might also want to try writing definitions in your own words and then checking your definitions with those in the text.

adolescence
age effects
age grade
age norms
aging
baby biographies
baby boom generation
bioecological model
biological aging
case study method
chronosystem
cohort
cohort effects
correlational method
correlation coefficient
cross-sectional design
culture
dependent variable
development
emerging adulthood
environment
ethnicity
ethnocentrism
evidence-based practice
exosystem
experiment
experimental control
functional magnetic resonance
    imaging (fMRI)
genes
gerontology

growth
hypothesis
independent variable
learning
life expectancy
life-span perspective
longitudinal design
macrosystem
maturation
mesosystem
meta-analysis
microsystem
naturalistic observation
nature-nurture issue
neuroplasticity
plasticity
population
quasi experiment
random assignment
random sample
research ethics
rite of passage
sample
scientific method
sequential design
social clock
socioeconomic status (SES)
storm and stress
structured observation
theory
time of measurement effect

1.   The relatively permanent changes in behavior that result from experiences or practice are referred to as _____.

2.   The _____ is a technique for systematically and objectively using observations to determine the merits of one's thinking.

3.   A(n) _____ is a research technique in which some aspect of the subject's environment is manipulated or altered see if there is any change in the subject's behavior.

4. Practitioners who base their activities and treatments on research are engaging in _____.

5. A(n) _____ is a testable prediction resulting from a theoretical position.

6. Standards of conduct that investigators must ethically follow in order to protect subjects from harm are _____.

7. The _____ is a research design that involves determining whether two or more variables are related.

8. A method that tests hypotheses by observing behaviors under naturally occurring conditions is called _____.

9. Systematic changes in a person occurring between conception and death are collectively referred to as _____.

10. A person or family's position in society is often measured by education level, occupational prestige, and income in a composite measure called _____.

11. A _____ is used to measure age-related change by studying participants from different age groups repeatedly over time.

12. A person's _____ consists of all the external physical and social conditions that can influence the person.

13. Being part of a group of people born about the same time and exposed to similar cultural and historical events constitutes a _____.

14. A technique that ensures that all research participants have an equal chance of being included in all experimental conditions is _____.

15. A _____ is a statistical value that represents the extent to which two variables are systematically related.

16. The physical changes that occur from conception to maturity are called _____.

17. Distinctive periods of the lifespan, usually delineated by ages, are called _____.

18. The historical events that occur when data are collected are referred to as _____.

19. In a _____, age-related differences are measured by simultaneously studying subjects from different age groups.

20. The _____ is an approach to the study of development that focuses on changes occurring from conception to death of a person.

21. The deterioration of individuals that eventually leads to their death is referred to as _____.

22. The _____ is a social setting that indirectly influences a child's development.

23. Expectations about how people should act at different ages are _____.

24. Changes that occur in a mature person are considered the _____ process.

25. A genetically programmed biological plan of development, relatively independent of effects of the environment, is _____.

26. The _____ refers to the large generation of people born from the end of WWII to about 1964.

27. The most immediate environment that a person experiences is the _____.

28. In an experiment, the _____ is the aspect of the environment that the investigator deliberately manipulates in order to discover what effect this has on behavior.

29. Psychologists develop _____, which are sets of rules or principles that describe and explain some behavior.

30. A subset of subjects from a larger population of interest is a _____.

31. A _____ is similar to an experiment, but participants are not randomly assigned to groups.

32. A technique that ensures that all factors besides the independent variable are controlled or held constant is _____.

33. The study of aging and old age is referred to as _____.

34. The _____ refers to the sense that life events should occur at a particular time, according to a schedule dictated by age norms.

35. In a _____, age-related changes are measured by repeatedly studying the same individuals over time.

36. In an experiment, the _____ is the aspect of behavior that is observed or measured in order to determine whether the independent variable had an effect.

37. A _____ is when participants are drawn from the larger population of interest such that all members of the population have an equal chance of being selected for the sample.

38. In a _____, the results of multiple studies addressing the same question are synthesized to produce overall conclusions.

39. Researchers sometimes use the technique of _____ to create conditions that will elicit the behavior of interest.

40. _____ refers to the ability to change in response to positive or negative experiences.

41. Researchers would like to be able to generalize their research findings to a _____ after studying a subset of this group.

42. The interrelationships between two or more microsystems are the _____ in Bronfenbrenner's bioecological model.

43. In research, the consequences of getting older are called _____.

44. The _____ concerns the question of whether development is primarily the result of biological or environmental forces.

45. The _____ is the largest cultural context in which development occurs.

46. The _____ model of development focuses on the influences of nature and nurture by examining a person's development within a series of environmental layers.

47. The transitional period between childhood and adulthood is known as the period of _____.

48. In Bronfenbrenner's bioecological model, the _____ characterizes the changes that occur in environmental systems over a person's lifetime.

49. G. Stanley Hall characterized adolescence as a turbulent period of _____.

50. The belief that one's own group and culture are superior to others' is _____.

51. Modern times have seen a delay of marriage and parenthood and an extended time of personal exploration, ushering in a period of development called _____.

Chapter One

52. A group with a shared understanding of how people in the group should behave and what they should believe has a common _____.

53. A published set of observations about the growth and development of a single child was the basis of early _____.

54. A group of people born at the same time or period of time belong to a _____.

55. A detailed analysis of an individual using multiple sources of data comprises the _____.

56. The hereditary material that is passed from parents to child at conception is called _____.

57. The brain is able to change in response to experience throughout the lifespan, a process known as _____.

58. A person's affiliation with a group based on shared heritage or traditions constitutes the person's _____.

59. A brain scanning technique that involves measuring blood flow in different parts of the brain during activity is the essence of _____.

60. In some cultures, shifts from one life status to another are marked by special rituals or _____.

61. The average number of years that a newborn can expect to live is that individual's _____.

MULTIPLE-CHOICE SELF-TEST

For each multiple-choice question, read all alternatives and then select the best answer.

1. A 65-year-old woman who feels as though it is time for her to become a grandmother is feeling the influence of
   a.   age grade.   c.   age norms.
   b.   social clock.   d.   physiological needs.

2. Development results from biologically programmed changes called _____ and from specific environmental experiences called _____.
   a.   aging; learning
   b.   learning; growth
   c.   maturation; learning
   d.   age changes; age differences

3. Urie Bronfenbrenner's bioecological approach to development contends that
   a. development is influenced by interacting environmental systems.
   b. the home environment is the only really important influence on development.
   c. children have a passive role in development and are unable to shape their futures.
   d. the environment has a similar effect on all children.

4. According to the bioecological approach to development, a person's most immediate environment is the _____.
   a. microsystem   c. exosystem
   b. mesosystem   d. macrosystem

5. The goals of developmental psychology are BEST described by which of the following?
   a. Developmental psychologists seek to modify behavior wherever possible.
   b. Developmental psychologists seek to identify behaviors that should be changed.
   c. Developmental psychologists seek to construct a single unifying theory to explain development.
   d. Developmental psychologists seek to describe and explain behavior, and where possible, optimize it.

6. One of the assumptions of the life-span perspective is that development is multidirectional. This means that
   a. development is caused by any number of factors and determining which cause is most influential can't be done.
   b. developmental changes are universal across most people.
   c. developmental outcomes can never be predicted.
   d. development at all ages consists of some gains and some losses, as well as some abilities that remain the same.

7. Another assumption of the lifespan perspective is that there is plasticity in development. This means that
   a. most of our acquisition of new skills will occur during infancy when our brains are not fully developed.
   b. developmental changes can occur in response to our experiences across the lifespan.
   c. development is never really complete.
   d. all skills can be developed at any time of the lifespan.

8. Ensuring that all subjects have an equal chance of participating in any of the experimental treatments is accomplished
   a. through experimental control.
   b. by selecting a random sample from the population.
   c. through random assignment to conditions.
   d. by administering a questionnaire.

9. Which of the following is an example of using naturalistic observation to collect data?
    a. Watching how children behave on their playground
    b. Asking participants to orally answer questions rather than fill out questionnaires
    c. Asking parents to keep track of their children's TV viewing habits
    d. Seeing how children behave when asked to play a game with unfamiliar children

10. Suppose you have one group of children role-play (children assume the role of someone else) while another group of children does not role-play. You then observe the level of empathy in children from both groups as they interact with other children. The independent variable would be
    a. whether children role-played or not.
    b. children's level of empathy.
    c. the relationship between role-playing and level of empathy.
    d. children's ability to role-play.

11. A positive correlation between viewing televised violence and aggressive behavior would indicate that
    a. children who watch less televised violence tend to be more aggressive.
    b. children who watch more televised violence tend to be more aggressive.
    c. increases in aggression are caused by watching more televised violence.
    d. watching televised violence is not related to level of aggressive behavior.

12. The major disadvantage of correlational studies is that
    a. they are costly and time-consuming.
    b. they do not allow researchers to make cause and effect conclusions.
    c. the conclusions are confounded by time-of-measurement effects.
    d. they have no clear dependent variables.

13. If you wanted to assess individual changes over time in prosocial behavior, you would need to use
    a. a longitudinal design.   c. a correlational design.
    b. a cross-sectional design.   d. an experimental design.

14. Cross-sectional designs provide information about age _____; longitudinal designs provide information about age _____.
    a. differences; changes   c. differences; differences
    b. changes; differences   d. changes; changes

15. Cross-sectional designs confound age effects with _____; longitudinal designs confound age effects with _____.
    a. cohort effects; cohort effects
    b. time of measurement effects; cohort effects
    c. cohort effects; type of measurement effects
    d. cohort effects; time of measurement effects

COMPARE DEVELOPMENTAL RESEARCH DESIGNS

For each of the major developmental designs, indicate the procedure used to conduct the study, the type of information that can be gained, and the major advantages and disadvantages. Use Table 1.4 on pages 24-25 of the text to check your answers.

	CROSS-SECTIONAL	LONGITUDINAL	SEQUENTIAL
Procedure			
Information Gained			
Advantages			
Disadvantages			

CRITICAL THINKING QUESTIONS

By answering the following questions, you will strengthen your understanding of the material in this chapter. These questions require higher-level thinking skills such as integration and application of concepts. Sample answers are provided for three of the questions. These illustrate one possibility, but there are other answers you could provide that might be just as good. For the other questions, you can check yourself by referring to the text (a hint is provided) or by asking a peer or your instructor to review your answer.

1. Many people in our society are interested in the possibility of "speeding up" some aspect of development, such as the ages when children can print or read. Similarly, parents are often concerned about providing appropriate learning experiences for their children to enhance their abilities. Design a study to test the possibility that some specific aspect of development can be accelerated. Indicate the type of design and the variables used to test this hypothesis.
   [Sample answer provided]

2.   Another current concern is the effect of divorce on children of all ages. Design a study to assess whether divorce has a negative impact on children at different ages. Specify the type of design needed for this question and how you would measure the impact of divorce.
    [Sample answer provided]

3.   The chapter notes that males, on average, are more aggressive than females. Using the framework of the nature-nurture issue, provide at least one possible explanation for the gender difference in aggression on both sides of the issue.
    [Sample answer provided]

4.   Suppose you would like to study how nutrition, both before birth and after birth, affects the three major areas of development: physical, cognitive, and psychosocial. How would you ethically conduct this study? Discuss factors that would need to be considered when designing an ethical study, and specify how you would define and measure your variables.
    [Hint: Review the section on "Protecting the rights of research participants?" and the discussion of the limitations of correlational experimental methods in the subsection on "The correlational method."]

5.   Bronfenbrenner notes the importance of studying development in its real context rather than in the artificial context of the laboratory. Describe the levels of context that can influence development.
    [Hint: Review the section on "Grasping the ecology of development."]

ANSWERS

Chapter Summary and Guided Review (fill in the blank)

1. cognitive	18. bioecological
2. psychosocial	19. microsystem
3. growth	20. mesosystem
4. biological aging	21. exosystem
5. aging	22. macrosystem
6. age grade	23. culture
7. rites of passage	24. chronosystem
8. social clock	25. description
9. ethnicity	26. explain
10. socioeconomic status (SES)	27. optimize
11. adolescence	28. evidence-based practice
12. emerging adulthood	29. baby biographies
13. nurture	30. case study
14. maturation	31. G. Stanley Hall
15. genes	32. storm and stress
16. environment	33. gerontology
17. learning	34. lifelong

35. multidirectional
36. plasticity
37. historical/cultural
38. theory
39. hypotheses
40. internal consistency
41. falsifiable
42. sample
43. random
44. verbal reports
45. naturalistic
46. structured
47. physiological
48. functional magnetic resonance imaging (fMRI)
49. case study
50. experiment
51. independent
52. dependent
53. random assignment
54. experimental control

55. quasi-experiment
56. correlational
57. correlational coefficient
58. causal
59. meta-analysis
60. cross-sectional
61. differences
62. longitudinal
63. changes
64. age effects
65. cohort
66. time of measurement
67. cohort
68. time of measurement
69. sequential
70. ethnocentrism
71. research ethics
72. informed consent
73. debrief
74. confidential

Review of Key Terms

1. learning
2. scientific method
3. experiment
4. evidence-based practice
5. hypothesis
6. research ethics
7. correlational method
8. naturalistic observation
9. development
10. socioeconomic status
11. sequential design
12. environment
13. cohort effects
14. random assignment
15. correlation coefficient
16. growth
17. age grades
18. time-of-measurement effects
19. cross-sectional design
20. life-span perspective
21. biological aging
22. exosystem
23. age norms

24. aging
25. maturation
26. Baby Boom generation
27. microsystem
28. independent variable
29. theories
30. sample
31. quasi-experiment
32. experimental control
33. gerontology
34. social clock
35. longitudinal design
36. dependent variable
37. random sample
38. meta-analysis
39. structured observation
40. plasticity
41. population
42. mesosystem
43. age effects
44. nature-nurture issue
45. macrosystem
46. bioecological

47. adolescence
48. chronosystem
49. storm and stress
50. ethnocentrism
51. emerging adulthood
52. culture
53. baby biographies
54. cohort

55. case study method
56. genes
57. neuroplasticity
58. ethnicity
59. functional magnetic resonance imaging (fMRI)
60. rites of passage
61. life expectancy

Multiple-Choice Self-Test

1. B (p. 5)	6. A (p. 12)	11. B (p. 19)
2. C (p. 7)	7. D (p. 18)	12. B (p. 20)
3. A (p. 9)	8. C (p. 15)	13. A (p. 22)
4. A (p. 9)	9. A (p. 15)	14. A (p. 24)
5. D (p. 10)	10. A (p. 18)	15. D (p. 25)

Critical Thinking Questions

1.   *You would need to use a longitudinal or sequential design to determine whether development could be accelerated. Acceleration is really looking at whether or not some experience produces change over time. A cross-sectional design wouldn't work because this would provide information about age differences but not about whether individuals change over time as a result of their experiences. Further, if you wanted to show that acceleration was* <u>caused</u> *by a particular program, you would need to use an experiment.*

Suppose you're interested in speeding up the age at which children read. After selecting a group of representative participants, these participants would be randomly assigned to either a treatment condition or the control group. In the treatment condition, children would spend one hour every day in a special program designed to foster reading, while children in the control condition would not get any special treatment. Children would begin the program when they were 18 months old and continue for at least 8 years. Both groups of children would be tested on their reading progress every 6 months until they were 9 or 10 years old. If children in the treatment group read at an earlier age and/or progressed faster once they started reading, then we could conclude that this particular aspect of development could be accelerated by this particular type of treatment.

You could also use a correlational study to study this question if you couldn't randomly assign children to different groups. To do this, you might measure the performance of children who were already in a special reading program and compare them to children in a regular reading program to see if one group tends to have higher reading scores than the other. The problem with this is that children in the two groups might have been different to begin with, which may account for why some of them were in the special reading group and others were not. Also, you wouldn't have control over what was in the program or how long it lasted.

2.   *Researchers would not be able to study this experimentally because it is not possible to randomly assign children to different levels of the variable* <u>divorce</u> *(divorced or together). Instead, researchers could use a correlational design to study this question. They could locate children who have experienced the divorce of their parents (or not), measure whatever aspects*

of behavior they are interested in, and then compare the responses or behaviors of the two groups. If the two groups are different, though, the researchers can't be sure that the divorce caused the differences because there are likely to be many other factors that differed between the two groups that were uncontrolled. And children whose parents end up getting divorced might have been different from the other kids even before the divorce. To determine this, researchers might start by testing a large number of children and then waiting to see if their parents get divorced at some point. The children could then be retested. This longitudinal study would allow researchers to compare pre- and post-measures of development in order to determine whether children of divorced parents become different from other kids after the divorce or whether they were different from other kids prior to the divorce.

In order to determine how divorce affects children of different ages, researchers would need to include children from different age groups. Children could be grouped into several age groups (e.g., preschoolers, elementary school-aged children, adolescents) or children of all ages could be included and then researchers could look to see if age correlates with one of their other measures for the two groups of children (divorced and non-divorced).

The measures used to assess children would depend on what it is the researchers are really interested in. If they are interested in cognitive development, they might want to use classroom grades. If they are interested in behavior, they might use school records to see if children have gotten into trouble or they might have teachers and parents complete a behavior inventory that asks about problem behaviors.

The effects of divorce will always be difficult to assess because there are many variables that go along with divorce that might influence development. For example, income often drops after parents divorce, and this might lead to changes in behavior rather than the divorce itself.

3.	*On the nature side, males may be more aggressive because something in their genes predisposes them to act more aggressively in response to certain conditions. Females, with their different genetic makeup (XX rather than XY chromosomes), respond less aggressively in the same situations. It may be that there are inherent chemical differences, such as greater testosterone in males, which lead to differences in expression of aggression. On the nurture side, parents and society expect males to be more aggressive, so perhaps they encourage and sanction greater aggression in boys than in girls. Parents may unintentionally (or even intentionally) reinforce their boys for their aggression, but punish their girls for behaving aggressively.*

CHAPTER TWO

THEORIES OF HUMAN DEVELOPMENT

OVERVIEW

This is an important foundational chapter for the rest of the text. The major developmental theories, which come up in most of the subsequent chapters, are introduced and evaluated here. Before getting into specific theories, the qualities of a good theory are discussed, as are the basic developmental issues that the theorists are trying to understand. These issues are assumptions about human nature, nature and nurture, activity and passivity, continuity and discontinuity, and universality and context-specificity.

The chapter includes Freud's psychoanalytic theory with its psychosexual stages and three personality structures, and Erikson's neo-Freudian psychoanalytic theory with its eight psychosocial stages. It covers the learning theories of Watson, Skinner, and Bandura, as well as Piaget's cognitive-developmental theory. Finally, the chapter introduces Gottlieb's epigenetic psychobiological systems view of development. You should be able to describe the distinct features of each theory, compare and contrast issues among the theories, and evaluate the contributions of each theory. A good understanding of these theories will be important as you read other chapters in the text.

LEARNING OBJECTIVES

After reading and studying the material in this chapter, you should be able to answer the following questions.

2.1 DEVELOPMENTAL THEORIES AND THE ISSUES THEY RAISE
1. What are the five basic issues in human development?

2.2 FREUD: PSYCHOANALYTIC THEORY
2. What are the distinct features of Freud's psychoanalytic theory? What are the strengths and weaknesses of the theory?

2.3 ERIKSON: NEO-FREUDIAN PSYCHOANALYTIC THEORY
3. How does Erikson's psychoanalytic theory compare to Freud's theory? What crisis characterizes each of Erickson's psychosocial stages?

2.4 LEARNING THEORIES
4. What are the distinct features of the learning theories covered in this chapter (Watson's classical conditioning, Skinner's operant conditioning, and Bandura's social-cognitive theory)? What are their strengths and weaknesses?

2.5   PIAGET: COGNITIVE-DEVELOPMENTAL THEORY

5.   What is Piaget's perspective on cognitive development? What are the strengths and weaknesses of Piaget's theory?

2.6   SYSTEMS THEORIES

6.   How do systems theories, in general, conceptualize development?

7.   What are the essential elements of Gottlieb's epigenetic psychobiological systems perspective of development? What are the strengths and weaknesses of the systems approaches to development?

2.7   THEORIES IN PERSPECTIVE

8.   How can we characterize the theories in general?

CHAPTER SUMMARY AND GUIDED REVIEW

The following summary provides an overview of the main points contained in this chapter of the text. Fill in the blanks with terms that appropriately complete the sentence. Scattered throughout the summary are questions in parentheses. These are meant to encourage you to think actively as you read and connect this summary to the more detailed information provided in the text.

2.1   DEVELOPMENTAL THEORIES AND THE ISSUES THEY RAISE

There are five basic issues concerning what humans are like and how development occurs. (***How do your views on these issues compare to the views of the major developmental theorists?***)

The Goodness-Badness of Human Nature

One issue concerns our assumptions about human nature. In particular, this issue questions whether people are inherently good or bad, or are born as (1) _____, meaning they are not inherently good or bad but develop according to their experiences.

Nature-Nurture

The most important issue concerns whether development results primarily from biological forces, called (2) _____, or environmental experiences, called (3) _____.

Activity-Passivity

A third issue concerns whether people actively produce developmental change or are more passively shaped by biological and/or environmental forces outside of their control.

Continuity-Discontinuity

A fourth issue is whether development is continuous or discontinuous. Continuity implies gradual and (4) _____ change, whereas discontinuity implies abrupt and (5) _____ change. Theorists who believe development is discontinuous often propose that development progresses through a series of (6) _____, or phases that are qualitatively distinct from one another.

Universality-Context Specificity

A final developmental issue is whether we all follow a common or (7) _____ path of development or whether we each follow different, context-specific paths of development.

2.2   FREUD: PSYCHOANALYTIC THEORY

Instincts and Unconscious Motives

Freud's psychoanalytic theory proposes that humans have inborn biological urges, called (8) _____, that must be satisfied. We are often unaware that these inborn urges motivate behavior because they are (9) _____.

Id, Ego, and Superego

Freud believed that there were three personality components. At birth, the personality consists of only the (10) _____, which seeks to satisfy a person's instincts. During infancy, the (11) _____ begins to develop and tries to realistically satisfy the demands of the id. The third component of the personality is the (12) _____, which begins to develop during early childhood and functions as a person's internalized moral standards. Problems may develop if the available (13) _____ is not evenly distributed among the three personality structures.

Psychosexual Development

As children mature, Freud believed that the psychic energy of the sex instinct, called the (14) _____, moves form one part of the body to another. These changes are reflected by progression through Freud's stages of (15) _____ development. During the first stage, the libido seeks pleasure through (16) _____ activities. This focus shifts to (17) _____ activities during the second psychosexual stage of development. Boys and girls become interested in their genitals and are influenced by the presence or absence of a penis during the (18) _____ stage of development. The psychic energy of the sex instinct becomes focused on socially appropriate activities such as schoolwork during the (19) _____ period. The (20) _____ stage is the final psychosexual stage and occurs with the onset of puberty. It is characterized by mature love with the goal of biological reproduction.

Freud emphasized the influence of inborn biological drives but also recognized that early experiences could have a long-term effect on personality development. During any psychosexual stage, conflict among the personality components may create anxiety that is alleviated by use of (21) _____. For example, if the psychic energy remains tied to an earlier stage of development, then a person may experience (22) _____ or arrested development. Another example is (23) _____, which involves returning to an earlier, less traumatic stage of development.

Strengths and Weaknesses

One of the criticisms of Freud's theory is that many of the concepts cannot be tested, which means the theory is not (24) _____. Freud also offered biased interpretations of many phenomena. Still, Freud's theory is valuable because it focused attention on unconscious motivation, early family experiences, and emotions.

2.3   ERIKSON: NEO-FREUDIAN PSYCHOANALYTIC THEORY

Erik Erikson was another psychoanalytic theorist, a neo-Freudian, who was distinct from Freud in several ways. Erikson focused less on sexual instincts than Freud and more on (25) _____ forces. He also had a more positive view of human nature and believed that development continued through adulthood. Erikson emphasized the rational ego more than the irrational id.

Psychosocial Stages

Erikson proposed that maturation and society together create eight life crises, which correspond to eight psychosocial stages of development. Each stage can be resolved positively or negatively, and unresolved crises can have an effect on later development. For example, in the first psychosocial stage, infants must learn to develop a sense of (26) _____. Adolescents struggle to develop a sense of (27) _____ as they try to define who they are. Adolescents who have trouble figuring out who they are experience (28) _____. Unlike Freud, Erikson extended his stages through adulthood. He believed that young adulthood is the time for establishing (29) _____ in a committed relationship. Middle-aged adults are concerned with whether or not they have produced something meaningful that will live on after them, which is an issue of (30) _____. In the last psychosocial stage, older adults try to find meaning in their lives and develop a sense of (31) _____ rather than despair.

Strengths and Weaknesses

Like Freud, Erikson's theory has been criticized because it is difficult to test. Erikson also does not adequately explain development. The theory has been praised for focusing attention on adolescent and adult development.

2.4   LEARNING THEORIES
Watson: Classical Conditioning

John Watson believed it was not possible to study unconscious motivations or mental processes and developed a branch of psychology called (32) _____. Watson believed that only overt behaviors were appropriate for study and that learned associations between a person's actions and external stimuli were the basis of human development. In classical conditioning, a stimulus that initially had no effect on an individual comes to elicit a response through its association with a stimulus that already produces the desired response. A stimulus that elicits the desired response without prior learning experiences is the (33) stimulus. A stimulus that produces the desired response only after being associated with a stimulus that always elicits the response is the (34) _____ stimulus. An unlearned response to an unlearned stimulus is the (35) _____ response, while a learned response to a conditioned stimulus is the (36) _____ response. (***Can you provide an example of classical conditioning that is not in the text?***)

Skinner: Operant Conditioning

B.F. Skinner demonstrated that existing behaviors become more or less probable depending on the consequences of the behaviors. This form of learning is called operant conditioning. One possible consequence is (37) _____, where something administered following a behavior strengthens that behavior. Behaviors could also be strengthened by removing something negative following the behavior, a process called (38)_____. (*Can you provide an example of this?*) Decreasing the strength of a behavior is accomplished either by adding something unpleasant following a behavior, which is called (39)_____, or removing something positive, which is (40)_____. [*Hint: To remember whether reinforcement or punishment is positive or negative, think of the action being performed. When something is added to the situation, it is positive (reinforcement or punishment), and when something is removed from the situation, it is negative (reinforcement or punishment).*] (*Can you describe ways to make the use of punishment effective as a discipline technique?*) Sometimes, a behavior is followed by no consequences, which eventually leads to (41)_____ because the behavior is not being reinforced.

Bandura: Social-Cognitive Theory

Albert Bandura, another learning theorist, emphasizes the importance of cognition. His social-cognitive theory makes the claim that humans are active processors of environmental information. Bandura believes that (42)_____ learning is the most important mechanism through which development occurs. Children can learn by watching others although they may not perform this behavior, a process termed (43)_____. Learners will be more likely to perform the behavior if they observe the model getting reinforced for his or her actions, referred to as (44)_____ reinforcement. Bandura has argued that humans exercise control over their environments and lives, a concept he calls (45)_____. Experience with a task leads people to form (46)_____, or the belief that they can effectively produce a desired outcome on this task. Bandura also believes that development occurs through a constant give-and-take relationship between a person and the environment, called (47)_____.

Strengths and Weaknesses

A strength of the learning theories is that precise hypotheses can be generated and tested. In addition, the principles apply to learning across the entire lifespan, and they are applicable to many developmental phenomenon. Learning theories have been criticized for not clearly showing that learning causes developmental changes and for not placing enough emphasis on (48)_____ factors.

2.5 PIAGET: COGNITIVE-DEVELOPMENTAL THEORY
Constructivism

Piaget focused on cognitive development and proposed that children actively construct their understanding of the world based on their experiences. Cognitive development results from the interaction of maturation and environment.

Stages of Cognitive Development

Piaget proposed four stages of cognitive development, which form what he called an (49)_____, meaning that children progress through the stages in order with no skipping. Infants are in the (50)_____ stage because they learn about the world through their sensory experiences and their motor responses to these experiences. Preschoolers are in the (51)_____ stage, which is characterized by use of (52)_____ and lack of logical thought. As a result, they fail to recognize that changing superficial features of an object does not alter the essential nature of the object, an awareness that Piaget called (53) _____. School-aged children are in the (54) _____ stage and can logically solve problems by applying a number of mental operations. They typically use a trial-and-error approach to solving problems. Adolescents are in the (55) _____ stage, which is characterized by systematic hypothesis testing and logical reasoning on abstract problems.

Strengths and Weaknesses

Piaget's theory has been very influential and his descriptions of cognitive development have largely been supported by research. However, he has been criticized for not adequately considering the influence of social factors on cognitive development. In addition, research suggests that cognitive development is not nearly as stage-like as Piaget proposed.

Other Perspectives on Cognitive Development

According to Vygotsky's view of cognitive development, development is influenced by the (56) _____ in which it occurs. The information-processing approach uses the computer as a metaphor for how the human mind works.

2.6 SYSTEMS THEORIES

Systems theories propose that development results from the ongoing interrelationships between a changing person and a changing environment.

Evolutionary Theory and Ethology

Inspired by Darwin's theory of evolution, the field of ethology studies the evolved behaviors of various species in their natural environments.

Gottlieb's Epigenetic Psychobiological Systems Perspective

Gottlieb's approach views development as a complex interaction between biological and environmental forces. According to this perspective, we are predisposed through our (57) _____ to certain developmental outcomes. The process through which nature and nurture interact and bring about outcomes is called (58) _____. Gottlieb notes that genes do not determine behavior; behaviors only emerge through an interaction of genes and environments.

Strengths and Weaknesses

Systems theories are valuable for pointing out the importance of the context of development. Most, however, are broad and not fully developed. Indeed, it may not be possible to develop a specific systems theory because at the very heart of these theories is the notion that development depends on the unique and continuous interactions between a person and his/her world.

2.7 THEORIES IN PERSPECTIVE

Theories can be grouped according to the broad assumptions they make about human development. Theorists such as Freud, Erikson, and Piaget believed in universal (59) _____, whereas Watson, Skinner, and Bandura did not. Learning theorists focus more on the (60) _____ than the person. The systems theories focus on both factors (***What are the implications of these basic assumptions for childrearing?***)

Below is a list of terms and concepts from this chapter. Use these to complete the following sentence definitions. You might also want to try writing definitions in your own words and then checking your definitions with those in the text.

activity-passivity issue
behaviorism
classical conditioning
concrete operations stage
conditioned response (CR)
conditioned stimulus (CS)
conservation
constructivism
continuity-discontinuity issue
defense mechanisms
developmental stage
eclectic
ego
Electra complex
epigenesis
epigenetic psychobiological systems
    perspective
ethology
evolutionary psychology
extinction
fixation
formal operations stage
human agency
id
identification
information-processing
    approach
instinct
latent learning
libido

negative punishment
negative reinforcement
observational learning
Oedipus complex
operant conditioning
positive punishment
positive reinforcement
preoperational stage
projection
psychoanalytic theory
psychosexual stages
psychosocial stages
reaction formation
reciprocal determinism
regression
repression
self-efficacy
sensorimotor stage
school refusal behavior
social-cognitive theory
sociocultural perspective
superego
systems theories
tabula rasa
unconditioned response (UCR)
unconditioned stimulus (UCS)
unconscious motivation
universality-context-specificity issue
vicarious reinforcement

1. With the defense mechanism of _____, a person reverts to an earlier, less traumatic stage of development.

2. According to a systems approach to development, nature and nurture interact in _____ to bring about development.

3. According to the school of psychology known as _____, researchers and theorists should focus on observations of overt behavior rather than unobservable mental processes.

4. In Piaget's _____ stage of cognitive development, school-aged children can reason logically about concrete problems.

5. According to _____, humans develop actively through a continuous reciprocal interaction between them and their environment, rather than being passively shaped by their environment.

6. The basic principle of _____ is that behaviors become more or less probable depending on the consequences they produce.

7. A form of learning in which a stimulus that initially had no effect on an individual comes to elicit a response through its association with a stimulus that already produces the desired response is _____.

8. The study of how different species evolve in their natural environments is called _____.

9. The _____ concerns whether humans are actively involved in their development or passively influenced by factors beyond their control.

10. According to Freud, the _____ is the most primitive component of personality, seeking immediate satisfaction of instincts.

11. A period of life characterized by a cohesive set of behaviors or abilities that are distinct from earlier or later periods is called a _____.

12. According to modern social-cognitive theory, humans deliberately control their environments and lives through a concept Bandura calls _____.

13. In classical conditioning, a stimulus that elicits the desired response without learning experiences is the _____.

14. Unconscious techniques used by the ego to protect itself from anxiety are _____.

15. The _____ perspective on development argues that development is a product of complex interactions between biological and environmental forces.

16. _____ is the belief that children have no inborn tendencies; instead, their outcome depends entirely on the environment in which they are raised.

17. Piaget's first stage of cognitive development during which infants learn about the world through their sensory experiences and their actions is the _____ stage.

18. A form of learning that results from watching the behavior of other people is _____.

19. In classical conditioning, an unlearned response to an unconditioned stimulus is the _____.

20. Theories stating that development arises from the ongoing interrelationships between a changing organism and a changing world are called _____.

21. We can decrease the likelihood of future responding with _____ or removing something pleasant from the situation.

22. Piaget believed in _____, that children actively build their own understanding of the world.

23. The question of whether development is smooth and gradual or somewhat abrupt is the focus of the _____.

24. The influence of information that is in memory but is not recalled at a conscious level is referred to as _____.

25. Freud's term for the sex instinct's psychic energy is _____.

26. Erikson's theory proposes eight _____ that represent conflicts between biological maturation and social demands.

27. The defense mechanism of _____ is when development becomes arrested because part of the libido remains tied to an earlier stage of development.

28. In Piaget's _____ stage of cognitive development, preschoolers are able to use symbols but lack logical reasoning.

29. Vygotsky's _____ of development maintains that cognitive development is shaped by the cultural context in which it occurs.

30. The personality component that seeks to realistically satisfy instincts is called the _____.

31. The Freudian term for a girl's feelings of love toward her father and rivalry with her mother is _____.

32. Decreasing the likelihood of future responses by administering something unpleasant is called _____.

33. In Piaget's _____ stage of cognitive development, adolescents can reason logically about abstract concepts and hypothetical ideas.

34. The personality component that contains values and morals learned from parents and society is called the _____.

35. In _____, a behavior is eliminated by removing its reinforcing consequences.

36. A person with a(n) _____ view believes that none of the major theories of human development can explain everything, but each has something to contribute to our understanding of human development.

37. With the defense mechanism of _____, people see their own personal motives reflected in others.

38. The theory that humans are active processors of information from the environment, rather than passive recipients of information from the environment is the _____.

39. A(n) _____ is an inborn biological force that motivates behavior.

40. According to the _____ theory, humans are driven by unconscious motives and emotions and shaped by early childhood experiences.

41. The _____ addresses whether developmental changes are common across people or are different for each person.

42. Children progress through the _____ as the libido shifts from one part of the body to another.

43. Any stimulus that increases the likelihood of a behavior occurring in the future when it is removed following the behavior is _____.

44. A learned response to a conditioned stimulus is a _____.

45. To increase the likelihood of a behavior in the future, we could use _____ by administering a pleasant stimulus following the behavior.

46. The Freudian defense mechanism in which a person expresses motives that are the opposite of his/her true motives is exhibiting _____.

47. Learning through observation can occur without a person actually performing the learned behavior, a phenomenon called _____.

48. In classical conditioning, the _____ produces the desired response only after it is associated with a stimulus that always elicits the response.

49. In the process of _____, children are influenced by observing another person receive reinforcement.

50. Developing the belief that you can effectively bring about a desired outcome is called _____.

51. A group of developmental theories that claim that changes over the lifespan occur through ongoing transactions between a changing organism and a changing world are collectively called _____ theories.

52. The understanding that changing superficial features of an object does not change the essential properties of the object is _____.

53. Applying evolutionary theory to understanding human thought and behavior is the field of _____.

54. A cognitive perspective that likens the human mind to a computer is the _____ approach.

55. Through the process of _____, children internalize the attitudes and behaviors of the same-sex parent.

56. The Freudian term for a boy's feelings of love toward his mother and fear of his father is _____.

57. A child's reluctance to go to school or remain at school, often associated with anxiety, is called _____.

58. With the defense mechanism of _____, unwanted or unacceptable thoughts or memories are pushed out of consciousness.

MULTIPLE-CHOICE SELF-TEST

For each multiple-choice question, read all alternatives and then select the best answer.

1. A theorist who believes that humans progress through developmental stages is likely to believe in
   a. discontinuous changes.   c. quantitative changes.
   b. continuous changes.   d. multiple paths of development.

2. The universality-context specificity issue concerns whether developmental changes
   a. are quantitative or qualitative in nature.
   b. are common to everyone or different from person to person.
   c. are multiply caused.
   d. follow universal paths determined by genetic factors or by environmental factors.

3. According to Freud's theory, the _____ must find ways of realistically satisfying the demands of the _____.
   a. superego; ego   c. id; ego
   b. superego; id   d. ego; id

4. Regression occurs when
    a.   a person reverts to an earlier stage of development.
    b.   a person pushes anxiety-provoking thoughts out of conscious awareness.
    c.   development becomes arrested because part of the libido remains tied to an earlier
         stage of development.
    d.   psychic energy is directed toward socially acceptable activities.

5. Which statement BEST characterizes Erikson's position on the nature-nurture issue?
    a.   He emphasized nurture more than nature.
    b.   He emphasized nature more than nurture.
    c.   He emphasized nature and nurture equally.
    d.   He didn't really take a stand on this issue.

6. According to Erikson, the main task facing adolescents is
    a.   developing a sense of identity.
    b.   achieving a sense of intimacy with another person.
    c.   mastering important academic tasks.
    d.   building a sense of self-confidence.

7. You turn on the can opener to open the dog's food, and the dog comes running into the
    room. In this example, food is the _____; the sound of the can opener is the
    _____; and running into the room in response to the sound is the _____.
    a.   unconditioned stimulus; conditioned stimulus; unconditioned response
    b.   conditioned stimulus; unconditioned stimulus; conditioned response
    c.   unconditioned stimulus; conditioned stimulus; conditioned response
    d.   conditioned stimulus; conditioned response; unconditioned response

8. A stimulus can serve as reinforcement or as punishment depending on whether it
    a.   is pleasurable or not (negative) for the subject receiving it.
    b.   increases or decreases the frequency of the behavior it follows.
    c.   occurs before or after the behavior in question.
    d.   is administered or taken away from the person.

9. Which of the following is an example of negative reinforcement?
    a.   Giving a child dessert as a reward for eating his/her vegetables at dinner
    b.   Paying a child for each "A" received on his or her report card
    c.   A parent stops nagging a child when the child finally cleans his or her room
    d.   Cutting a child's television viewing by 30 minutes each time the child misbehaves

10. Which of the following is <u>necessary</u> in order to learn through observation?
    a.   Observing the model get a reward or punishment for his/her actions
    b.   Being provided with an opportunity to imitate the model's actions immediately
         after the observation
    c.   Hearing the model describe the consequences of his/her actions
    d.   Observing and remembering the model's actions

11.   Which of the following explanations for developmental change would a social-learning theorist be most likely to give?
        a.   Children are unconsciously motivated by internal conflict.
        b.   Children observe the world around them and actively process this information.
        c.   Children are passively influenced by environmental rewards and punishments.
        d.   Children actively construct an understanding of the world through interactions with their environment.

12.   Piaget would be most likely to make which one of the following statements?
        a.   Children learn best by observing people around them.
        b.   Children actively construct an understanding of the world by interacting with the world around them.
        c.   Children are genetically predisposed to act in certain ways and seek out environments that are compatible with their genetic makeups.
        d.   Children are unconsciously propelled from one stage to another by maturational forces.

13.   A child in Piaget's preoperational stage is able to solve problems
        a.   that are concrete by using logical reasoning.
        b.   that are abstract by using logical reasoning.
        c.   using symbols.
        d.   through their sensory experiences and their actions.

14.   Of the following, Piaget has been MOST criticized for his belief that
        a.   sexual instincts propel children from one stage of development to the next.
        b.   children are actively involved in their development.
        c.   cognitive development occurs gradually throughout the lifespan.
        d.   cognitive development occurs through an invariant sequence of coherent stages.

15.   Which of the following theoretical perspectives places the greatest emphasis on the interaction of biological and environmental forces?
        a.   Freud's psychoanalytic theory
        b.   Learning theory
        c.   Erikson's neo-Freudian psychoanalytic theory
        d.   Gottlieb's epigenetic psychobiological systems theory

COMPARE THEORIES ON BASIC DEVELOPMENTAL ISSUES

For this exercise, first summarize the essential message of each theory. Then, on the next page, indicate each theory's position on the five basic issues of human development. Check yourself using Table 2.4 on page 56 of the text.

ESSENTIAL MESSAGE OF EACH THEORY

Psychoanalytic Theory: Freud's Psychosexual Theory
Psychoanalytic Theory: Erikson's Psychosocial Theory
Learning Theory: Skinner's Behavioral Theory
Learning Theory: Bandura's Social-Cognitive Theory
Cognitive-Developmental Theory: Piaget's Constructivism
Systems Theory: Gottlieb's Epigenetic Psychobiological Perspective

POSITION ON BASIC ISSUES	PSYCHOANALYTIC THEORIES		COGNITIVE-DEVELOPMENTAL THEORY
	FREUD—PSYCHOSEXUAL THEORY	ERIKSON—PSYCHOSOCIAL THEORY	PIAGET—CONSTRUCTIVISM
Nature—Nurture			
Human Nature—Good or Bad			
Activity—Passivity			
Continuity—Discontinuity			
Universality--Context-Specificity			

POSITION ON BASIC ISSUES	LEARNING THEORIES		SYSTEMS THEORIES
	SKINNER—LEARNING THEORY	BANDURA—SOCIAL-COGNITIVE THEORY	GOTTLIEB—EPIGENETIC PSYCHOBIOLOGICAL
Nature—Nurture			
Human Nature—Good or Bad			
Activity—Passivity			
Continuity—Discontinuity			
Universality--Context-Specificity			

CRITICAL THINKING QUESTIONS

By answering the following questions, you will strengthen your understanding of the material in this chapter. These questions require higher-level thinking skills such as integration and application of concepts. Sample answers are provided for three of the questions. These illustrate one possibility, but there are other answers you could provide that might be just as good. For the other questions, you can check yourself by referring to the text (a hint is provided) or by asking a peer or your instructor to review your answer.

1. Consider the problem of shyness. Many children and adults in our society are socially shy to a significant degree and express anxiety in many everyday, social situations. How would each of the theorists in this chapter interpret or explain the development of this condition?
    [Sample Answer provided]

2. In what ways do the learning theory explanations of development conflict with the psychoanalytic explanations of development?
    [Sample Answer provided]

3. Freud and Piaget are often considered to be the "great stage theorists" of developmental psychology. Discuss ways in which Freud and Piaget are similar in their views of development and ways in which they differ.
    [Sample Answer provided]

4. How do the learning theories of Watson, Skinner, and Bandura differ from the cognitive-developmental theory of Piaget?
    [Hint: Review sections on "Learning theories" and "Piaget: Cognitive-developmental theory" as well as Table 2.4, which compares all of the theories.]

5. Gottlieb's theory is called the epigenetic psychobiological systems approach to development. What ideas about development are conveyed by this perspective?
    [Hint: Review section on "Systems theories."]

ANSWERS

Chapter Summary and Guided Review (fill in the blank)

1. tabula rasa
2. nature
3. nurture
4. quantitative
5. qualitative
6. stages
7. universal
8. instincts
9. unconscious
10. id
11. ego
12. superego
13. psychic energy
14. libido
15. psychosexual
16. oral
17. anal
18. phallic
19. latency
20. genital
21. defense mechanisms
22. fixation

23. regression
24. falsifiable
25. societal
26. trust
27. identity
28. role confusion
29. intimacy
30. generativity
31. integrity
32. behaviorism
33. unconditioned stimulus (UCS)
34. conditioned stimulus (CS)
35. unconditioned response (UCR)
36. conditioned response (CR)
37. positive reinforcement
38. negative reinforcement
39. positive punishment
40. negative punishment
41. extinction

42. observational
43. latent
44. vicarious
45. human agency
46. self-efficacy
47. reciprocal determinism
48. biological
49. invariant sequence
50. sensorimotor
51. preoperational
52. symbols
53. conservation
54. concrete operations
55. formal operations
56. context
57. genes or genetic endowment
58. epigenesis
59. stages
60. environment

Review of Key Terms

1. regression
2. epigenesis
3. behaviorism
4. concrete operations
5. reciprocal determinism
6. operant conditioning
7. classical conditioning
8. ethology
9. activity/passivity issue
10. id
11. developmental stage
12. human agency
13. unconditioned stimulus (UCS)
14. defense mechanisms
15. epigenetic psychobiological systems
16. tabula rasa
17. sensorimotor stage
18. observational learning
19. unconditioned response (UCR)
20. contextual/systems theories
21. negative punishment
22. constructivism
23. continuity/discontinuity issue
24. unconscious motivation
25. libido

26. psychosocial stages
27. fixation
28. preoperational stage
29. sociocultural perspective
30. ego
31. Electra complex
32. positive punishment
33. formal operations stage
34. superego
35. extinction
36. eclectic
37. projection
38. social-cognitive theory
39. instinct
40. psychoanalytic
41. universality/context-specificity issue
42. psychosexual stages
43. negative reinforcement
44. conditioned response
45. positive reinforcement
46. reaction formation
47. latent learning
48. conditioned stimulus (CS)
49. vicarious reinforcement
50. self-efficacy

51. systems theories
52. conservation
53. evolutionary psychology
54. information-processing approach

55. identification
56. Oedipus complex
57. school refusal behavior
58. repression

Multiple-Choice Self-Test

1. A (p. 34)
2. B (p. 35)
3. D (p. 37)
4. A (p. 39)
5. C (p. 41)

6. A (p. 41)
7. A (p. 42)
8. B (p. 43-44)
9. C (p. 43-44)
10. D (p. 45)

11. B (p. 46)
12. B (p. 48)
13. C (p. 49)
14. D (p. 50)
15. D (p. 52-54)

Critical Thinking Questions

Freud might say that shyness is used as a defense mechanism to protect the ego from anxiety caused by the superego. A shy child becomes inhibited through regression to early stages of development. Perhaps the shy child was punished for sucking his or her thumb too long in the oral stage or was punished for toilet training accidents during the anal stage. Early experiences may cause the child to develop a strong superego, which in turn leads the child to become inhibited and withdrawn in the quest to satisfy the need for perfection and acceptance in society. Whatever the specific cause, the child is not consciously aware of these motivating factors.

According to *Erikson*, a child may become shy as a result of not adequately resolving a life crisis in one of the eight psychosocial stages. For example, in the trust vs. mistrust stage, shyness could result because the parent is unresponsive to the child's needs, and the child does not form a trusting relationship to others. In autonomy vs. shame and doubt, the child may not learn to be autonomous; instead, the child may feel doubtful of his/her abilities and not very comfortable trying new things. In initiative vs. guilt, the caregiver may have been too protective, inhibiting the child's initiative and interactive skills. The child may feel guilty whenever he/she tries to do something new and end up not initiating things.

According to *Piaget*, children construct their own understanding of the world through their interactions with their environment. Thus, the child interprets his/her experiences in a way that leads the child to be shy. To avoid disequilibrium, people act in ways that are consistent with their cognitive understanding of events. The child decides that shyness is an adaptive way of interacting with the world. Perhaps the infant in the sensorimotor stage did not have adequate opportunity to explore the environment, leading to shyness because of lack of experience. Or a child in the preoperational stage who has had a bad experience may reason that all experiences are bad and withdraw from seeking new ones.

Based on *learning theories*, people learn by forming associations between behaviors and consequences. *Watson* might argue that shyness is a conditioned response that has resulted from previous pairings of an unconditioned stimulus (something automatically elicited an unconditioned response, in this case, feelings of shyness) with a stimulus that is now conditioned to prompt feelings of shyness. *Skinner* would say that a person who is shy was either rewarded for being shy or punished for being outgoing. For example, the parent might reward the child for quiet activities like reading a book or punish child for being loud. According to *Bandura*, a child may model an adult who is shy and rewarded in some way.

Systems theorists believe that development arises from the ongoing interrelationships between a changing organism and a changing world: changes in a person will affect his/her *environment, and changes in the environment will affect that person. According to <u>Gottlieb</u>, development results from a complex interaction of nature and nurture. Biological factors interact with environmental factors at both the species level and the individual level. We begin life with genetic predispositions that have been formed as a result of gene-environment interactions of previous generations. These genetic predispositions then interact with the individual's environments over a lifetime to determine outcomes. A person might be shy because he/she has been genetically predisposed to shyness and then ended up in environments that fostered this predisposition.*

2.   *Psychoanalytic theories place greater emphasis on nature than do the learning theories. According to Freud's psychoanalytic theory, development is driven by biology; children are propelled through the psychosexual stages according to a biological plan. Erikson, another psychoanalytic theorist, believed that biology interacts with environment to create the eight psychosocial conflicts that confront people throughout the lifespan. In contrast, the learning theorists focus almost exclusively on the role of the environment. Another difference between the two types of theories is their position on the continuity and discontinuity issue. The psychoanalytic theorists, Freud and Erikson, believe that development is discontinuous. They both propose that humans go through stages of development; during each stage, we are different from how we are in other stages. The learning theorists believe that development is continuous over the lifespan. At different points of the lifespan, we may have more or less of something, but we are not qualitatively different. Another difference is their position on the universality and context specificity issue. The psychoanalytic theorists believe that there are universal changes in development, reflected in the stages that we all go through. Development, therefore, is somewhat predictable. The learning theorists believe that development is context specific; there are not universal stages that everyone goes through. Development depends very much on the specific experiences and environments that we each experience. Psychoanalytic theorists are likely to clash with learning theorists by claiming that developmental changes are 1) influenced largely by nature (Freud) or by nature and nurture equally (Erikson); 2) stagelike; and 3) universal rather than specific to the individual.*

3.   *Piaget and Vygotsky were developing their theories at about the same time, but Vygotsky had the misfortune to die young, whereas Piaget worked on his theory for much of his 84 years. As a result, Piaget's theory is much more developed than Vygotsky's. Both theorists believed that children are actively involved in their development and in creating an understanding of the world. Piaget, though, focused more on the individual in isolation. That is, Piaget believed that children learned about their world by independently exploring it and interacting with physical objects. By interacting with toys, for example, they learn about the toys' properties. Vygotsky focused more on the social interactions of the person. Thus, he believed that children learned more by interacting with others than they did by interacting with toys. Piaget believed that cognitive development was largely an internal process, whereas Vygotsky placed greater emphasis on the sociocultural context in which development occurred. Because of this focus on the culture, Vygotsky believed that development varies across social as well as historical contexts. Piaget believed that development is largely universal—it is the same across social and historical contexts.*

CHAPTER THREE

GENES, ENVIRONMENT, AND DEVELOPMENT

OVERVIEW

As the title suggests, this chapter is about both genetic and environmental contributions to development. In addition to describing how parents pass along their genes to their children, the chapter examines how genes interact with environments to make each of us unique with respect to intellectual and psychological attributes. Interestingly, genes can influence the kinds of environments we are exposed to, and environments can affect the expression of genetic factors. Note the point made in the second half of the chapter: people do not inherit traits, they inherit predispositions for traits that may or may not arise depending on the environmental influences.

One of the most interesting findings reported in the chapter is that siblings do not become similar to one another as a result of growing up in the same family and sharing similar experiences. Instead, nonshared environmental experiences are more important in creating individual differences among family members. This may help you understand why you and your siblings are so different from one another on some basic personality characteristics.

An important lesson from this chapter concerns the logic of the methods used to study genetic and environmental influences, and the pattern of the findings. The methods, including twin and adoption studies, can be used to demonstrate both genetic and environmental influences, not just genetic factors. You should understand the pattern of findings that would show a genetic influence, an environmental influence, and interaction effects, even if you do not know actual correlation coefficients or concordance values.

LEARNING OBJECTIVES

After reading and studying the material in this chapter, you should be able to answer the following questions.

3.1   EVOLUTION AND SPECIES HEREDITY
1.   What do evolution and species heredity contribute to our understanding of universal patterns of development?

3.2   INDIVIDUAL HEREDITY
2.   What are the basic workings of individual heredity, including the contributions of genes, chromosomes, the zygote, and the processes of mitosis and meiosis? Note the difference between genotype and phenotype.

3.   How are traits passed from parents to offspring? What is an example of how a child could inherit a trait through each of the three mechanisms described in the text?

4.   What methods are used to screen for genetic abnormalities? What are the advantages and disadvantages of using such techniques to test for prenatal problems? What are some abnormalities that can currently be detected with genetic screening?

3.3   STUDYING GENETIC AND ENVIRONMENTAL INFLUENCES

5.   How do scientists compare the contributions of heredity and environment to behavioral characteristics? Describe the logic of the methods, as well as strengths and weaknesses of each method.

6.   How can concordance rates help researchers estimate the influences of heredity and environment? How do genes, shared environment, and nonshared environment contribute to individual differences in traits?

3.4   SELECTED FINDINGS

7.   How do genes and environments contribute to individual differences in intellectual abilities, personality and temperament, and psychological disorders?

8.   What do researchers mean when they talk about the heritability of traits? Which traits are more strongly heritable than others?

3.5   GENES AND ENVIRONMENT CONSPIRING

9.   What is an example that illustrates the concept of a gene-environment interaction?

10.   What are three ways that genes and environments correlate to influence behavior?

11.   What are the major controversies surrounding genetic research?

CHAPTER SUMMARY AND GUIDED REVIEW

The following summary provides an overview of the main points contained in this chapter of the text. Fill in the blanks with terms that appropriately complete the sentence. Scattered throughout the summary are questions in parentheses. These are meant to encourage you to think actively as you read and connect this summary to the more detailed information provided in the text.

3.1   EVOLUTION AND SPECIES HEREDITY

Although people are quite different from one another, all members of a species share some commonalities because of (1) _____. (***Can you provide examples of this common genetic endowment in humans?***) Charles Darwin's theory of evolution tries to explain how characteristics of species change or evolve over generations. His theory has three main points:

- There is genetic variation in a species.
- Some genes are "better" or aid in (2) _____ more than others.
- Those genes that are more useful will be passed along to offspring more so than genes that are less useful. This is the principle of (3) _____. Evolution involves interactions of genes and environments. Genes that are adaptive in one environment may not be adaptive in another environment. Through (4) _____, we "inherit" proven methods of adapting to our environment and we then pass along what we have learned about adaptation to future generations.

3.2   INDIVIDUAL HEREDITY

Genes can contribute to differences between individuals through the process of individual heredity. A new life begins at (5) _____ when a woman's egg cell is fertilized by a man's sperm.

The Genetic Code

Once the genetic material from sperm and egg cells merge, the new cell formed from this union is called a (6) _____. This new cell has 46 threadlike (7) _____, each made up of thousands of (8) _____, or segments of DNA molecules.

The single cell formed at conception begins to divide through a process called (9) _____, which results in daughter cells with the same 46 chromosomes as the mother cell. The sperm and ova result from the process of (10) _____so that they each have only 23, or half, of the original cell's chromosomes.

Our understanding of genetics has been greatly enhanced by the (11) _____, designed to decipher the genetic code. *(What are some of the findings that have emerged from this work?)*

Although biological siblings share the same parents, their genetic makeup is unique, partly due to the phenomenon of (12) _____in which parts of chromosomes are exchanged during cell division. Twins that are (13) _____ develop from one zygote and share 100% of their genes. On the other hand, twins that result from two separate ova fertilized by different sperm, called (14) _____, are no more genetically similar than siblings. Siblings and fraternal twins share, on the average, half of their genes.

A child's sex is determined by whether or not the sperm that fertilizes the egg carries an X or Y chromosome. The chromosome pair of a female consists of (15) _____ chromosome(s) and for a male, the pair has (16) _____ chromosome(s).

Translation and Expression of the Genetic Code

Genes provide a blueprint for development, but environmental factors exert a strong influence on how genes are expressed. A person's genetic makeup is called his/her (17)_____, whereas the actual outward characteristics a person shows are part of his/her (18) _____. All cells contain the same genes but (19) _____, the activation of certain genes in particular cells at particular times, determines our traits.

Mechanisms of Inheritance

There are three main mechanisms of inheritance. One way to inherit is through a single pair of genes. Each gene of the pair can be either dominant or (20) _____. If one gene in the pair is (21) _____, then the characteristic associated with this gene will express itself. In order for a (22) _____ trait to express itself, a person would need to receive a matched pair, one from each parent. (*What is an example of this?*)

Another pattern of inheritance occurs when a dominant gene in a pair does not completely mask the effects of the recessive gene. This pattern is called (23) _____. If neither gene dominates the other but both influence a trait, (24) _____ is said to be operating. (*Can you provide examples of characteristics inherited through each of these mechanisms?*)

Some traits are influenced by genes on the sex chromosomes, rather than on the other 22 pairs of chromosomes and are called (25) _____. (*Why are males more likely*

Chapter Three

than females to inherit a trait through this mechanism?) Many human characteristics are influenced by more than one pair of genes and so are transmitted through the mechanism of (26) _____ inheritance. (*Can you provide examples of characteristics inherited through this mechanism?*)

Mutations

Occasionally, a new gene appears that was not passed from parent to child but results from a mutation. Some mutations are actually beneficial and become more common through the process of (27) _____. (*What is an example of a trait that probably started as a result of mutation?*)

Chromosome Abnormalities

A chromosomal abnormality that results from an extra 21st chromosome is called (28) _____. (*Why are older women at greater risk for having a child with such chromosomal abnormalities?*) Females with a missing X chromosome have a condition known as (29) _____ syndrome. Males who inherit an extra X chromosome are said to have (30) _____ syndrome. (*What characteristics are associated with each of these chromosomal abnormalities?*) A common sex-linked disorder that causes mental retardation is (31) _____.

Genetic Diagnosis and Counseling

Genetic counseling provides information to parents who are concerned about the possibility of genetic birth defects. Genetic disorders that they might be tested for include (32) _____ disease, a recessive disorder that results from odd-shaped blood cells that deliver less oxygen than normal cells, leading to a number of debilitating symptoms. Individuals who have one dominant and one recessive gene for a recessive trait or disorder are called (33) _____. These individuals do not express the trait but can pass it on to their offspring. Another disorder that parents might be concerned about, caused by a single dominant gene and associated with motor problems, personality changes, and cognitive declines, is (34) _____ disease. (*What are the pros and cons of genetic screening techniques?*)

Prenatal detection of abnormalities often begins with an (35) _____, which constructs a visual image of the fetus by passing sound waves over the womb. In another procedure called (36) _____, fetal cells are extracted from amniotic fluid and analyzed for chromosomal abnormalities. Similar information can be gained from a procedure called (37) _____ in which fetal cells are extracted from the chorion membrane surrounding the fetus. For some couples, preimplantation genetic diagnosis can be used to screen for genetic abnormalities and then a healthy egg can be selected and implanted.

3.3 STUDYING GENETIC AND ENVIRONMENTAL INFLUENCES

The field of study concerned with the extent to which genetic and environmental differences among people are responsible for differences in their traits is (38) _____. Scientists in this field often use (39) _____ estimates, which provide information about the amount of variability between people that can be attributed to the genetic differences among those people. Even traits that are highly heritable are still influenced by environmental factors.

Experimental Breeding

One way to study the influence of genes on animal behavior is to deliberately mate animals and see whether certain traits are more or less likely following this (40) _____. (***What have researchers learned from doing these sorts of studies?***)

Twin, Adoption, and Family Studies

Experimental breeding cannot be used with humans, so researchers use twin and adoption studies to study the influences of genes and environments. (***Can you identify some cautions regarding interpretation of findings from twin and adoption studies?***) If heredity influences a trait, (41) _____ twins should be more similar on the trait than (42) _____ twins. If adopted children resemble their adoptive parents more than they resemble their biological parents on some trait, then the trait must be influenced by (43) _____ factors.

Estimating Influences

To estimate the influence of genetic and environmental factors on traits, researchers may calculate the (44) _____ rate, which indicates the percentage of pairs who both have the trait if one of them has it. For traits that vary numerically, such as height or intelligence, they may also use (45) _____.

Behavioral geneticists try to estimate how various factors contribute to individual differences observed in a trait. Finding that identical twins score more similarly on a trait than do fraternal twins suggests variation due to (46) _____ differences. The fact that siblings raised together in the same home score more similarly on a trait than siblings raised apart would indicate the influence of the shared (47) _____. Finding that genetically identical pairs who are raised together are not perfectly similar would indicate the influence of (48) _____ factors.

Molecular Genetics

Molecular genetics is the analysis of specific genes and their effects. A major goal of molecular genetics is to determine how much variation in a trait is due to genes and how much is due to environment. For example, researchers are studying the apoE4 gene, which has been linked to (49) _____.

3.4 SELECTED FINDINGS

Intellectual Abilities

Research on intellectual abilities shows the influence of genes, and shared and nonshared environments. (***Can you describe the patterns of these findings?***) Identical twins tend to become more similar to one another in mental ability after 18 months of age and tend to follow the same course of mental development. Fraternal twins tend to become less similar to one another over the years. (***Can you explain why this pattern emerges?***) Overall, research shows that the most important environmental influence is the (50) _____ component.

Temperament and Personality

The tendency to respond in predictable ways is called temperament and is considered a precursor to later personality. Individual differences in temperament during infancy seem to be related to (51) _____ differences among infants. In addition, the influence of (52) _____ environmental factors contribute to individual differences in temperament. (***What pattern of findings would support this conclusion?***) These influences help explain why siblings, who share, on average, 50% of their genes and grow up in the same home, can be so different.

Psychological Disorders

Psychological problems are also influenced by genetic and environmental factors. Some individuals may be genetically predisposed to developing a disorder involving disturbances in logical thinking and behavior called (53) _____. Psychological disorders are not inherited directly; people inherit (54) _____ to develop traits. (***What may determine whether individuals will develop a psychological disorder?***)

The Heritability of Different Traits

Although all traits are influenced to some extent by genes, some traits are more heritable than others. (***Which traits are more heritable, and which ones are less heritable?***)

Influences on Heritability

Estimates of heritability vary depending on the sample studied; heritability is not a fixed quality. Age and environmental factors such as socioeconomic status influence heritability.

3.5   GENES AND ENVIRONMENT CONSPIRING

Genes operate throughout a person's lifespan, interacting with environmental factors. Modern psychologists examine how heredity and environment work together.

Gene-Environment Interactions

The expression of a person's genotype depends on the person's environment, and how people respond to their environment depends on their genotype.

Gene-Environment Correlations

There are three models for how genes and environments are correlated. In a(n) (55) _____ genotype/environment correlation, the child and the child's environment are both influenced by the parents' genotypes. In a(n) (56) _____ genotype/environment correlation, a child's (57) _____ triggers certain responses from other people. In a(n) (58) _____ genotype/environment correlation, children actively seek out (59) _____ that suit their particular genotype. (***Can you provide examples of each type of genotype/environment correlation?***)

Genetic Influences on Environment

Research shows that individuals can indeed actively shape their environments, which in turn, influence them. Environmental and genetic factors constantly influence one another and are influenced by each other. Research on gene-environment correlations suggests that the family is a vehicle for expressing the common genetic code of family members. (***Can you give an example that illustrates what this means?***)

Controversies Surrounding Genetic Research

Some experts worry about potential dangers arising from genetic technology, such as cloning or attempting to improve the human race by altering genetic traits. Others believe that the benefits of gene technology outweigh the pitfalls. There are still many questions to answer regarding the process through which genotypes are translated into phenotypes, called (60) _____.

REVIEW OF KEY TERMS

Below is a list of terms and concepts from this chapter. Use these to complete the following sentence definitions. You might also want to try writing definitions in your own words and then checking your definitions with those in the text.

adoption study	Huntington's disease
allele	identical twins
amniocentesis	incomplete dominance
behavioral genetics	karyotype
carrier	Klinefelter syndrome
chorionic villus sampling (CVS)	maternal blood sampling
chromosome	meiosis
chromosome abnormalities	mitosis
codominance	molecular genetics
conception	mutation
concordance rate	natural selection
crossing over	nonshared environmental influences
cultural evolution	phenotype
DNA	phenylketonuria (PKU)
dominant gene	polygenic trait
Down syndrome	preimplantation genetic diagnosis
fragile X syndrome	recessive gene
fraternal twins	schizophrenia
gene-environment correlation	selective breeding
gene-environment interaction	sex-linked characteristic
gene expression	shared environmental influences
gene therapy	sickle-cell disease
genetic counseling	single gene-pair inheritance
genotype	species heredity
hemophilia	stem cell
heritability	temperament
Human Genome Project	Turner syndrome
	twin study

ultrasound   Y chromosome
X chromosome   zygote

1.   A person's _____ consists of his/her genetic makeup.

2.   Threadlike structures containing genetic material are called _____.

3.   A fertilized egg cell is a _____.

4.   The genetic endowment common to all members of a particular species is _____.

5.   Two individuals who develop as a result of one fertilized egg splitting in two are called
      _____.

6.   When a child receives too many or too few chromosomes at conception,
      _____ occurs.

7.   A common cause of mental retardation resulting from an abnormality on the X
      chromosome is called _____.

8.   The gene in a dissimilar pair that typically does not express itself in that person's
      phenotype is called the _____.

9.   The presence of the _____ determines a child's biological sex.

10.   The field of _____ involves the analysis of specific genes and their effects.

11.   Comparing adopted children to their biological parents and to their adopted parents is
      done to separate genetic from environmental influences and is called _____.

12.   Interventions that somehow alter a person's genetic makeup constitute _____.

13.   Two individuals who developed at the same time but from two different fertilized eggs
      are _____.

14.   The gene in a dissimilar pair that usually expresses itself phenotypically is called the
      _____.

15.   Cell division that results in two cells identical to the one original cell occurs through the
      process of _____.

16.   Some couples undergo _____ so that their physician can select and then
      implant only fertilized eggs that do not have chromosomal or genetic abnormalities.

17. A person's _____ reflects the expression of their genotype in conjunction with environmental influences.

18. The moment a woman's egg is fertilized by a man's sperm is called _____.

19. According to _____, genes that promote adaptation to one's environment will be passed to offspring more often than genes that do not promote adaptation.

20. A disorder involving disturbances in logical thinking, emotional expression, and social behavior is _____.

21. In a procedure called _____, fetal cells are removed from the amniotic sac by inserting a needle through the mother's abdomen in order to test chromosomal makeup.

22. The activation of certain genes in particular cells of the body at particular times is _____.

23. A chromosome disorder resulting from an extra 21st chromosome is _____.

24. A female who receives only one X chromosome has a condition called _____.

25. A _____ refers to the interrelationship between one's genes and one's environment.

26. Providing information to people regarding the likelihood of genetically based problems in their unborn children is the purpose of _____.

27. A disorder resulting in dementia, emotional problems, loss of motor control, and premature death is _____.

28. Cell division that results in four cells, each with half the number of chromosomes as in the one original cell, occurs through the process of _____.

29. According to the concept of _____, the influence of our genes depends on the experiences we have, and the experiences we have depend on the genes we have.

30. A _____ is a photograph of an individual's chromosomes organized into groups.

31. Experiences that are unique to an individual are called _____.

32. The phenomenon in which parts of chromosomes are exchanged during cell division is called _____.

33. A _____ results in a change in the structure or arrangement of one or more genes, resulting in a new phenotype.

34. _____ occurs when one pair of genes determines the presence or absence of a trait.

35. A disorder in which blood cells cluster together and distribute less oxygen than normal cells is _____.

36. A male who receives an extra X chromosome has a condition called _____.

37. Experiences that individuals have in common because they live in the same home environment are _____.

38. In the inheritance pattern of _____, the dominant gene in a pair is not able to totally mask the effects of the recessive gene.

39. The _____ statistic represents the amount of variability in a trait within a large group of people that can be linked to genetic differences among those people.

40. Deliberately mating animals with certain genotypes in order to determine if it is possible to produce offspring with certain characteristics is the goal of _____.

41. In the inheritance pattern of _____, neither gene in a pair is able to completely dominate the other, and both express themselves.

42. Each gene has alternate forms, called _____, that reside in a particular location on the chromosome and together determine the expression of a trait.

43. A trait that is influenced by single genes located on the sex chromosomes is referred to as a _____.

44. A characteristic that is influenced by multiple genes is called a _____.

45. Individuals who are _____ do not express a trait but can pass the trait on to their offspring.

46. A disorder in which a critical enzyme needed to metabolize phenylalanine is missing is _____.

47. In a procedure called _____, fetal cells from the chorion are removed by inserting a catheter through the mother's vagina in order to test chromosomal makeup.

48. The _____ is a sex chromosome that, when matched with another like it, results in a female child.

49.   The tendency to respond in predictable ways is part of a person's _____.

50.   The probability that one of a pair of twins will show a given characteristic, given that the other twin has the characteristic, is represented with the statistic _____.

51.   A genetic disorder that causes gradual deterioration of the nervous system is called _____.

52.   A(n) _____ is a procedure to detect fetal growth and characteristics by passing sound waves over the mother's abdomen.

53.   The scientific study of the extent to which genetic and environmental differences within a species are responsible for differences in traits is referred to as _____.

54.   Through _____, it may be possible to analyze fetal cells that have slipped through the placenta and into the mother's blood.

55.   A method that attempts to separate genetic and environmental influences by determining whether identical twins differ from fraternal twins, when both pairs are raised together, is the basis of the _____.

56.   A sex-linked disorder that limits the blood's ability to clot is called _____.

57.   The _____ is a massive attempt to decipher the human genetic code.

58.   Passing along proven methods of adapting to the environment from one generation to the next is the process of _____.

59.   Strands of _____, consisting of chemical sequences, make up each chromosome.

60.   Cells that have the potential to become many different specialized cells are _____.

MULTIPLE-CHOICE SELF TEST

For each multiple choice question, read all alternatives and then select the best answer.

1.   All children tend to walk and talk at about 12 months of age. This universal pattern of development results from
        a.   the crossing over phenomenon.
        b.   societal expectations.
        c.   species heredity.
        d.   single gene-pair inheritance.

2. A zygote
   a. merges with a sperm cell at conception to form a fertilized cell.
   b. is a cell that will split and develop into fraternal twins.
   c. contains only the sex chromosomes.
   d. is a fertilized egg cell.

3. A person's phenotype is most accurately described as
   a. a person's genetic inheritance.
   b. the outcome of the interaction between a person's genotype and a particular environment.
   c. the result of the union between a sperm cell and egg cell.
   d. those characteristics that do not have a genetic basis.

4. Suppose two people are carriers for thin lips, which is a recessive trait. Each one of their children would have a _____ chance of expressing this trait in their phenotype.
   a. 25%   c. 75%
   b. 50%   d. 100%

5. Incomplete dominance results when
   a. two different genes in a pair are both expressed in a compromise of the two genes.
   b. one gene in a pair cannot completely mask the effects of the other gene.
   c. several gene pairs contribute to the expression of a trait.
   d. both parents are carriers for a particular trait.

6. In X-linked traits,
   a. males and females are equally likely to express (i.e., have or show) the trait.
   b. males are carriers of the trait but do not always express the trait.
   c. females can express the trait but do so much less often than males.
   d. females and males typically carry but do not express the trait.

7. A person is a carrier for a genetic disorder if she/he
   a. does not show the disorder and cannot pass on the disorder to offspring.
   b. does not show the disorder but can pass on the disorder to offspring.
   c. shows the disorder but cannot pass on the disorder to offspring.
   d. shows the disorder and can pass on the disorder to offspring.

8. Down syndrome occurs when
   a. a child receives too few chromosomes.
   b. a male receives an extra X chromosome.
   c. there is an abnormality associated with one of the sex chromosomes.
   d. a child receives an extra 21st chromosome.

9. The goals of genetic counseling include all of the following EXCEPT
   a. identify traits that parents might be carrying.
   b. calculate probabilities that a particular trait might be transmitted to children.
   c. make decisions for the couple about whether to terminate or continue a pregnancy.
   d. provide information about characteristics and treatment of genetic disorders.

10. Heritability refers to
    a. the amount of variability in a group's trait that is due to genetic differences between people in the group.
    b. the degree to which an individual's characteristics are determined by genetics.
    c. the degree of relationship between pairs of individuals.
    d. a person's genetic makeup.

11. Some people have criticized the logic of twin studies because
    a. identical twins are always the same biological sex while fraternal twins are not.
    b. identical twins are more likely to participate in this type of study than fraternals.
    c. identical twins are treated more similarly than fraternal twins, making it difficult to separate environmental from genetic factors.
    d. it is not always possible to accurately identify twins as fraternal or identical.

12. Which of the following statements is FALSE regarding genetics and intellectual ability?
    a. Intellectual development in infancy is only weakly influenced by individual heredity and environment.
    b. Identical twins become more similar with age in their intellectual performance, while fraternal twins become less similar.
    c. Both identical and fraternal twins become more similar in intellectual performance with increasing age.
    d. Genes influence the course of intellectual development.

13. With regard to individual differences in intellectual ability, research suggests that
    a. genes, shared environmental influences, and nonshared environmental influences contribute equally across the lifespan.
    b. shared environmental influences have the largest impact across the entire lifespan.
    c. genetic influences become more influential and shared environmental influences become less influential with age.
    d. shared and nonshared environmental influences become more influential and genes become less influential with age.

14. Research shows that
    a. people directly inherit many psychological disorders.
    b. people inherit predispositions to develop psychological disorders.
    c. psychological disorders have no genetic basis.
    d. having a parent with a psychological disorder means that the child of that person will also have the disorder.

15. The concept of an evocative genotype/environment correlation suggests that
    a. parents select environments for their children, and their selection is determined by genetic factors.
    b. children's genotypes trigger certain reactions from other people.
    c. children seek out environments that suit their particular genotypes.
    d. genotypes limit the range of possible phenotypic outcomes.

REVIEW GENETIC AND ENVIRONMENTAL CONTRIBUTIONS TO TRAITS

This exercise helps you interpret data concerning genetic and environmental contributions to human traits. Review the section on "Intellectual abilities" on pages 82-83 of the text and take a look at the following table of correlations of intelligence scores (taken from Table 3.5 of the text) to help answer the questions.

Relationship between Pairs	Raised Together	Raised Apart
Identical Twins	.86	.72
Fraternal Twins	.60	.52
Biological Parent & Child	.42	.22
Adopted Parent & Child	.19	—

1. Which correlation(s) show a genetic influence? Would you characterize this influence as slight, moderate, or strong? Why?

2. Which correlation(s) show the influence of the environment on intelligence? Would you characterize this influence as slight, moderate, or strong? Why?

3. Are genetic or environmental forces more evident in IQ differences? Use the correlations to support your answer.

4. How do shared and nonshared environmental influences on intelligence change across the lifespan?

5. Do genetic influences on variations in IQ increase or decrease with age?

CRITICAL THINKING QUESTIONS

By answering the following questions, you will strengthen your understanding of the material in this chapter. These questions require higher-level thinking skills such as integration and application of concepts. Sample answers are provided for three of the questions. These illustrate one possibility, but there are other answers you could provide that might be just as good. For the other questions, you can check yourself by referring to the text (a hint is provided), or by asking a peer or your instructor to review your answer.

1. Consider a characteristic such as humor. What evidence would you need to collect to convince someone that this trait is influenced by genetic factors? What evidence would you need to show the effects of shared and nonshared environmental influences on humor?
    [Sample answer provided]

2.   How can you account for the findings that identical twins become more similar to one
       another in mental ability as they get older, and fraternal twins become less similar to one
       another in mental ability as they get older?
       [*Sample answer provided*]

3.   What measures are currently available to screen for chromosomal and genetic
       abnormalities? Evaluate the pros and cons of these techniques for couples considering
       having a baby.
       [*Sample answer provided*]

4.   How can you explain the intriguing finding that biological siblings who share, on
       average, 50% of the same genetic material and grow up in the same home, turn out to
       have such different personalities?
       [*Hint: Review the section in the text on "Temperament and personality," paying
       particular attention to the part in which this very question is posed.*]

5.   How can genes influence the environments that people live in and how can environments
       influence genes?
       [*Hint: Review the section of the text on "Heredity and environment conspiring."*]

ANSWERS

Chapter Summary and Guided Review (fill in the blank)

1. species heredity	23. incomplete dominance
2. adaptation	24. codominance
3. natural selection	25. sex-linked
4. cultural evolution	26. polygenic
5. conception	27. natural selection
6. zygote	28. Down syndrome
7. chromosomes	29. Turner
8. genes	30. Klinefelter
9. mitosis	31. fragile X syndrome
10. meiosis	32. sickle cell
11. Human Genome Project	33. carriers
12. crossing over	34. Huntington's
13. identical	35. ultrasound
14. fraternal	36. amniocentesis
15. 2 X	37. chorionic villus sampling (CVS)
16. 1 X and 1 Y	38. behavioral genetics
17. genotype	39. heritability
18. phenotype	40. selective breeding
19. gene expression	41. identical
20. recessive	42. fraternal
21. dominant	43. environmental
22. recessive	44. concordance

Chapter Three

45. correlation coefficients
46. genetic
47. shared environment
48. nonshared environmental
49. Alzheimer's disease
50. nonshared
51. genetic
52. nonshared

53. schizophrenia
54. predispositions
55. passive
56. evocative
57. genotype
58. active
59. environments
60. epigenesis

Review of Key Terms

1. genotype
2. chromosomes
3. zygote
4. species heredity
5. identical twins
6. chromosome abnormalities
7. fragile X syndrome
8. recessive gene
9. Y chromosome
10. molecular genetics
11. adoption study
12. gene therapy
13. fraternal twins
14. dominant gene
15. mitosis
16. preimplantation genetic diagnosis
17. phenotype
18. conception
19. natural selection
20. schizophrenia
21. amniocentesis
22. gene expression
23. Down syndrome
24. Turner syndrome
25. gene-environment correlation
26. genetic counseling
27. Huntington's disease
28. meiosis
29. gene-environment interaction
30. karyotype

31. nonshared environmental influences
32. crossing over
33. mutation
34. single gene-pair inheritance
35. sickle cell disease
36. Klinefelter syndrome
37. shared environmental influences
38. incomplete dominance
39. heritability
40. selective breeding
41. codominance
42. allele
43. sex-linked characteristic
44. polygenic trait
45. carriers
46. phenylketonuria (PKU)
47. chorionic villus sampling (CVS)
48. X chromosome
49. temperament
50. concordance rate
51. Tay-Sachs disease
52. ultrasound
53. behavioral genetics
54. maternal blood sampling
55. twin study
56. hemophilia
57. Human Genome Project
58. cultural evolution
59. DNA
60. stem cells

Multiple-Choice Self-Test

1. C (p. 64)
2. D (p. 66)
3. B (p. 69)
4. A (p. 70-72)
5. B (p. 73)

6. C (p. 73)
7. B (p. 76)
8. D (p. 74)
9. C (p. 75-77)
10. A (p. 79)

11. C (p. 79)
12. C (p. 82-83)
13. C (p. 82-83)
14. B (p. 85)
15. B (p. 88)

1.   *To show that humor is influenced by genetic factors, you could show that identical twins raised apart are similar to one another on some measure of humor, and more similar than fraternal twins or other siblings who are raised together. Because the only thing the identical twins raised apart have in common is their genetic makeup, any similarities among them must be due to their genetic similarity. One way to demonstrate influences of the shared environment is to show that sibling pairs raised together are more similar to one another than sibling pairs raised apart. The influence of nonshared environmental influences would be evident if identical twins raised together were dissimilar on humor.*

2.   *Research on intellectual ability suggests that genetic influences actually increase over the lifespan rather than decrease. During infancy, fraternal twins are about as similar to one another on mental ability as identical twins are to one another. This is true despite the fact that identical twins share 100% of the same genetic material, whereas fraternal twins share, on average, 50% of the same genetic material. Starting around 18 months of age, identical twins become more similar to one another, with correlations of about 0.85 in childhood and adolescence. In contrast, fraternal twins become less similar to one another, with correlations of about 0.54 in adolescence. This difference in the pattern of scores for fraternal and identical twins indicates that heritability of mental ability increases. Genetic differences between people in a group play a large role in observed differences in their mental ability.*

At the same time, shared environmental influences decrease in importance across the lifespan. Siblings growing up in the same home often seem similar to one another because they are strongly influenced by their parents, who determine what they wear, what their rooms look like, what they do, etc. Young children's lives are strongly controlled by their parents, but as they get older, this parental (shared environmental) influence lessens. This may occur because children begin to express their unique, and genetically influenced, personalities and intellects. They seek out environments that are most compatible with their true selves. They no longer go to music classes because their parents want them to and take them, but they sign themselves up for soccer or computer camp because that's what they enjoy or are good at. Identical twins are likely to select similar environments for themselves because the same genes influence their choices. Fraternal twins are less likely to seek out similar environments because of their greater genetic variability. The different experiences make fraternal twins (and other siblings) increasingly different from one another.

3.   *There are several tests used during pregnancy that can reveal some genetic conditions. Many pregnancies are monitored with ultrasound, which uses sound waves to scan the womb and create a visual image of the developing fetus. Physical abnormalities and growth problems may be detected with an ultrasound. Some women undergo amniocentesis in which a needle is inserted into the abdomen and cells are extracted from the amniotic fluid. These cells can be examined microscopically to determine the sex of the fetus as well as abnormalities of the chromosomes. Amniocentesis, for example, can indicate whether a fetus has the normal array of 46 chromosomes, arranged in 23 pairs. A third 21st chromosome indicates the presence of Down syndrome. Because of safety concerns, amniocentesis can't be performed until at least the 15th week of pregnancy. The same information can be derived a little earlier in pregnancy by using chorionic villus sampling, which involves collecting cells from the chorion by going through the mother's vagina and cervix. For parents who are worried that they will pass along a known genetic defect to their children, preimplantation genetic diagnosis is an option. This involves fertilizing an egg with a sperm in a laboratory and then conducting DNA tests on the fertilized egg. Eggs that don't contain the genetic abnormality can then be implanted in the mother's womb. Many people have concerns about preimplantation genetic diagnoses because parents might use it just to eliminate traits they don't like rather than traits that are life-threatening or harmful. Testing the mother's blood might also yield some information about fetal development. The mother's blood might contain fetal cells that have slipped through the placenta, but then again, it might not, or it might contain cells from a previous pregnancy. This form of testing is best when combined with other indicators of genetic defects.*

CHAPTER FOUR

PRENATAL DEVELOPMENT AND BIRTH

OVERVIEW

This chapter begins by discussing the dramatic changes that take place during the prenatal period and the environmental factors that can influence prenatal development. These include maternal conditions such as age, emotional state, and nutritional condition, along with outside factors—called teratogens—that can adversely affect development. The environment surrounding birth (the perinatal environment) is also discussed, with attention to complicating factors and to the parent's experience of the birth process. As you read about all the things that could potentially harm a developing fetus, keep in mind that the vast majority of pregnancies and deliveries are normal, with no complications. Finally, the early environment of the newborn (the neonatal period) is discussed in this chapter, including risks to development such as low-birth-weight as well as factors associated with resilience.

LEARNING OBJECTIVES

After reading and studying the material in this chapter, you should be able to answer the following questions.

4.1   PRENATAL DEVELOPMENT
1.   How does development unfold during the prenatal period from conception until the time of birth?

2.   How does prenatal behavior of the fetus relate to postnatal behavior of the infant?

4.2   PRENATAL ENVIRONMENT
3.   How and when do various teratogens affect the developing fetus? How can you summarize the effects of teratogens during the prenatal period?

4.   How do maternal age, emotional state, and nutrition affect prenatal and neonatal development? What about the father's state—can this influence development?

4.3   PERINATAL ENVIRONMENT
5.   What is the typical perinatal environment like? What hazards can occur during the birth process?

6.   What is the birth experience like from the mother's and father's perspectives, and from different cultural perspectives?

4.4 NEONATAL ENVIRONMENT

7. What are the advantages of breast feeding? Are there disadvantages of breast feeding?

8. How can at-risk newborns be identified? What treatments are available to optimize development of at-risk babies?

9. To what extent are the effects of the prenatal and perinatal environments long lasting? What factors influence whether effects are lasting?

CHAPTER SUMMARY AND GUIDED REVIEW

The following summary provides an overview of the main points contained in this chapter of the text. Fill in the blanks with terms that appropriately complete the sentence. Scattered throughout the summary are questions in parentheses. These are meant to encourage you to think actively as you read and connect this summary to the more detailed information provided in the text.

4.1 PRENATAL DEVELOPMENT

Conception

Conception occurs when a sperm fertilizes an egg cell, forming a single cell called a (1) _____, which begins to divide and replicate. Couples who are unable to get pregnant after a year of trying to do so are experiencing (2) _____. This is equally likely to arise from issues associated with the male as well as with the female partner and can often be treated. For instance, doctors can inject sperm directly into a woman's uterus in a procedure called (3) _____. In another procedure termed (4) _____, eggs are removed from a woman's uterus, combined with sperm in a laboratory, and then placed in a woman's uterus in hopes that one will implant and flourish.

Prenatal Stages

Prenatal development is divided into three stages. First is the (5) _____ period, which lasts from conception until implantation of the (6) _____ in the wall of the uterus. At this point, the period of the (7) _____ begins and lasts through the eighth week of prenatal development. Many pregnancies are lost during these early weeks, often before they are recognized, a situation referred to as (8) _____. During the first 2 months, every major organ forms in the process of (9) _____. The layers of the embryo become distinct, with an outer layer forming the amnion and the (10) _____, which attaches to the uterine wall. Eventually, this becomes the lining of the (11) _____, a tissue that is fed by blood vessels from the mother. This tissue connects the embryo to the umbilical cord, and these structures provide nutrients and oxygen for the embryo. The brain begins to emerge at 3-4 weeks when the neural plate folds up to form the (12) _____. Failure of the tube to close completely at the bottom can lead to (13) _____ in which the spinal cord is not fully encased by the protective spinal column. Failure to close at the top of the tube can lead to the lethal defect of (14) _____.

The process of sexual differentiation begins during the 7th and 8th prenatal weeks with development of male testes or female ovaries from an undifferentiated tissue. The testes will then secrete (15) _____, which will stimulate development of a male internal reproduction system, or in its absence, the internal reproduction system of a female.

The third stage of prenatal development is the (16) _____, which lasts from the 9th week of pregnancy until birth. The number of neurons increases dramatically during this period. They migrate to their final location and take on specialized functions. Before becoming specialized, cells are called (17) _____ and have the potential to take on any function. At about 24 weeks, the fetus may be able to survive outside the womb, making this the age of (18) _____. The last trimester brings rapid weight gain for the fetus; brain cells increase in number and size and some develop an insulating cover called (19) _____. Fetal behavior becomes increasingly organized, resembling organized patterns of waking and sleeping known as (20) _____. Prenatal behavior patterns correlate with later infant patterns, demonstrating continuity in development.

4.2   PRENATAL ENVIRONMENT

The mother's womb is the physical environment prior to birth. The prenatal environment can have lasting effects on development, both negative and positive.

Teratogens

A teratogen is any environmental agent that can produce abnormalities in a developing fetus. A time when the developing embryo or fetus is particularly sensitive to environmental influences is called a (21) _____. Effects of teratogens are worse with greater exposure. Outcomes are influenced by maternal and fetal genetic makeup as well as quality of pre- and postnatal environments. One category of teratogens includes drugs. A mild tranquilizer called (22) _____, used years ago to combat morning sickness, caused serious deformities that varied depending on when the drug was taken during pregnancy. Smoking, and even exposure to second-hand smoke, can lead to growth retardation and other developmental delays. Smoking also increases the risk of (23) _____, when a sleeping baby unexpectedly stops breathing and dies. (***How have researchers attempted to determine whether adverse effects of maternal smoking during pregnancy are due to nature or nurture?***) Children whose mothers drank alcohol during pregnancy may exhibit a cluster of symptoms called (24) _____. There is no known amount of alcohol that is entirely safe to consume during pregnancy, although the severity of FAS symptoms depends on the amount of alcohol consumed. The illegal stimulant drug (25) _____ also leads to a number of pre- and postnatal complications, including possible long-term deficits in cognitive, language, and social development. (***What other environmental conditions or maternal conditions can adversely affect prenatal development?***)

Numerous diseases can adversely affect prenatal development. German measles or (26) _____ is most damaging to the developing organism during the first trimester and can cause a variety of defects. Elevated blood glucose levels can lead to   (27) _____ and can increase chances of premature delivery and other adverse prenatal complications. A sexually transmitted disease called (28) _____ results in similar problems but has its greatest impact on development during the middle and later stages of pregnancy. Another sexually transmitted disease caused by the human immunodeficiency virus, (29) _____, can be passed from mother to infant prior to, during, or after birth.

A number of environmental hazards, such as radiation and pollutants, can also adversely affect prenatal development. Although some pollutants known to be hazardous have been restricted, they still exist in the environment. For example, older houses may expose children to high levels of (30) _____ in paint.

The Mother's State

A number of factors associated with the prenatal environment can influence growth and development. Mothers who are younger than 17 years or older than about 40 years are more likely to experience complications. (***What is one possible reason for this increased risk associated with mother's age?***) Especially devastating are fetal deaths late in pregnancy, termed (31) _____. Mothers who experience prolonged and severe (32) _____ during their pregnancies increase the risk of harm to the fetus. (***What mechanisms might explain how this factor influences fetal development?***) Maternal nutrition can also impact negatively on the developing fetus, particularly if malnutrition occurs during the (33) _____ trimester of pregnancy. Insufficient amounts of folic acid or folate in the mother's diet can lead to (34) _____.

The Father's State

A father's (35) _____ can influence the quality and quantity of his sperm, leading to fertility problems and genetic defects.

4.3   THE PERINATAL ENVIRONMENT

The perinatal environment is the environment surrounding birth and includes drugs administered to the mother, delivery practices, and the immediate social environment following birth. Birth consists of three stages that are, in order of occurrence, (36) _____, (37) _____, and (38) _____. Maternal-fetal specialists, called (39) _____, work with women experiencing high-risk pregnancies and deliveries.

Possible Hazards

During birth, lack of adequate oxygen or (40) _____ can result in brain damage or a neurological condition called (41) _____ that is associated with trouble controlling muscle movements. (***What are some of the potential outcomes for an infant/child who experienced lack of oxygen at birth?***) Another birth complication can result if the fetus is not positioned in the typical head-down position, but instead is positioned feet or buttocks first, called a (42) _____ presentation. Some fetuses are delivered by (43) _____, in which an incision is made in the mother's abdomen and uterus so that the fetus can be removed. Delivery methods and medications administered to the mother during delivery can affect the outcome of the delivery process.

The Mother's Experience

The cultural and social environment surrounding birth can have an impact on the mother's experience of birth. Mothers who receive (44) _____ and are prepared for the birth generally have a more positive experience than other mothers. Some mothers may experience (45) _____, or feelings of sadness, irritability, and depression following a birth. (***What are possible effects of this on the infant?***)

The Father's Experience

Like mothers, fathers experience the birth of a baby as a significant life event, and often feel stressed during delivery and engrossed by the baby after birth. Some fathers even experience some of the same pregnancy symptoms as their partner, called (46) _____.

Sibling Adjustment

In many families, it is not just the mother/father who must adjust to a new baby; there may be older children who need to adjust to the birth of a sibling. Numerous factors, including age, gender, and personality, influence sibling adjustment to this major life event.

4.4   THE NEONATAL ENVIRONMENT

The first month after birth is referred to as the (47) _____ period. There are large cultural differences in how parents interact with their babies during this period.

Breast or Bottle?

Breast feeding is recommended by all major health organizations. Breast milk contains optimal (48) _____ for infants and helps protect them from (49) _____. Despite its benefits to mother and child, not all women breast feed or they discontinue breast feeding earlier than is recommended. (*What are some reasons why more women do not breast feed or breast feed only briefly?*)

Identifying At-Risk Newborns

Some newborns are thought to be (50) _____ or in jeopardy for some reason. To measure general well-being of an infant, the (51) _____ test is administered immediately and at five minutes after birth. (*Can you list the five characteristics assessed by this test?*)

One group of at-risk infants are those born small or with (52) _____. Low birth weight is associated with certain teratogens, poverty, and births of multiples. These babies may experience respiratory problems because their premature lungs have not yet produced enough (53) _____ to function normally. Skin-to-skin contact, or (55) _____, benefits development of these tiny babies, as does therapeutic massage.

Risk and Resilience

Even if infants experience prenatal or perinatal complications, studies show that some are (55) _____; they can get back on track and develop normally. There may be some (56) _____ factors that help prevent at-risk infants from developing problems. Success seems to depend on the child's personal resources or (57) _____ makeup as well as having a favorable postnatal (58) _____. (*What does research indicate with respect to outcomes for these infants?*)

REVIEW OF KEY TERMS

Below is a list of terms and concepts from this chapter. Use these to complete the following sentence definitions. You might also want to try writing definitions in your own words and then checking your definitions with those in the text.

acquired immune deficiency syndrome
   (AIDS)
age of viability
amnion
anencephaly

anoxia
Apgar test
artificial insemination
at risk
blastocyst

breech presentation
cerebral palsy
Cesarean section
chorion
couvade
critical period
differentiation
embryonic period
fetal alcohol syndrome (FAS)
fetal period
germinal period
infertility
in vitro fertilization (IVF)
kangaroo care
Lamaze method
low birth weight (LBW)
miscarriage
myelin

neonatal
organogenesis
perinatal environment
perinatologist
placenta
postpartum depression
prenatal environment
rubella
spina bifida
still birth
sudden infant death syndrome
    (SIDS)
surfactant
syphilis
teratogen
testosterone
thalidomide

1. During the process of _____, all major organs begin to take shape.

2. An inability to get pregnant after a year of trying to do so is termed _____.

3. A mild tranquilizer that typically results in birth defects when taken during pregnancy is _____.

4. Symptoms in children whose mothers drank alcohol during their pregnancy are collectively referred to as _____.

5. Loss (death) of a fetus late in pregnancy is termed _____.

6. Often caused by anoxia, _____ is a neurological problem associated with trouble controlling muscle movements.

7. The _____ is the third prenatal phase, lasting from the 9th week until birth.

8. A medical specialist who focuses on maternal-fetal issues associated with pregnancy and delivery is a _____.

9. Failure of the respiratory system causing the death of a sleeping baby is known as _____.

10. Spontaneous loss of a pregnancy in its early stages, prior to when survival outside the womb is possible, is a _____.

11. A substance that helps infants breathe by preventing the air sacs of the lungs from sticking together is _____.

12. During a procedure called _____, sperm is injected into a woman's uterus.

13. Using a procedure called _____, eggs are fertilized in a laboratory dish and the fertilized eggs are then placed in a woman's uterus.

14. _____ is the first prenatal period, lasting from conception to implantation of the blastula in the wall of the uterus.

15. _____ is a membrane surrounding the amnion that attaches to the uterine lining to gather nourishment for the embryo.

16. The point at about the 24th prenatal week when survival outside the uterus may be possible is called the _____.

17. The weeks following the birth of a baby are referred to as the _____ period.

18. The disease caused by the HIV virus that destroys the immune system is called _____.

19. A period of time during which the developing organism is particularly sensitive to environmental influences is a _____.

20. _____ is a viral infection that can cause a number of serious birth defects if contracted by the mother during the first trimester of pregnancy.

21. The primary male hormone secreted by the testes is _____.

22. A hollow ball of cells formed from the repeated cell division of the zygote is called a _____.

23. Any environmental agent that can produce abnormalities in a developing embryo or fetus is referred to as a _____.

24. A test used to assess a newborn's heart rate, respiration, color, muscle tone, and reflexes immediately and five minutes after birth is the _____.

25. A cluster of symptoms including feelings of sadness, irritability, resentment, and depression that some new mothers experience shortly after a birth is _____.

26. The physical environment of the womb is the _____.

27. The tissue connecting the mother and embryo that provides oxygen and nutrients and eliminates waste products is called _____.

28. A fluid-filled, watertight membrane surrounding the embryo is the _____.

29. A sexually transmitted infection that is most damaging during the middle and later stages of pregnancy and can result in blindness, deafness, heart problems, or brain damage is _____.

30. In a _____, a baby is born feet or buttocks first.

31. The events surrounding birth are collectively referred to as the _____.

32. Resting a newborn on his/her parent's chest to provide skin-to-skin contact is a technique called _____.

33. A lack of adequate oxygen to the brain, which can result in brain damage, occurs with _____.

34. The second prenatal period, lasting from implantation of the blastula to the end of the 8th week of prenatal development is _____

35. Some babies are delivered by _____, a surgical procedure in which an incision is made in the mother's abdomen and uterus so that the baby can be removed.

36. A method of prepared childbirth in which parents learn a set of mental exercises and relaxation techniques is termed _____.

37. Infants who are thought to be likely candidates for developing problems make up the category of _____ infants.

38. Failure of the neural tube to close at the top of the tube causes _____ in which the main portion of the brain fails to develop.

39. The insulating cover on some neurons that facilitates transmission of signals is called _____.

40. Newborns with _____ are smaller than average and are at risk for complications.

41. Some fathers-to-be develop some of the same symptoms as their pregnant partner, an experience called _____.

42. The specialization of cells into distinct functions occurs through the process of _____.

43. A defect in the formation of the spinal column that allows part of the spinal cord to protrude causes _____.

For each multiple choice question, read all alternatives and then select the best answer.

1.   Infertility is defined as
    a.   the period of time prior to conception.
    b.   loss of a pregnancy early in the prenatal period.
    c.   implantation of the zygote in the fallopian tube rather than the uterus.
    d.   inability to get pregnant after a couple has tried to do so for at least a year.

2.   The single cell that is formed by the union of a sperm cell and egg cell is called a(n)
    a.   blastocyst.   c.   zygote.
    b.   embryo.   d.   germ cell.

3.   All major organs begin to form between the 2nd and the 8th week after conception. This
        period of time is called the
    a.   embryonic period.   c.   fetal period.
    b.   germinal period.   d.   age of viability.

4.   The placental barrier
    a.   supports the developing embryo with oxygen and nutrients from the mother.
    b.   blocks dangerous substances from reaching the developing embryo.
    c.   allows maternal blood to pass to the developing embryo.
    d.   is replaced by the umbilical cord at the end of the germinal period.

5.   The presence or absence of testosterone affects the process of sexual differentiation in
    a.   males only.
    b.   females only.
    c.   males and females.
    d.   neither males nor females.

6.   Which of the following accurately represents the process of sex differentiation during the
        prenatal period?
    a.   Sex differentiation is determined at conception by the inheritance of X and Y
            chromosomes.
    b.   Males and females begin with different tissue at conception that evolves into
            different reproductive systems
    c.   Sex differentiation begins around the 7th or 8th week with the development of
            male and female external genitalia.
    d.   Males and females begin with identical tissue that can evolve into male or female
            reproductive systems depending on genetic and hormonal factors.

7.   The age of viability refers to
       a.   the age at which a woman is still able to conceive.
       b.   the point at which a fetus has a reasonable chance of survival outside the womb.
       c.   the point at which the brain and respiratory system are completely formed and
              functional.
       d.   the point at which all the major organs can be identified.

8.   A critical period is a time when
       a.   a fetus can survive outside the womb.
       b.   conception occurs.
       c.   the brain forms.
       d.   a developing organ is particularly sensitive to environmental influences.

9.   Which of the following is NOT a generalization about the effects of teratogens?
       a.   The greater the exposure to a teratogen, the more likely that serious damage will
              occur.
       b.   The effects of teratogens are worse during the time when organs are rapidly
              developing.
       c.   Effects of teratogens are not affected by the quality of the postnatal environment.
       d.   Not all fetuses are equally affected by the same teratogen.

10.   Mothers who smoke cigarettes during pregnancy are at risk of having children with all of
       the following problems EXCEPT
       a.   limb (leg and arm) malformations and auditory defects.
       b.   growth retardation leading to low birth weight.
       c.   respiratory problems.
       d.   behavioral and conduct problems.

11.   Prolonged and severe emotional strain experienced by a mother during pregnancy can
       result in
       a.   a miscarriage.
       b.   prolonged and painful labor.
       c.   a baby who is irritable and has irregular habits.
       d.   all of the above

12.   It is most important for mothers to consume ample amounts of protein, vitamins, and
       calories during
       a.   the first trimester.   c.   the third trimester.
       b.   the second trimester.   d.   before becoming pregnant.

13.   Serious anoxia during the birth process is associated with
       a.   low birth weight.
       b.   cerebral palsy.
       c.   sudden infant death syndrome.
       d.   irritability at birth and mild cognitive deficits.

14.	The experience of childbirth
a.	is universal.
b.	is influenced by cultural factors.
c.	determines the quality of postnatal life.
d.	can be predicted by the experience of pregnancy.

15.	Longitudinal studies of at risk babies
a.	show that most of these babies continue to have problems throughout their lives.
b.	show that most of these children never develop any problems regardless of their experiences.
c.	show that babies at greater risk have a better prognosis because they receive more medical care than babies at less risk.
d.	suggest that children can outgrow their problems when placed in favorable environments.

CRITICAL THINKING QUESTIONS

By answering the following questions, you will strengthen your understanding of the material in this chapter. These questions require higher-level thinking skills such as integration and application of concepts. Sample answers are provided for three of the questions. These illustrate one possibility, but there are other answers you could provide that might be just as good. For the other questions, you can check yourself by referring to the text (a hint is provided), or by asking a peer or your instructor to review your answer.

1.	What advice concerning prenatal care would you give to a woman who has just learned that she is two months pregnant? Provide justification for your answer.
[*Sample answer provided*]

2.	How can the material in this chapter be used to illustrate the <u>interaction</u> of nature and nurture?
[*Sample answer provided*]

3.	Outline the basic developments occurring during each trimester of pregnancy.
[*Sample answer provided*]

4.	How can we structure the environment to optimize development?
[*Hint: There is information about this throughout the chapter, including things that mothers can do (or avoid) while pregnant and things that can be done during and after birth. Also review the section on "Risk and resilience."*]

5.	An increasing number of older women are giving birth to healthy babies. Considering material covered in Chapters 3 and 4, what challenges must these women overcome in order to experience healthy pregnancies and deliveries?
[*Hint: You will want to review the sections on "Chromosome abnormalities" and "Genetic diagnosis and counseling" from Chapter 3 as well as the sections on "Conception" and "Prenatal environment" from Chapter 4. In particular, note the research on how maternal age influences her pregnancy.*]

ANSWERS

Chapter Summary and Guided Review (fill in the blank)
1. zygote
2. infertility
3. artificial insemination
4. in vitro fertilization
5. germinal
6. blastula
7. embryo
8. miscarriage
9. organogenesis
10. chorion
11. placenta
12. neural tube
13. spina bifida
14. anencephaly
15. testosterone
16. fetal period
17. stem cells
18. viability
19. myelin
20. infant states
21. critical period
22. thalidomide
23. sudden infant death syndrome
24. fetal alcohol syndrome
25. cocaine
26. Rubella
27. diabetes
28. syphilis
29. AIDS
30. lead
31. still births
32. stress
33. third (or last)
34. neural tube defects
35. age
36. perinatologists
37. contractions
38. delivery of baby
39. delivery of placenta
40. anoxia
41. cerebral palsy
42. breech
43. Cesarean section
44. social support
45. postpartum depression
46. couvade
47. neonatal
48. nutrition
49. infections
50. at-risk
51. Apgar
52. low birth weight
53. surfactant
54. kangaroo care
55. resilient
56. protective
57. genetic
58. environment

Review of Key Terms
1. organogenesis
2. infertility
3. thalidomide
4. fetal alcohol syndrome
5. still birth
6. cerebral palsy
7. fetal period
8. perinatologist
9. sudden infant death syndrome
10. miscarriage
11. surfactant
12. artificial insemination
13. in vitro fertilization (IVF)
14. germinal period
15. chorion
16. age of viability
17. neonatal
18. acquired immune deficiency syndrome
19. critical period
20. rubella
21. testosterone
22. blastocyst
23. teratogen

24. Apgar test
25. postpartum depression
26. prenatal environment
27. placenta
28. amnion
29. syphilis
30. breech presentation
31. perinatal environment
32. kangaroo care
33. anoxia

34. embryonic period
35. Cesarean section
36. Lamaze method
37. at risk
38. anencephaly
39. myelin
40. low birth weight (LBW)
41. couvade
42. differentiation
43. spina bifida

Multiple-Choice Self-Test

1. D (p. 96)
2. C (p. 97)
3. A (p. 97)
4. A (p. 97)
5. C (p. 98)

6. D (p. 98)
7. B (p. 101)
8. D (p. 103)
9. C (p. 103)
10. A (p. 105-106)

11. D (p. 114)
12. C (p. 115)
13. B (p. 117)
14. B (p. 120)
15. D (p. 128)

Critical Thinking Questions

1.   *I would first note that the vast majority of pregnancies and deliveries are without complications. However, there are a number of things that a woman should be aware of that may affect prenatal development. The first three months are especially important because this is when all the major fetal organs develop (organogenesis). Diseases, such as rubella and drugs such as the prescription thalidomide or the illegal cocaine, can adversely affect the fetus, leading to long-term problems. Maternal nutrition is important, especially during the third trimester when the fetus should be putting on weight and brain development is taking place. Heavy alcohol consumption can lead to a cluster of symptoms, both physical and behavioral, that can plague a child for years. Other factors can influence prenatal development, but women do not always have control of these factors, such as pollution in the air or water and their own age. Finally, these things are risk factors and do not automatically lead to developmental problems. There are large individual differences in their effects, which are influenced by the child's personal resources (e.g., genetic makeup) and the postnatal environment.*

2.   *Prenatal development provides a good illustration of the interaction of nature and nurture. Many environmental factors have the potential to adversely affect development during the prenatal period. Whether, and to what extent, these factors affect a particular fetus depends on the* nature *(e.g., the genetic makeup) of the mother and her unborn child. For example, drinking alcohol during pregnancy can have serious health consequences such as fetal alcohol syndrome (FAS). But there is no single amount of alcohol that is safe for all women. Some babies might exhibit signs of FAS after their mothers consumed small amounts of alcohol during the first trimester. Another baby may be unaffected, even though his mother consumed larger amounts of alcohol throughout pregnancy. Some women and their unborn babies may have genetic makeups that are more resistant to the harmful byproducts of alcohol.*

     Another example is stress. High levels of stress during pregnancy could potentially influence the growth of the fetus because stress releases different levels of hormones in the mother's body. But the same environmental stress might debilitate one woman yet have little effect on another woman. One woman may have inherited a personality that is resistant to stress—she is sturdy and stoic in the face of problems. But another woman might have inherited a personality that leads her to "fall to pieces" at the slightest problem.

So while many environmental factors could influence prenatal development, the nature of the mother and the fetus play a large role in how these factors express themselves. For this reason, it is difficult to say that one factor will affect all pregnancies the same way.

3.   *Pregnancy can be divided into three trimesters, each characterized by amazing changes in the developing child.*

First trimester
- *Includes the germinal period*
  - *Conception and implantation into the wall of the uterus*
  - *Rapid cell division*
- *Includes the embryonic period*
  - *Formation of all major organs during a process of organogenesis (approximately weeks 3 to 8 after conception)*
  - *Heart begins to beat*
  - *The brain is formed from the neural tube*
  - *Sexual differentiation takes place leading to different sex organs for males and females*

Second trimester
- *Continued proliferation and differentiation of neurons*
- *Fetus begins to be more active and mother may begin to feel fetal movements*
- *Sensory organs begin to function by end of second trimester*
- *Reaches the age of viability toward the end of the second trimester; survival outside the womb might be possible*

Third trimester
- *Fetus increases in size, puts on weight*
- *Much brain growth occurs and important neural connections are made*
- *Behavior is increasingly organized*

CHAPTER FIVE

HEALTH AND PHYSICAL DEVELOPMENT

OVERVIEW

This chapter has a great deal of useful information about health and physical changes across the lifespan. It begins with an overview of the endocrine and nervous systems, which act in concert to produce physical growth and facilitate physical behavior. You will learn that there is a tremendous amount of brain growth during the prenatal period and the first two years of life. Brain development, though, is by no means "set in stone" at the end of infancy. The brain continues to be responsive to experiences, and can change to adapt to these experiences, across the lifespan.

This chapter covers the maturation of the reproductive system during adolescence and its changes during adulthood. The discussion of how adolescents interpret and react to the changes of puberty is particularly interesting. Physical behaviors across the lifespan, including motor skills, are also explored in this chapter. One of the most valuable lessons about physical behavior may be one regarding adults: healthy, active adults show little decline in physical and psychological functioning. This contradicts stereotypes of older adults as physically unfit.

Finally, this chapter explores the major health issues that arise during each of the major developmental periods. These include congenital malformations that may be present at birth, accidents throughout childhood, and nutritional problems. Adults face a fairly wide array of health problems, but exercise—both physical and mental—can help slow the effects of aging.

LEARNING OBJECTIVES

After reading and studying the material in this chapter, you should be able to answer the following questions.

5.1 BUILDING BLOCKS OF GROWTH AND DEVELOPMENT

1. How do the workings of the endocrine and nervous systems contribute to growth and development across the lifespan? To what extent are cells responsive to the effects of experience?

2. What is lateralization? How does it affect behavior?

3. How does the brain change with aging?

4. What principles underlie growth? What are examples of each principle?

5. How can we apply a lifespan developmental approach to our understanding of health?

5.2 THE INFANT

6. What is the difference between survival and primitive reflexes? What are examples of each type of reflex? What other capabilities do newborns have?

7. How do locomotion and manipulation of objects evolve during infancy? What factors influence the development of an infant's motor skills?

8. What health issues should be considered during the first two years of life?

5.3 THE CHILD

9. How are children's motor skills advanced relative to those of infants?

10. What factors influence children's health? How can health be optimized during childhood?

5.4 THE ADOLESCENT

11. What physical changes occur during adolescence? What factors contribute to sexual maturity of males and females? What psychological reactions accompany variations in growth spurt and the timing of puberty?

12. What health issues may confront adolescents?

5.5 THE ADULT

13. What physical changes occur during adulthood? What are the psychological implications of the physical changes that occur with aging?

14. What health concerns arise as adults age? How can the health of older adults be preserved?

CHAPTER SUMMARY AND GUIDED REVIEW

The following summary provides an overview of the main points contained in this chapter of the text. Fill in the blanks with terms that appropriately complete the sentence. Scattered throughout the summary are questions in parentheses. These are meant to encourage you to think actively as you read and connect this summary to the more detailed information provided in the text.

5.1 BUILDING BLOCKS OF GROWTH AND DEVELOPMENT

Growth is influenced by both genetic and environmental factors. Individuals who inherit a digestive disorder that interferes with the ability to absorb nutrients, called (1) _____, may not reach their full growth potential. Such individuals are often malnourished and their growth is slowed, but with appropriate treatment, they can get back on track, demonstrating (2) _____.

The Endocrine System

Physical development in humans is driven by the endocrine and nervous systems. The endocrine glands secrete chemical substances called (3) _____ directly into the bloodstream. These substances regulate growth and development. One of these glands, the

(4) _____, regulates other glands and secretes (5) _____ hormone, which stimulates rapid growth and development of body cells. Growth and development are also influenced by the (6) _____ gland. A male fetus develops male reproductive organs when a gene on his Y chromosome triggers development of testes, which in turn secrete a male hormone called (7) _____. This hormone, along with others that are collectively called (8) _____, stimulate the adolescent growth spurt and development of male sex organs. In females, the ovaries produce larger quantities of the primary female hormone, (9) _____, which along with progesterone, is responsible for development of female sex organs and for regulating menstrual cycles. In addition, the (10) _____ glands secrete androgen-like hormones that contribute to the maturation of bones and muscles.

The Nervous System

    The nervous system is made up of billions of nerve cells, or (11) _____. The connection point between neurons is called a (12) _____. By releasing neurotransmitters across this space, neurons can stimulate or inhibit another neuron's action. During development, axons of some neurons become covered by a protective substance in the process of (13) _____, which improves transmission of neural impulses. Early in life, the brain exhibits responsivity or (14) _____ in response to experiences. (**How can normal and abnormal experiences affect the brain?**)

    Brain growth continues beyond infancy, with increased myelination of neurons and specialization. Specialization of the two hemispheres of the cerebral cortex is called (15) _____. Specialization of the brain is evident at birth and becomes stronger throughout childhood. (**What is an example of specialization of the hemispheres?**) Brain development continues through adolescence and may be responsible for advances in adolescent thinking. Changes in the brain during adolescence may also contribute to the increased (16) _____ seen during this period.

    There is some degeneration of the nervous system with aging. Yet the brain is able to generate new neurons throughout the lifespan with the process of (17) _____. The aging brain also shows some ability to change in response to experiences and develop new abilities, illustrating (18) _____. (**How can the aging brain be characterized by both degeneration and plasticity?**)

Principles of Growth

    Several principles underlie the pattern of growth. Growth occurs from the head to the tail, or in a (19) _____ direction. As a result, the head of a newborn is more fully developed than the trunk and legs. Growth also proceeds from the center outward, or in a (20) _____ direction. (**What is an example of this principle of growth?**) According to the (21) _____ principle, physical development proceeds from responses that are global to ones that are differentiated and integrated.

A Lifespan Model of Health

    Health can be viewed from a lifespan developmental model. Accordingly, health is a (22) _____ process that changes in response to choices throughout life. Like all aspects of development, health is influenced by both genetic and environmental factors. Health is (23) _____ and involves both gains and losses. Finally, health occurs in a sociohistorical context, with (24) _____ being especially important.

6.2   THE INFANT

Rapid Growth
Physical growth during infancy is rapid and occurs in bursts.

Newborn Capabilities
Newborns can produce a number of unlearned and automatic responses to stimuli called (25) _____. (***Can you provide examples of some unlearned responses that are essential to survival?***) Some (26) _____ reflexes do not seem to have functional value in our culture and typically disappear during the first year of life. (***Can you provide examples of this type of reflex? What is the significance of the presence and then the absence of these reflexes?***)

Another strength of newborns is the presence of organized patterns of daily activity such as sleep-week cycles called (27) _____. There are individual differences in how much time infants spend in each state, although newborns spend about 70% of their time asleep and only 2-3 hours a day actively taking in their environments. Half of a newborn's sleep time is spent in active, irregular sleep called (28) _____ sleep. This percentage decreases across the lifespan to about 20%. (***What are possible explanations for this change across the lifespan?***) Newborns also have well-developed sensory systems and can learn from their experiences.

Physical Behavior
The average age when half of infants have mastered a skill is the (29) _____ for the skill. Motor behaviors develop according to the cephalocaudal and proximodistal principles. They master (30) _____ skills using large muscle groups before (31) _____ skills that require precise motor control. (***What are some examples of how the orthogenetic principle guides the development of motor skills?***) Infants use a variety of methods to move from one place to another, demonstrating (32) _____. Most infants begin walking at about (33) _____ months of age.

Initially, infants hold objects in a clumsy palm-to-fingers manner called the (34) _____. By around 9 to 12 months, infants can pick up objects using only their thumb and one other finger in a (35) _____ grasp. This development occurs sometime after infants have gained control of their arms and hands and thus is an example of the (36) _____ direction of development. Acquisition of motor skills is largely directed by (37) _____, although experience affects the (38) _____ at which infants progress through the sequence of motor milestones. (***How do sleep position and "walker" use affect crawling and walking?***)

According to Thelen's (39) _____ approach, motor development is influenced by infants' use of feedback from different movements. Before a new motor skill emerges, infants often engage in (40) _____, when they repeat individual components of the skill. In this view, motor skills emerge from a combination of maturation and experience.

Health and Wellness
Some infants are born early or (41) _____ and struggle with health issues during their first months and beyond. Most deaths during the first year of life are caused by

(42) _____ present at birth that may have arisen from either genetic factors or prenatal events.

5.3 THE CHILD
Steady Growth
Growth from infancy to adolescence is slow but steady, and continues to be guided by cephalocaudal and proximodistal principles.

Physical Behavior
Children learn to control their movements in a (43) _____ environment, extending earlier skills mastered in a stationary environment. Motor skills are refined during childhood, and eye/hand coordination improves. Children also respond faster, or have better (44) _____ as they develop.

Health and Wellness
Children's health is influenced by their parent's education level and (45) _____, as well as their own eating habits. The leading cause of death during childhood is (46) _____, particularly those involving motor vehicles. Good health can be fostered with good nutrition and physical activity, but today's lifestyles often make it difficult to follow healthy recommendations. An estimate of body fat derived from a person's weight and height called (47) _____ can indicate whether someone is in a healthy range. An increasing number of children are 20% or more overweight, meeting the criteria for (48) _____.

5.4 THE ADOLESCENT
Adolescents experience significant physical changes as they go through (49) _____ and become sexually mature.

The Growth Spurt
Adolescents experience rapid growth, called the (50) _____. Females typically begin their growth spurt about two years before males. (*What are the typical ages of rapid growth for males and females?*)

Sexual Maturation
Starting in middle childhood, the adrenal glands increase production of adrenal androgens in a process of (51) _____, a precursor to puberty. Puberty for girls is marked by (52) _____, their first menstruation, at about 12 or 13 years of age. For boys, the event typically used to mark puberty is (53) _____ or first ejaculation, which occurs around 13 or 14 years of age. There is large variation in the timing of sexual maturation. Rate of development is largely determined by (54) _____ factors, although environment also plays a role in timing of maturation, as indicated by the (55) _____ or the tendency for earlier maturation and larger body size in industrialized societies.

Emotional responses to puberty are mixed for males and females, but tend to be stronger in females. (*How do pubertal changes affect parent-child relations?*) The psychological impact of being an early versus a late developer is different for males and females. Early maturation often has advantages for (56) _____ over their later-maturing peers. (***What are some*** *of these advantages and are they long-lasting?*) Early development is not really an advantage for girls and may in fact be a disadvantage. Late maturers of both sexes often experience some anxiety, but late-maturing (57) _____ seem to experience the most disadvantages. For children who are small for age, entering puberty late but otherwise growing at a near-normal rate, their (58) _____ may lead to emotional stress until they catch up to their peers.

Physical Behavior

Advances in strength and physical competence continue throughout adolescence. Gender differences emerge as boys' physical performance continues to increase while girls' physical performance levels off or declines. Biological differences in muscle mass may account for some of this difference, but (59) _____ also contributes.

Health and Wellness

For most, adolescence is a period of peak physical fitness and health. An increasing number of teens, though, are overweight and experience health problems as a result. In particular, being overweight can increase a person's risk for (60) _____, or high levels of sugar in the blood. The leading causes of death during adolescence are accidents and violence, including (61) _____. Adolescents may also compromise their health with lifestyle choices such as smoking cigarettes or drinking (62) _____.

5.5   THE ADULT
Typical Changes

Although physical aging occurs over most of the lifespan, outward signs are often not noticed until one's (63) _____. Wrinkles, thinning and graying hair, and extra weight are common physical changes in middle age. Older adults lose muscle mass, largely because they are less active than younger adults.

The average older adult has poorer physical functioning than younger adults, although not all older people experience declines in physical functioning. Many organ systems show a decrease in (64) _____, which is the ability to respond to demands for above-normal output. A majority of adults over the age of 65 have some sort of chronic impairment. Nonetheless, many older adults report that they are in good health.

Negative stereotypes about older adults can lead to prejudice against them or (65) _____. Older adults strive to avoid being classified in the "old" category. Despite some physical declines, most older adults have a good sense of well-being.

The Reproductive System

Hormone levels fluctuate in both sexes across the lifespan, although hormone changes typically affect women more than men. Some women experience (66) _____, a cluster of symptoms including breast tenderness and irritability, just before menstruation. Both premenstrual and menstrual symptoms are affected by biological factors and social factors. (*What are some of the social factors that contribute to symptoms?*)

The end of menstrual periods occurs sometime during midlife and is called (67) _____. The lower levels of female hormones that are produced may result in vaginal dryness and (68) _____ for some women. Some women have psychological symptoms such as irritability and depression in connection with menopause. Some symptoms may be severe enough to warrant treatment with (69) _____, but side effects of this treatment have reduced its popularity.

Men also experience loss of reproductive capacity, but more gradually than women, during a period of time referred to as (70) _____.

Slowing Down

A number of physical behaviors are carried out at a (71) _____ pace as we get older. Slowing is quite variable among adults and relates to exercise of physical skills.

Disease, Disuse, or Abuse?

Chronic disease often contributes to some of the declines among older adults. In addition, declines in physical functioning may relate to (72) _____ of the body, as well as to abuses of the body.

Health and Wellness

Some older adults may experience extreme bone loss or (73) _____, leaving bones fragile. (*What can be done to prevent this disease?*) Other adults have a joint problem called (74) _____ that may limit their activities.

Successful Aging

The "Nun Study" has shown that longevity and health are influenced by (75) _____ level. At every age studied, those with greater education had lower risk of death. The study also showed that (76) _____, both physical and mental, contributed to longer and healthier lives.

REVIEW OF KEY TERMS

Below is a list of terms and concepts from this chapter. Use these to complete the following sentence definitions. You might also want to try writing definitions in your own words and then checking your definitions with those in the text.

adolescent growth spurt	gross motor skills
adrenarche	growth hormone
ageism	hormone replacement therapy (HRT)
androgens	hot flashes
andropause	lateralization
body mass index (BMI)	locomotion
catch-up growth	menarche
celiac disease	menopause
cephalocaudal principle	myelination
congenital malformations	neurogenesis
constitutional growth delay	neuron
developmental norm	obesity
diabetes	orthogenetic principle
dynamic systems theory	osteoarthritis
endocrine gland	osteoporosis
estrogen	pincer grasp
fine motor skills	pituitary gland

plasticity
premenstrual syndrome (PMS)
proximodistal principle
puberty
reaction time
reflex(es)
REM sleep

reserve capacity
rhythmic stereotypies
secular trend
semenarche
synapse
ulnar grasp

1. Male hormones, including testosterone, that trigger the adolescent growth spurt and development of male sex organs are collectively called _____.

2. Unlearned and automatic responses to stimuli are called _____.

3. Children show mastery of _____ when they engage in movements that require precise control of their hands or feet.

4. Located at the base of the brain, the _____ is an endocrine gland that is responsible for regulating other glands and producing growth hormone.

5. According to the _____, growth proceeds in a head to tail direction.

6. Cells that have not yet been committed to a particular function and have the capacity to be shaped by experience are said to be in a state of _____.

7. Specialization of the left and right hemispheres of the cerebral cortex is referred to as _____.

8. The rapid increase in growth at the end of childhood is the _____.

9. Aging of the male reproductive system is known as _____.

10. The _____ is the tendency for earlier maturation and larger body size in industrialized societies over time.

11. A disease resulting from a loss of minerals, causing deterioration of bone tissue is _____.

12. Some women experience _____, a cluster of symptoms including breast tenderness, a bloated feeling, irritability, and moodiness that occur just before menstruation.

13. Secreted by the pituitary gland, _____ stimulates growth and development of body cells.

14. Some children may experience _____ and get back on their genetically programmed growth course after a growth delay.

15. Some women may experience _____, which are sudden, brief, and unpredictable sensations of warmth that may be followed by a cold shiver.

16. The process of generating new neurons is called _____.

17. A(n) _____ is a ductless gland that secretes hormones directly into the bloodstream.

18. A female hormone secreted by the ovaries that stimulates development of female sex organs and regulates menstrual cycles is _____.

19. According to the _____, growth proceeds from the central portions of the body to the extremities.

20. The _____ is evident when children use their thumb in opposition to one other finger in order to pick up and manipulate objects.

21. The point when a person reaches sexual maturity and acquires secondary sexual characteristics is called _____.

22. A _____ is the basic cell of the nervous system that transmits and receives signals.

23. Movement from one place to another is accomplished through various methods of _____.

24. A _____ represents the average age when half of all infants can master a particular skill.

25. A girl's first menstrual period is referred to as _____.

26. The space between the axon of one neuron and the dendrites of another neuron is the _____.

27. An active, irregular sleep pattern that includes rapid eye movements and is associated with brain-wave activity resembling wakefulness is _____.

28. The process of _____, which coats the axon of some neurons with a waxy substance, facilitates transmission of neural impulses.

29. Women experience _____ when their menstrual periods end sometime during midlife.

30. The testes secrete a male hormone called _____.

31. The ability of an organ system to respond to a request for excess output is known as its
    _____.

32. Children who are small for their age and enter puberty later than their peers, yet are
    growing at a near-normal rate may be experiencing _____.

33. According to the _____, growth proceeds from being global and
    undifferentiated to being increasingly specific, differentiated, and integrated.

34. Children use their _____ when they run or otherwise make movements that
    involve large muscle groups.

35. Infants often hold objects by pressing their palm against their outer fingers, a clumsy grip
    called the _____.

36. According to the _____, children use sensory feedback to their movements to
    develop more sophisticated behavior patterns.

37. The speed with which people can respond to a task is their _____.

38. Prejudice against older adults, or _____, can result from the negative
    stereotypes that people hold.

39. Some women take _____ to reduce the symptoms associated with
    menopause.

40. A measure of body fat known as the _____ is calculated from a person's
    height and weight.

41. Some older adults experience _____, a joint problem that results from
    gradual deterioration of the protective cartilage surrounding bones.

42. Before a new motor skill emerges in its full form, infants often engage in
    _____ or repetitive movements of parts of the skill.

43. A boy's first ejaculation is referred to as _____.

44. Defects from genetic factors or prenatal events that are present at birth are collectively
    called _____.

45. Being 20% or more overweight is considered _____.

46. Slow growth may occur in children with _____, a genetic condition in which
    glutens cause an immune response that damages the small intestine.

47.   Increased production of adrenal hormones starting around 6 to 8 years of age marks the period of _____.

48.   The health condition of _____ is characterized by high levels of sugar in the blood.

MULTIPLE-CHOICE SELF-TEST

For each multiple choice question, read all alternatives and then select the best answer.

1.   Which structure is considered the "master gland" of the endocrine system?
       a.   Thyroid gland   c.   Adrenal gland
       b.   Hypothalamus   d.   Pituitary gland

2.   Plasticity ensures that the brain
       a.   can recover from any sort of damage.
       b.   receives the maximum benefits from stimulation throughout the lifespan.
       c.   is not influenced by adverse environments.
       d.   is responsive to individual experiences.

3.   Lateralization is a process by which
       a.   one hemisphere takes over some functions of the other hemisphere after brain damage to the other hemisphere has occurred.
       b.   specialization of the functions of the left and right hemisphere occurs.
       c.   neurons in the brain develop rapidly.
       d.   neurons are covered by a myelin sheath.

4.   As the body ages from childhood to adulthood, the brain
       a.   develops more neurons.
       b.   begins to form a myelin sheath around many neurons.
       c.   grows longer dendrites that may form new connections with other neurons.
       d.   releases large quantities of neurotransmitters.

5.   The cephalocaudal principle predicts that
       a.   growth of the brain and spinal cord will be the last to occur.
       b.   growth will proceed from bones and cartilage to internal organs.
       c.   growth will proceed from head to tail.
       d.   growth will proceed from the midline to the extremities.

6.   Based on the cephalocaudal principle of growth, infants typically can _____ before they can _____.
       a.   stand; roll over
       b.   roll over; control their arms or hands
       c.   walk backward; walk up steps
       d.   sit; walk

7. The primitive reflexes
   a. are essential to survival.
   b. disappear sometime during infancy.
   c. include rooting, sucking, and swallowing.
   d. protect the infant from various adverse conditions.

8. Research on infant states suggests that
   a. there is large variability in amount of time infants spend in different states.
   b. infants are remarkably similar in the amount of time spent in different states.
   c. increased age brings an increase in the number of behavioral states that infants can experience.
   d. neurological health can be predicted by amount of time spent in different states.

9. The developmental norm for grasping small objects is _____ months of age, and the developmental norm for standing alone is _____ months of age.
   a. 6; 18   c. 4; 11
   b. 2; 6   d. 12; 8

10. According to the dynamic systems approach,
    a. motor movements unfold according to a strict genetic plan.
    b. children adjust their movements in response to sensory feedback.
    c. children learn to walk by watching the movements of those around them.
    d. motor movements are correlated with mental capabilities.

11. Which of the following hormone(s) trigger the adolescent growth spurt?
    a. Progesterone   c. Activating hormones
    b. Androgens   d. Thyroxine

12. The secular trend refers to
    a. earlier maturation and decreased body size from generation to generation.
    b. later maturation and decreased body size from generation to generation.
    c. historical changes in life expectancy from generation to generation.
    d. earlier maturation and increased body size from generation to generation.

13. Regarding the timing of maturation,
    a. Sheila, who matures early, is likely to be more popular than Mary, who matures late.
    b. Bill, who matures late, is likely to be more academically skilled than Mark, who matures early.
    c. Tom, who matures early, is likely to be confident and poised relative to Steve, who matures late.
    d. Mike, who matures "on time," is likely to be viewed most favorably by his parents and teachers, relative to other boys in his class who mature early or late.

14. The apparent decline of physical performance of females by the end of adolescence
    a.   is a myth not supported by any data.
    b.   results largely from socialization differences between males and females.
    c.   results from an overall decline in the proportion of muscle mass relative to fat.
    d.   is similar to the decline that occurs in males.

15. Menopause is a time when
    a.   women no longer ovulate or menstruate.
    b.   most women experience mood swings for extended periods of time.
    c.   women continue to ovulate but do not menstruate.
    d.   women experience an increase in hormone levels.

CRITICAL THINKING QUESTIONS

By answering the following questions, you will strengthen your understanding of the material in this chapter. These questions require higher-level thinking skills such as integration and application of concepts. Sample answers are provided for three of the questions. These illustrate one possibility, but there are other answers you could provide that might be just as good. For the other questions, you can check yourself by referring to the text (a hint is provided), or by asking a peer or your instructor to review your answer.

1.   Suppose you are in charge of writing a newsletter for adults who are approaching retirement age. In one issue of the newsletter, you want to write an informative article on physical changes that these adults might experience as they age. What would this article say?
      [*Sample answer provided*]

2.   What are the psychological implications of the timing of puberty?
      [*Sample answer provided*]

3.   What changes occur in the nervous system early in life and late in life?
      [*Sample answer provided*]

4.   What are perhaps two of the most important lifestyle choices you can make to improve your health across the lifespan?
      [*Hint: Review the subsections on "Health and wellness" in the sections on The Child, The Adolescent, and The Adult.*]

5.   What are the greatest risks to health and wellness at each period of the lifespan and how could each risk be reduced?
      [*Hint: Review the subsections on "Health and wellness" in the sections on The Infant, The Child, The Adolescent, and The Adult.*]

ANSWERS

Summary and Guided Review (fill in the blank)

1. celiac disease
2. catch-up growth
3. hormones
4. pituitary
5. growth
6. thyroid
7. testosterone
8. androgens
9. estrogen
10. adrenal
11. neurons
12. synapse
13. myelination
14. plasticity
15. lateralization
16. risk-taking
17. neurogenesis
18. plasticity
19. cephalocaudal
20. proximodistal
21. orthogenetic
22. life-long
23. multidimensional
24. socioeconomic status
25. reflexes
26. primitive
27. behavioral states
28. REM
29. developmental norm
30. gross motor
31. fine motor
32. locomotion
33. twelve
34. ulnar
35. pincer
36. proximodistal
37. maturation
38. rate
39. dynamic systems
40. rhythmic stereotypies
41. prematurely
42. congenital malformations
43. changing
44. reaction times
45. socioeconomic status
46. accidents
47. body mass index (BMI)
48. obesity
49. puberty
50. growth spurt
51. adrenarche
52. menarche
53. semenarche
54. genetic
55. secular trend
56. males
57. males
58. constitutional growth delay
59. socialization
60. diabetes
61. suicide
62. alcohol
63. 40s
64. reserve capacity
65. ageism
66. premenstrual syndrome
67. menopause
68. hot flashes
69. hormone replacement therapy
70. andropause
71. slower
72. disuse
73. osteoporosis
74. osteoarthritis
75. education
76. activity

Review of Key Terms

1. androgens
2. reflexes
3. fine motor skills
4. pituitary gland
5. cephalocaudal principle
6. plasticity
7. lateralization
8. adolescent growth spurt

9. andropause
10. secular trend
11. osteoporosis
12. premenstrual syndrome (PMS)
13. growth hormone
14. catch-up growth
15. hot flashes
16. neurogenesis
17. endocrine gland
18. estrogen
19. proximodistal principle
20. pincer grasp
21. puberty
22. neuron
23. locomotion
24. developmental norm
25. menarche
26. synapse
27. REM sleep
28. myelination

29. menopause
30. testosterone
31. reserve capacity
32. constitutional growth delay
33. orthogenetic principle
34. gross motor skills
35. ulnar grasp
36. dynamic systems theory
37. reaction time
38. ageism
39. hormone replacement therapy (HRT)
40. body mass index (BMI)
41. osteoarthritis
42. rhythmic stereotypies
43. semenarche
44. congenital malformations
45. obesity
46. celiac disease
47. adrenarche
48. diabetes

Multiple-Choice Self-Test

1. D (p. 135)
2. D (p. 139)
3. B (p. 139)
4. C (p. 140)
5. C (p. 141)

6. D (p. 141)
7. B (p. 143)
8. A (p. 143)
9. C (p. 145; 148)
10. B (p. 149)

11. B (p. 155)
12. D (p. 157)
13. C (p. 158-159)
14. B (p. 159-160)
15. A (p. 164)

Critical Thinking Questions

1.   *Worried about a few physical changes as you approach retirement? Well, it's not as bad as you may have heard. Sure, you have a few wrinkles, some gray hair, and a little extra weight around the middle. It will probably take you longer to do the things you sped through as a young adult. For women, menopause may mean hot flashes and vaginal dryness, making intercourse more painful. Old age may also bring a loss of bone mass, or osteoporosis, which can lead to fractures and seriously erode quality of life. Unfortunately, statistics indicate that a majority of older adults have some sort of chronic impairment, such as arthritis. Despite this, a majority of older adults report that their health is actually quite good, suggesting that they take impairments in stride or find ways to work around them.*

The good news is that if you take care of yourself and remain healthy and active, you can look forward to a satisfying old age. Older adults who are disease free perform just as well on many physical tasks as younger adults. Many older adults perform tasks more slowly because they are out of shape; continuing to exercise may reduce this disadvantage of aging. In many ways, the saying, "use it or lose it," applies to the physical functioning of older adults.

2.   *The psychological effects of the timing of puberty are different for boys and girls. In general, boys who mature earlier than their peers experience some advantages. They are rated as more socially competent, self-assured, and popular. However, early-maturing boys are likely to get involved in substance abuse earlier than other boys. Early maturation for boys may be largely advantageous because it makes them look more mature, whether or not they really are. Late-maturing boys experience several disadvantages, including being less self-assured. They score somewhat lower on achievement tests and are more likely to have behavior problems.*

Early-maturing girls may experience several disadvantages. They may feel awkward if they are one of the only girls in their peer group to develop breasts. While boys going through puberty might welcome the increase in size, deepening of their voices, and sexual maturity, girls going through puberty often don't feel the same way about getting larger and becoming sexually mature. In addition, parents and society seem to be more uncomfortable with girls' emerging sexuality than with boys' emerging sexuality. This may help explain why girls who mature early experience some problems with self-esteem. Another problem for early-maturing girls is that they tend to socialize with older peers, which exposes them to dating, drinking, and sex at an earlier age than their on-time peers. Girls who mature late may experience some anxiety, wondering when they will catch up to their peers. But for the most part, there are no significant disadvantages for late-maturing girls, like there are for late-maturing boys.

In sum, early-maturing girls and late-maturing boys experience more problems than other adolescents. But the influence of the timing of puberty also depends on other individual characteristics, such as personality, and how the individual interprets the events of puberty.

3.   *Early in life, the nervous system changes in significant ways. The process of myelination is occurring rapidly during infancy and then tapers off throughout childhood and adolescence. Myelination enables neurons to send and receive messages more efficiently. The young brain is also responsive to the individual's experiences and can develop in a variety of ways, showing plasticity. The greatest period of plasticity is infancy, when the brain is vulnerable to damage, but also is more capable of recovering from damage than it will be later in life. The young brain is becoming increasingly organized with areas specialized for specific functions. Lateralization of the brain also occurs early in life. This means that the two hemispheres of the brain do not develop identically, but develop in different ways to specialize in different functions. Once it reaches maturity, it is more difficult for an area of the brain that is dedicated to one function to pick up another function.*

At the other end of the age spectrum, there is some gradual and mild degeneration within the nervous system. Neurons are lost and there is reduced functioning of many of the remaining neurons. The protective myelin covering many neurons begins to deteriorate, leading to a general slowing of the older nervous system. In addition, there are often decreases in levels of some neurotransmitters, which can lead to a variety of problems depending on the type of neurotransmitter. There is still some plasticity in the older brain, though, especially for individuals who remain active and mentally involved.

CHAPTER SIX

SENSATION, PERCEPTION, AND ATTENTION

OVERVIEW

You should take note of the point at the beginning of this chapter: sensation and perception are at the very heart of human functioning. Without sensation and perception, there would be no meaningful cognitive activity or social interactions, no enjoyable walks through the neighborhood, and no ability to appreciate music or food. The centrality of sensation and perception makes it important to understand changes in these processes across the lifespan.

Many significant changes in perceptual processes occur during infancy, with few changes during childhood, adolescence, and early adulthood. During middle and older adulthood, there are again some notable changes in perceptual processes. Thus, there is weighty coverage of vision, hearing, taste, smell, touch, temperature, and pain in the sections on "The Infant" and "The Adult." Additionally, the section on infants discusses several clever methods of assessing infants' perceptual abilities. The section on children concentrates on the development of attention processes as well as problems of attention, including research on attention deficit hyperactivity disorder.

LEARNING OBJECTIVES

After reading and studying the material in this chapter, you should be able to answer the following questions.

6.1   ISSUES OF NATURE AND NURTURE
1.   What are the views of constructivists and nativists on the nature/nurture issue as it relates to sensation and perception?

6.2   THE INFANT
2.   How are perceptual abilities of infants assessed?

3.   What are infants' visual capabilities? What sorts of things do infants prefer to look at?

4.   What are the auditory capabilities of infants? What do researchers know about infants' abilities to perceive speech?

5.   What are the taste and smell capabilities of infants? To what extent are infants sensitive to touch, temperature, and pain?

6.   To what extent can infants integrate their sensory experiences? What is an example of cross-modal perception?

7.   What role do early experiences play in development of perceptions? What factors contribute to normal visual perception?

6.3   THE CHILD

8.   What changes occur in attention throughout childhood?

9.   What are the main features and likely causes of attention deficit disorder?

6.4   THE ADOLESCENT

10.   How can hearing loss be minimized across the lifespan, beginning with adolescence?

6.5   THE ADULT

11.   What changes occur in visual capabilities and visual perception during adulthood?

12.   What changes in auditory capabilities and speech perception occur during adulthood?

13.   What changes occur in taste and smell, and in sensitivity to touch, temperature, and pain during adulthood?

CHAPTER SUMMARY AND GUIDED REVIEW

The following summary provides an overview of the main points contained in this chapter of the text. Fill in the blanks with terms that appropriately complete the sentence. Scattered throughout the summary are questions in parentheses. These are meant to encourage you to think actively as you read and connect this summary to the more detailed information provided in the text.

The process by which sensory receptors detect stimuli and transmit it to the brain is called
(1) _____, and the process of interpreting this information is called
(2) _____. These processes are at the center of human understanding.

6.1   ISSUES OF NATURE AND NURTURE

One issue concerning perceptual development is whether infants are born with knowledge or need to acquire all knowledge through their senses. The position that infants begin life as blank slates is on the (3) _____ side of this issue and is held by (4) _____, who believe that we build an understanding of the world. On the other side of the issue, the
(5) _____ argued that infants are born with knowledge, which represents the
(6) _____ side of the nature/nurture issue.

6.2   THE INFANT

Assessing Sensory and Perceptual Abilities

Infants' perceptual capabilities are often assessed by measuring decreased responding to a stimulus that has been presented repeatedly, a technique called (7) _____. (***Can you explain the rationale of this approach?***) Another technique is to present two stimuli to infants and measure their (8) _____, which shows that they can discriminate the two stimuli. Sometimes, researchers measure electrical activity of the brain in response to stimulation, a technique called (9) _____. Infants can also be taught to respond a certain way when a particular stimulus is presented; their response to a second stimulus can then be measured to determine whether they perceive the stimuli to be similar or different. This learning technique is called (10) _____.

Vision

A newborn's ability to perceive visual detail, or their (11) _____, is poor. This may result from problems with visual (12) _____, which refers to the changing shape of the lens of the eye to bring objects at varying distances into focus. Young infants can visually detect differences in stimuli and prefer to look at (13) _____ stimuli such as faces. (*Is the apparent preference for faces really a preference for faces? Why or why not?*) Young infants tend to be attracted to patterns that have light-dark transitions or (14) _____, stimuli that move, and stimuli that are moderately complex. In general, we can conclude that infants prefer to look at what they can see well.

At around 2 months of age, infants begin to visually explore the entire field of a figure or form, rather than just an exterior border of the figure. They also begin to prefer (15) _____ faces over scrambled facial features. This might suggest that infants are beginning to form (16) _____ for familiar objects.

Another aspect of visual perception is perception of 3D space or (17) _____. Infants develop the ability to perceive an object as its same size despite changes in the retinal image of the object as its distance from the eyes changes, known as (18) _____. Depth perception has been assessed using an apparatus called the (19) _____, which has an apparent drop-off. Early research showed that infants of crawling age perceived depth, demonstrated by avoiding the drop-off. A major limitation of this technique was that infants needed to be able to crawl. By modifying the testing procedures, researchers have tested infants as young as 2 months and found that while these young infants can perceive the visual cliff, they have not yet learned to (20) _____ drop-offs.

An important perceptual task for infants is learning to distinguish one object from another. To organize the world of objects, infants use common motion, or the expectation that all parts of an object will move in the same direction at the same time, as a cue to establish the boundaries of objects. In addition, infants seem to be equipped with organized systems of knowledge, called (21) _____, that help them understand their world.

Hearing

Newborns' auditory capabilities are well developed. Infants are able to discriminate basic speech sounds, or (22) _____, early in life. In fact, unlike adults, infants can discriminate speech sounds of languages not spoken in the home. Familiarity with voices begins to develop prenatally, and newborns are able to recognize their mothers' voices. (*Can you describe how this has been studied?*) Infants can also discriminate between rhythmic music and non-rhythmic noise soon after birth.

The Chemical Senses: Taste and Smell

The sense of taste and the sense of smell, also called (23) _____, are well developed at birth. Both of these senses rely on detection and interpretation of (24) _____. Infants show distinct taste preferences and those who are breast fed can recognize their mothers on the basis of smell. Flavor preferences are very responsive to the effects of (25) _____.

Touch, Temperature, and Pain

Newborns are sensitive to tactile stimulation and may respond with reflexes if touched in certain areas. Newborns are also sensitive to temperature and to pain. The intensity of a painful

experience can be communicated by the quality of an infant's (26) _____.
Research suggests that infants learn from experience to anticipate pain with certain stimuli.

Integrating Sensory Information

Putting together information from different senses can help an infant make sense of the world. Some senses seem to be integrated earlier than others. For example, touch and vision, as well as vision and hearing, seem to be linked very early.

The ability to recognize through one sense modality an object that is familiar through another sense modality is called (27) _____. (*Can you provide an example of this?*) Not all forms of this occur reliably until 4-7 months of age.

Influences on Early Perceptual Development

The presence of such significant early perceptual capabilities suggests that (28) _____ plays a role in perceptual development. Early experiences are also necessary for normal development and there seems to be a window of time, or (29) _____, when particular experiences are especially important to normal perceptual development. Infants need to be exposed to a variety of (30) _____ stimulation for neurons in the visual areas of the brain to develop normally. Infants also need to be exposed to movement in their environment, especially if they are not able to move. Some infants are not able to receive normal visual experiences because they are born with clouded lenses or (31) _____. The earlier this problem can be corrected, the better an infant's chances for normal perceptual development. Even after correction, there may be some later problems with visual perception due to (32) _____ effects in which the brain has been sensitized by the early visual deprivation.

Infants actively seek and explore their environments, which means they typically expose themselves to appropriate sensory experiences. According to Eleanor Gibson, infants progress through three phases of exploratory behavior. For the first few months, they explore their immediate surroundings by taking in information through their (33) _____. From about 5 to 7 months, they explore (34) _____ with their eyes and hands. Once they learn to crawl, they are able to explore the larger environment around them. Finally, the way we perceive and interpret sensory experiences varies across cultures. (*What are some examples of these variations?*)

6.3   THE CHILD
The Development of Attention

Although much of sensory and perceptual development is complete by the end of infancy, children need to develop better (35) _____, the selective focusing of perception and cognition on some particular aspect of the environment. Attention span increases during childhood, and attention becomes more (36) _____. (*What evidence is there to support this conclusion?*) In addition, visual search becomes more (37) _____ or exhaustive during childhood.

Problems of Attention

A common disorder, attention deficit hyperactivity disorder (ADHD), may be diagnosed if a child displays regular inattention, often acts before thinking or is (38) _____, and is restless or (39) _____. Symptoms of ADHD typically persist across the lifespan, although expression of the symptoms may change with age. ADHD is likely caused by different brain chemistry, although why the chemistry differs is unclear. Treatment for ADHD often involves prescribing (40) _____ to increase activity in the parts of the brain involved in attention and concentration. In combination with this, (41) _____ treatment is also beneficial.

6.4   THE ADOLESCENT

Attention

Attention span continues to increase during adolescence as those parts of the brain involved in attention become fully myelinated. Adolescents also become more efficient at ignoring (42) _____ information so that they can focus their attention more effectively. Adolescents tend to use more efficient strategies for scanning visual displays.

Hearing

The auditory sense should be at peak levels of performance during adolescence. However, some adolescents will sustain damage to their hearing through exposure to (43) _____. The most common symptom of damage to the auditory system is (44) _____ or ringing sounds in one or both ears. (***What measures can be taken to protect hearing?***)

Another Look at the Chemical Senses

The perception of a savory or "brothy" flavor named (45) _____ may influence food preferences. Adolescents may be more adventuresome than children when it comes to trying new foods.

Sensitivity to smell varies somewhat by gender, with (46) _____ generally displaying greater sensitivity.

6.5   THE ADULT

Sensory and perceptual capabilities gradually decline with age. There are increases in (47) _____, which means that a higher level of stimulation is needed for sensory detection as we age. Older people may also have trouble processing sensory information.

Vision

A number of changes occur within the eye as we age. Older people tend to be less sensitive to dim light, and the process of adjusting to low light levels, (48) _____, does not function as well for older people. Many adults experience a loss of near vision starting in their 40s from a condition called (49) _____ caused by thickening of the lens. The ability to clearly see details, known as (50) _____, normally decreases with age. Significant decreases, however, are usually associated with pathological conditions. One such condition is (51) _____, in which the lens of the eye becomes opaque and limits the amount of light entering the eye. Blurry vision and loss of vision from the center of the visual field are symptoms of age-related (52) _____. Loss of peripheral vision can result from (53) _____, a group of disorders that involve deterioration of the cells of the retina. Vision loss may also occur from (54) _____ in which there is increased fluid pressure in the eye, which can eventually lead to blindness. (***What are some implications of these changes in visual capabilities?***)

Research shows that older adults perform worse on visual search tasks than younger adults, particularly when there are numerous distractions. Older adults have the greatest difficulties processing visual information in situations that are (55) _____ and (56) _____, but have few problems with familiar or simple tasks.

Hearing

Hearing problems are often associated with aging. One common problem is decreased sensitivity to high-frequency sounds, a condition called (57) _____. Older adults seem to have more trouble with speech perception than younger adults, especially under poor listening conditions, such as a great deal of (58) _____. As with visual perception, older adults perform better on auditory tasks that are familiar or meaningful to them.

Aging of the Chemical Senses

Sensory thresholds for some tastes increase with age. Taste for (59) _____ substances does not seem to change markedly across the lifespan. Sensitivity to odors and the ability to discriminate between them are highest from childhood to middle adulthood and then decline in old age. Decreases in taste and smell can affect recognition of different foods, although losses in the sense of (60) _____ seem to contribute more to problems of food recognition.

Touch, Temperature, and Pain

Sensitivity to touch and changes in temperature decrease with age. Sensitivity to pain seems to both increase and decrease in older adults. Older adults are less likely to report mild forms of pain, but are likely to report stronger forms of pain stimulation as being especially painful.

The Adult in Perspective

The most serious age changes in perception occur with vision and hearing. Most older adults suffer some losses, although overall levels are fairly good.

REVIEW OF KEY TERMS

Below is a list of terms and concepts from this chapter. Use these to complete the following sentence definitions. You might also want to try writing definitions in your own words and then checking your definitions with those in the text.

age-related macular degeneration
attention
attention deficit hyperactivity
    disorder (ADHD)
cataracts
cochlear implant
constructivists
contour

cross-modal perception
dark adaptation
glaucoma
habituation
intuitive theories
nativists
olfaction
orienting system

perception   sensory threshold
phoneme   size constancy
presbycusis   tinnitus
presbyopia   umami
retinitis pigmentosa (RP)   visual accommodation
selective attention   visual acuity
sensation   visual cliff
sensitive period

1.   A group of hereditary disorders called _____ involve the gradual
      deterioration of the cells of the retina.

2.   The process of _____ produces changes in the shape of the lens to bring
      objects at varying distances into focus.

3.   Someone who believes that infants enter the world with knowledge that permits them to
      perceive meaningful patterns in the world is a(n) _____.

4.   The tendency to perceive an object as its same size despite changes in the retinal image
      of the object as its distance from the eyes changes is called _____.

5.   The detection of stimuli by the sensory receptors and the transmission of this information
      to the brain is the process of _____.

6.   Sense of smell, which is mediated by receptors in the nasal passage, is also called
      _____.

7.   The _____ is an apparatus with an apparent drop-off that is used to assess
      early depth perception.

8.   The point at which a minimum level of stimulation can be detected by a sensory system
      is its _____.

9.   Decreased responding to a repeatedly presented stimulus is _____.

10.   The basic unit of speech is a _____.

11.   The process of _____ involves interpreting sensory input.

12.   The ability to recognize through one sensory modality an object that is familiar through
      another is called _____.

13.   A savory or "brothy" flavor often present in protein-rich foods is _____.

14.   The dark and light boundaries or transitions of a perceptual pattern are the
      _____ of the pattern.

15. A _____ is a device that permits amplification of sound by directly stimulating the auditory nerve with electrical impulses.

16. The process of _____ selectively focuses perception and cognition on some aspect of the environment.

17. The sharpness of the visual system, or its ability to perceive detail, is _____.

18. The process of adjusting to lowered levels of light is called _____.

19. Vision loss may occur in _____ when cells in the retina that are responsible for central vision are damaged.

20. A decreased ability to focus on objects that are close to the eye occurs in the condition of _____.

21. Focusing perception or cognition on something specific is known as _____.

22. Opaque or cloudy areas in the lens of the eye that decrease the amount of light reaching the retina result in _____.

23. A person who believes that infants enter the world with no knowledge of the world and learn everything through their senses is a(n) _____.

24. Increased fluid pressure in eye is a symptom of _____.

25. Problems in hearing that result from aging, such as decreased sensitivity to high-frequency sounds, are called _____.

26. The ability to deliberately focus on one thing while ignoring other things is _____.

27. A window of time when an individual has greater plasticity or ability to be influenced by experiences is _____.

28. A ringing in one or both ears following exposure to loud noise is called _____.

29. An attention system that reacts to events rather than deliberately seeking out and focusing on events is a _____.

30. A serious attention problem characterized by inattention, impulsivity, and sometimes hyperactivity is labeled _____.

For each multiple choice question, read all alternatives and then select the best answer.

1. Sensation refers to _____ of stimuli, while perception refers to _____ of this information.
   a. detection; interpretation
   b. sense; the value
   c. interpretation; detection
   d. recognition; the use

2. Nativists argue that a child is
   a. born knowing nothing and learns through interaction with the environment.
   b. born with knowledge and is very similar to an adult in terms of perceptual ability.
   c. influenced intellectually by genetics, maturation and the environment.
   d. learns mainly through cultural experiences.

3. Suppose you repeatedly present a stimulus until an infant loses interest in it. This technique is known as
   a. visual accommodation.
   b. color discrimination.
   c. visual acuity.
   d. habituation.

4. Which of the following is TRUE about young infants' visual capabilities?
   a. Infants are not able to perceive color until sometime during the second half of the first year.
   b. Infants as young as 2 months can detect details of a patterned stimulus as well as adults.
   c. Infants are fairly good at detecting differences in brightness.
   d. Infants' visual systems are at their peak performance.

5. Newborns appear to have a preference for viewing human faces. This probably reflects
   a. an innate ability to recognize faces.
   b. a preference for patterned stimuli with contour and some complexity.
   c. the fact that infants will learn to look at what they have been reinforced for in the past.
   d. the fact that infants can focus only on faces.

6. At around 2 or 3 months of age, infants prefer to look at "normal" faces as opposed to faces that have been distorted in some way. This suggests that infants
   a. cannot really detect a difference between them.
   b. have organized their perceptions according to Gestalt principles.
   c. prefer the simplest form or pattern.
   d. are developing mental representations of what a normal face looks like.

7.	Two-month-olds tested on the visual cliff typically show a slower heart rate on the deep side than on the shallow side of the cliff. This suggests that 2-month-olds
	a.	are afraid of falling off the apparent cliff.
	b.	detect a difference between the two sides of the visual cliff.
	c.	perceive size constancy.
	d.	have learned to avoid potential drop-offs.

8.	Normal hearing in young infants is different from normal hearing in adults in that infants
	a.	are better able to hear soft sounds and whispers.
	b.	have more difficulty discriminating between speech sounds.
	c.	are unable to localize sound.
	d.	can distinguish between all speech sounds, including those not used in the language of adults around them.

9.	An infant who sucks on an object and then recognizes this object visually is showing evidence of
	a.	selective attention.
	b.	habituation.
	c.	cross-modal perception.
	d.	recognition of the object's distinctive features.

10.	Research findings with animals suggest that, in order for normal perceptual development to occur, infants
	a.	must be able to actively move through their environment.
	b.	must be able to watch movement in the environment.
	c.	must be exposed to patterned stimulation.
	d.	both b and c

11.	Attention deficit hyperactivity disorder is
	a.	diagnosed on the basis of too much motor activity.
	b.	a problem with attention and impulsivity or hyperactivity.
	c.	a mismatch between a child's learning style and his/her class format.
	d.	a problem with the sensory and perceptual systems.

12.	Which of the following can we conclude from research on causes of attention deficit hyperactivity disorder?
	a.	Most cases of ADHD can be traced to problems related to premature birth.
	b.	ADHD is caused by overly strict parenting and rigid classroom environments.
	c.	ADHD children show different brain chemistry profiles than children without ADHD.
	d.	Diets high in sugar and fats have increased the rates of ADHD among children.

13.	The point at which a dim light can still be detected is termed
	a.	dark adaptation.	c.	visual accommodation.
	b.	sensory threshold.	d.	visual acuity.

14.   Most age-related hearing problems originate in the
       a.   hearing center of the brain.
       b.   auditory nerves and receptors.
       c.   structures of the middle ear.
       d.   outer ear membrane.

15.   When speaking to people who are hard of hearing, the speaker should
       a.   elevate the voice—shout if necessary.
       b.   talk directly into the person's ear so they can hear better.
       c.   repeat what was just said instead of rewording the misunderstood statement.
       d.   make sure the hearing impaired person can see him/her.

CRITICAL THINKING QUESTIONS

By answering the following questions, you will strengthen your understanding of the material in this chapter. These questions require higher-level thinking skills such as integration and application of concepts. Sample answers are provided for three of the questions. These illustrate one possibility, but there are other answers you could provide that might be just as good. For the other questions, you can check yourself by referring to the text (a hint is provided), or by asking a peer or your instructor to review your answer.

1.   In light of their sensory and perceptual abilities, what do young infants know about the people and world around them?
      [*Sample answer provided.*]

2.   How can researchers measure an infant's perceptual abilities?
      [*Sample answer provided.*]

3.   What sensory and perceptual changes can an older adult expect? What implications do these changes have with respect to an older adult's lifestyle?
      [*Sample answer provided.*]

4.   Discuss the likely outcomes for an infant born with congenital cataracts that preclude any sort of visual stimulation.
      [*Hint: Review the section in the text on "Influences on early perceptual development."*]

5.   Reports suggest that today's teens and young adults will experience high rates of auditory problems as they get older. What are the likely causes of this and what can be done to reduce the growing incidence of hearing loss?
      [*Hint: Review the section in the text on hearing under "The Adolescent."*]

ANSWERS

Chapter Summary and Guided Review (fill in the blank)

1. sensation
2. perception
3. nurture
4. constructivists
5. nativists
6. nature
7. habituation
8. preferential looking
9. evoked potentials
10. operant conditioning
11. visual acuity
12. accommodation
13. patterned
14. contour
15. normal
16. mental representations (or schemata)
17. depth
18. size constancy
19. visual cliff
20. fear
21. intuitive theories
22. phonemes
23. olfaction
24. chemical molecules
25. learning
26. cries
27. cross-modal perception
28. nature
29. sensitive period
30. patterned
31. cataracts
32. sleeper
33. senses
34. objects
35. attention
36. selective
37. systematic (or detailed)
38. impulsive
39. hyperactive
40. stimulants
41. behavioral
42. irrelevant
43. loud noise
44. tinnitus
45. umami
46. females
47. sensory thresholds
48. dark adaptation
49. presbyopia
50. visual acuity
51. cataracts
52. macular degeneration
53. retinitis pigmentosa (RP)
54. glaucoma
55. novel
56. complex
57. presbycusis
58. background noise
59. sweet
60. smell

Review of Key Terms

1. retinitis pigmentosa
2. visual accommodation
3. nativist
4. size constancy
5. sensation
6. olfaction
7. visual cliff
8. sensory threshold
9. habituation
10. phoneme
11. perception
12. cross-modal perception
13. umami
14. contour
15. cochlear implant
16. attention
17. visual acuity
18. dark adaptation
19. age-related macular degeneration
20. presbyopia

21. attention
22. cataracts
23. constructivist
24. glaucoma
25. presbycusis
26. selective attention

27. sensitive periods
28. tinnitus
29. orienting system
30. attention deficit hyperactivity disorder

Multiple-Choice Self-Test

1. A (p. 174)
2. B (p. 174)
3. D (p. 175)
4. C (p. 177-178)
5. B (p. 177-178)

6. D (p. 178-179)
7. B (p. 179-180)
8. D (p. 182-183)
9. C (p. 186)
10. D (p. 187)

11. B (p. 190)
12. C (p. 191-193)
13. B (p. 198)
14. B (p. 202)
15. D (p. 203)

Critical Thinking Questions

1.   *Infants actually know a lot more than previously thought. They can recognize their mother's voice, and if they are breast fed, they can recognize her by smell. They can see people and objects that are close to them, particularly if what they are looking at has sharp light-dark contrasts or bold patterns. This means that infants can see their parents' faces fairly well when parents are interacting with them. Infants seem to like looking at human faces more than other patterned stimuli, but this seems to be because the features of faces are interesting. Show them a picture of a scrambled face, and they will look at it almost as long as they look at a "normal" face. Objects in the environment that move are interesting to infants, as long as the movement is not too fast. Finally, infants like to look at things that are somewhat, but not overly, complex. As they mature, they prefer increasing complexity. The bottom line is that infants like to look at things that they can see well.*

2.   *Testing infants is challenging because they can't communicate in the same ways as children and adults do. Researchers have used habituation and preferential looking tasks to learn a great deal about what infants know about the world around them. In habituation, the infant is exposed repeatedly to a stimulus (e.g., a picture or a sound). At first, they are interested and pay attention to the stimulus, but eventually, they get bored with the same stimulus being presented over and over, and they look away. The researcher then switches to a different stimulus. If the infant detects that this new stimulus is different from the old one, they will once again pay attention. Researchers can vary characteristics of the stimuli and measure how long it takes infants to become bored or for their attention to be recaptured. Preferential looking is similar, except that researchers present two stimuli at the same time and measure how long the infant looks at each one. If the infant does not detect any difference between the two stimuli, then there shouldn't be any difference in looking times. But if the infant detects a difference, he will presumably look longer at the one that he finds more interesting. A few researchers also measure electrical activity of the infant's brain while he/she is exposed to a stimulus. By noting differences in the pattern of electrical activity of the brain, researchers can infer what was detected and what the infant's preferences are. Finally, researchers have taken advantage of the fact that infants can learn through operant conditioning. They condition the infant to perform a simple action (e.g., sucking on a pacifier or turning his/her head) when he/she detects a particular stimulus. Then the researcher presents a second stimulus and measures whether the*

infant performs the action (suggesting that he/she does not detect a difference between the two stimuli) or not (suggesting that that he/she DOES detect a difference).

3.   *Most, but not all, adults can expect some sensory and perceptual declines as they get older. Sensory thresholds increase, which means that sensory stimulation needs to be stronger (e.g., noises need to be louder and odors need to be stronger) in order for them to be detected. Even when sensations are detected, the older adult may have more trouble processing the information or integrating it. Thus, it may be more difficult for the older adult to make sense of the world. In practical terms, a majority of older adults have vision problems and wear corrective lenses. Many of them have hearing problems and could benefit from hearing aids. Their taste buds aren't as sensitive as they once were, so they often end up putting more salt or seasonings on their food. Their sense of smell is also diminished, so they may use more perfume and don't detect potentially harmful smells as well as when they were younger. These changes make it more challenging for adults to get out; it limits their driving ability. Social interactions are more difficult when hearing and vision are diminished. Older adults with uncorrected problems may become socially isolated because they are increasingly uncomfortable in social situations.*

CHAPTER SEVEN

COGNITION

OVERVIEW

This chapter covers two major views on cognitive development. First up is Piaget's constructivist theory, which views intelligence as a basic life function that helps us adapt to our environment. To master this theory, you will need to understand *what* develops, as well as *how* this development occurs in the Piagetian perspective. "What" develops are the cognitive schemes or structures; this growth is reflected in children's progression through Piaget's four stages of development: sensorimotor, preoperations, concrete operations, and formal operations. The "how" of development occurs through the processes of organization and adaptation, and is motivated by cognitive disequilibrium.

In addition to the *what* and *how*, you need to have some sense of how the theory has fared in light of the decades of research that have been conducted on children's thinking. Piaget's theory stops short of being a lifespan theory; Piaget did not propose any new stages beyond formal operations in adolescence. As discussed in the chapter, though, other researchers have looked at cognitive changes during adulthood.

The second perspective covered in this chapter comes from Vygotsky, who viewed cognitive development as a product of social interactions and the child's sociocultural context. Vygotsky believed that children learn problem-solving skills from knowledgeable partners who guide them to more advanced levels of skill in the child's zone of proximal development. The textbook provides a discussion of Vygotsky's contributions and how they differ from Piaget's.

LEARNING OBJECTIVES

After reading and studying the material in this chapter, you should be able to answer the following questions.

7.1   PIAGET'S CONSTRUCTIVIST APPROACH
1.   How do organization, adaptation, and disequilibrium guide development?

7.2   THE INFANT
2.   What are the major achievements of the sensorimotor stage, and how do infants progress toward these achievements?

7.3   THE CHILD
3.   What are the characteristics and limitations of preoperational thought?

4.   What are the major characteristics and limitations of concrete operational thought?

7.4   THE ADOLESCENT

5.   What are the main features of formal operational thought?

6.   What are several implications of the emergence of formal operational thought during the adolescent period?

7.5   THE ADULT

7.   In what ways might adult thought be more advanced than adolescent thought?

8.   How well do cognitive skills hold up in old age?

7.6   PIAGET IN PERSPECTIVE

9.   What are the limitations and challenges to Piaget's theory of cognitive development?

7.7   VYGOTSKY'S SOCIOCULTURAL PERSPECTIVE

10.   What is the main theme of Vygotsky's theory of cognitive development?

11.   How does social interaction contribute to cognitive development according to Vygotsky's theory?

12.   In what ways are Vygotsky and Piaget similar and different in their ideas about cognition?

CHAPTER SUMMARY AND GUIDED REVIEW

The following summary provides an overview of the main points contained in this chapter of the text. Fill in the blanks with terms that appropriately complete the sentence. Scattered throughout the summary are questions in parentheses. These are meant to encourage you to think actively as you read and connect this summary to the more detailed information provided in the text. .

The activity of knowing and the process of acquiring knowledge and solving problems is called (1) _____.

7.1   PIAGET'S CONSTRUCTIVIST APPROACH

Piaget examined how children come to know reality. He was especially interested in the common mistakes that children of different ages made and believed that these responses reflected different levels or (2) _____ of thinking. He used a question-and-answer technique called the (3) _____ to determine the process of children's thinking. This method allows for flexibility but is not standardized for all children.

What Is Intelligence?

According to Piaget, intelligence is a basic life function that helps a person (4) _____ to the environment. Further, people are actively involved in their own development. As knowledge is gained, people form cognitive structures, or (5) _____, which are organized patterns of action or thought that allow us to interpret our experiences. Infants' schemes are action-oriented, while preschool-aged children develop (6) _____ schemes. Older children can manipulate symbols in their heads to solve problems.

How Does Intelligence Develop?

Schemes develop through two innate processes. Children combine existing schemes into more complex schemes through the process of (7) _____. (**What is an example of this process?**) By adjusting to the demands of the environment, children demonstrate the second process of (8) _____. This adjustment occurs through (9) _____, by which new experiences are interpreted in terms of existing schemes, and through (10) _____, in which existing cognitive schemes are modified to account for new experiences. (**What are examples of each of these processes?**) When we encounter new experiences, the conflict between new information and old understanding creates (11) _____, which stimulates cognitive growth. Piaget believed that humans actively create their understanding of the world in a process called (12) _____.

Major cognitive changes are organized into four distinct stages. Thinking in each stage is qualitatively different from thinking in the other stages. Progress through the stages occurs in an (13) _____ sequence, or unchanging order for all children, although the (14) _____ of progress may vary from child to child.

7.2 THE INFANT

According to Piaget, infants are in the (15) _____ stage, which has six substages and is dominated by behavioral schemes.

Substages of the Sensorimotor Stage

Through six substages of sensorimotor development, infants gradually progress from relying on innate reflexes to using mental symbols to guide future behavior. Initially, infants react to stimulation with (16) _____. From approximately 1 to 4 months, infants repeat actions involving their own bodies in the substage of (17) _____. From 4 to 8 months of age, infants in the substage of (18) _____ repeat actions involving objects in their environment. After this, they combine these actions in order to achieve simple goals in the substage of (19) _____. At around 12 months, they begin to experiment with objects in a variety of ways in the substage of (20) _____. By 18 months, infants experience the (21) _____ when they can use one object to represent another one. (**Can you trace the development of a behavior, such as play, through the sensorimotor substages?**)

The Development of Object Permanence

One of the important achievements of the sensorimotor stage is the understanding that objects continue to exist even though not directly experienced, an understanding that Piaget termed (22) _____. Infants in substage four (8-12 months) will search for a concealed object if they watched as it was hidden, but if the object is then hidden in a new location, infants in this substage typically make the (23) _____ error. Not until substage six (18-24 months) when infants are capable of mental representation can they follow invisible displacements of objects. Recent research suggests that infants have a rudimentary understanding of object permanence earlier than Piaget claimed. (**Why is object permanence an important concept for infants to develop?**)

The Emergence of Symbols

Piaget referred to the ability to use one thing to represent objects or experiences as the (24) _____.

7.3   THE CHILD
The Preoperational Stage

According to Piaget, preschool-aged children are in the preoperational stage of cognitive development where children use symbolic reasoning but not logical reasoning. As children get a little older, some may use this ability to invent (25) _____. Preschoolers typically focus on the most obvious features of a task, or what has (26) _____. Children in this stage do not understand that certain properties of a substance or object remain the same despite superficial changes in appearance; that is, they lack (27) _____. There are several reasons for this. They have trouble focusing on two or more dimensions of a problem at the same time, demonstrating (28) _____. Instead, preoperational children engage in (29) _____ where they focus on a single aspect of the problem when more are relevant. In addition, preoperational children struggle with mentally reversing an action and have trouble with (30) _____ or the processes of change from one state to another, so their thought is static. (***Try writing responses to one of the conservation problems that demonstrate each of these concepts from a preoperational child's perspective.***)

Piaget also believed that preoperational children viewed the world from their own perspective and had trouble recognizing other points of view, displaying (31) _____. Finally, preoperational children have difficulty relating subclasses of objects to the whole class of objects because they tend to center on the most perceptually salient feature of the task, and so they have trouble solving (32) _____ problems.

Piaget seems to have underestimated what the preschool-aged child can do. Recent research suggests that such children understand simple conservation concepts and classification systems, and they are not as egocentric as Piaget claimed. Nonetheless, preschool-aged children do rely more on their perceptions to solve tasks than do older children.

The Concrete Operations Stage

School-aged children (roughly 7 to 11 years) are in Piaget's third stage of cognitive development—concrete operations. They have mastered the (33) _____ operations that were absent from preoperational thought. (***What are these mental operations?***) This allows concrete operational children to solve conservation tasks, although they don't solve all types at the same time, which Piaget described as (34) _____. They can also mentally order items along a quantifiable dimension, an operation called (35) _____, and have mastered a cognitive operation that allows children to recognize the relationships among elements in a series, termed (36) _____. (***What are examples of problems that children can solve by applying each of these operations?***) Finally, concrete operational children understand that subclasses are included in a whole class allowing them to solve (37) _____ problems.

7.4   THE ADOLESCENT
The Formal Operations Stage

According to Piaget, adolescents are entering the stage of formal operations. Like concrete operational children, adolescents can reason logically about objects. They can also apply their

mental actions to ideas, extending their reasoning to non-concrete, or (38) _____
concepts. This facilitates "what if" questions or (39) _____ reasoning.

Formal operational thinkers also use systematic problem-solving strategies, rather than trial-and-error approaches often used by children in earlier stages. One type of reasoning that formal operational thinkers might use is (40) _____, where individuals reason from general ideas to specific implications of these ideas. They are also increasingly able to (41) _____ or separate prior knowledge from current task demands.

Implications of Formal Thought

Mastery of formal operational thought takes place over several years and is often quite slow. There are several implications of formal operational thought. On the positive side, formal operational thought may be related to achieving a sense of identity and to advances in (42) _____ reasoning. On the other hand, formal operational thought may lead to a period of confusion or rebellion because of all the questions about life that formal operational thinkers can generate. Specifically, formal operational adolescents may have trouble separating their own thoughts and emotions from those of others, experiencing (43) _____. According to Elkind, this emerges in two forms. One is the (44) _____, which involves confusing your own thoughts with those of a hypothetical audience. (***Can you provide an example of this phenomenon?***) A second form is the (45) _____, which is a tendency to think that your thoughts or feelings are unique and that others cannot possibly experience the same thoughts or feelings.

7.5   THE ADULT

Piaget believed that formal operational thought was mastered by most 15- to 18-year-olds, however more recent research suggests otherwise.

Limitations in Adult Cognitive Performance

Many adults do not reason at the formal operational level. Although average intelligence contributes to formal operational thought, formal education is an important factor as well. (***Can you explain why this is the case?***) Further, we tend to apply formal operational thought to areas with which we have some (46) _____ and knowledge.

Growth beyond Formal Operations?

Despite the fact that formal operational thought is not completely mastered by all adults, some researchers believe that Piaget did not go far enough with cognitive development and have proposed growth beyond formal operations, that is, (47) _____ thought. One suggestion is that adults are more likely than adolescents to use (48) _____ thinking, which means that they believe that knowledge depends on the subjective perspective of the person with the knowledge. (***What does Perry's work with college students indicate about changes in thought throughout college?***). Adults may also be better able to uncover and resolve (49) _____ between ideas, and to think about entire systems of ideas.

Aging and Cognitive Skills

Cross-sectional studies with older adults suggest that they perform poorly on concrete and formal operational tasks. Older adults may approach tasks using different styles of thinking that are useful in everyday life, but not on laboratory-type tests.

7.6   PIAGET IN PERSPECTIVE

Piaget's Contributions

   Piaget's contributions to developmental psychology are enormous. His theory has stimulated a tremendous amount of research, and his insights about development—such as active involvement in one's own development and sequencing of cognitive development—continue to guide our understanding of children's thinking.

Challenges to Piaget

   Piaget's contributions must be viewed in the context of various challenges to the theory. One criticism of Piaget is that he (50) _____ the cognitive abilities of young children. Piaget has also been criticized for blurring the distinction between competence and (51) _____. Some researchers do not believe that development is best characterized by a series of broad, coherent (52) _____ or qualitative changes in thinking. Piaget has also been criticized for describing development but not really (53) _____ development. Others have criticized Piaget for not giving enough attention to the role of (54) _____ influences on cognitive development.

7.7   VYGOTSKY'S SOCIOCULTURAL PERSPECTIVE

   Vygotsky developed a theory of cognitive development that emphasizes the sociocultural context of development and the influence of social interactions.

Culture and Thought

   Culture and historical context shape what people know and how they think.

Social Interaction and Thought

   Social interactions that foster cognitive growth typically take place in what Vygotsky called the zone of (55) _____ development. This is the difference between what learners can do (56) _____ and what they can do with assistance. Vygotsky believed that children learned through (57) _____ as they interacted with more skilled thinkers or problem solvers. This is similar to the idea of providing structure or (58) _____ to support children's learning.

The Tools of Thought

   According to Vygotsky, the primary means of passing on successful problem-solving strategies is through (59) _____. Vygotsky noted that young children often talked to themselves when working on a problem, and he believed this (60) _____ guided the child's thoughts and behaviors. Through social interactions, (61) _____ speech is eventually transformed into (62) _____ speech. (*How is this different from Piaget's view of early speech and thought?*)

Evaluation of Vygotsky

   Vygotsky has been criticized for placing too much emphasis on (63) _____ (recall that Piaget was criticized for *not enough* emphasis on this). Unlike Piaget, Vygotsky believed that different social and historical contexts create differences in cognitive development. Vygotsky thought that adults were more important to children's cognitive development. This is different from Piaget's view because Piaget believed that (64) _____ were especially important to children's learning.

Cognition

REVIEW OF KEY TERMS

Below is a list of terms and concepts from this chapter. Use these to complete the following sentence definitions. You might also want to try writing definitions in your own words and then checking your definitions with those in the text.

A-not-B error
accommodation
adaptation
adolescent egocentrism
assimilation
centration
class inclusion
clinical method
cognition
conservation
coordination of secondary schemes
decentration
decontextualize
dialectical thinking
egocentrism
equilibration
guided participation
horizontal décalage
hypothetical-deductive reasoning
imaginary audience

imaginary companions
object permanence
organization
perceptual salience
personal fable
postformal thought
primary circular reaction
private speech
relativistic thinking
reversibility
scaffolding
scheme (schema)
secondary circular reaction
seriation
static thought
symbolic capacity
tertiary circular reaction
transformational thought
transitivity
zone of proximal development

1. The tendency to view the world from one's own perspective and to have trouble recognizing other points of view is called _____.

2. A method of learning through interaction with others who provide aid and support is _____ in Vygotsky's theory.

3. According to Piaget, the inborn tendency to combine existing schemes into new and more complex schemes is _____.

4. Understanding that objects continue to exist even when those objects are no longer directly experienced is called _____.

5. Adolescents sometimes create a(n) _____ when they confuse their own thoughts with the thoughts of a hypothetical audience.

6. In Piaget's theory, _____ is an inborn tendency to adjust to the demands of the environment.

7. The _____ is often made by 8- to 12-month-old infants who successfully find an object hidden at one location and then continue to search at this location after watching the object being hidden at a second location.

8. Cognitive development that may emerge after formal operations is referred to as _____.

9. The process of interpreting new experiences in terms of existing cognitive structures is called _____.

10. The sensorimotor substage of _____ is when infants repeat interesting actions relating to their own bodies.

11. The ability to understand changes from one state to another is called _____.

12. The _____ is the difference between what one can do independently and what one can do with assistance.

13. Preschoolers often show _____ when they focus on the most obvious features of a task.

14. The process of mentally "undoing" an action is called _____.

15. _____ speech is not directed toward another person but helps direct the speaker's thoughts and behaviors.

16. Children in Piaget's preoperational stage have trouble with conservation tasks because they have _____, a focus on endpoints of the problem rather than on the transformation that occurred.

17. The process of modifying existing cognitive structures in order to understand or adapt to new experiences is _____.

18. Piaget used an interview technique called _____, in which a child's response to each question determines the next question.

19. Reasoning from general ideas or hypotheses to specific implications and then systematically testing these implications is the basis of _____ reasoning.

20. The sensorimotor substage of _____ involves experimenting with toys and actions out of curiosity and enjoyment.

21. Piaget used the term _____ to refer to a balanced mental state.

22. An organized pattern of thought or action used to interpret our experiences is called a _____ in Piaget's theory.

23. Teens may exhibit _____ when they fail to differentiate their own thoughts and feelings from those of other people.

24. The ability to use images, words, or gestures to represent objects and experiences emerges with the development of _____.

25. A cognitive operation called _____ allows children to mentally order items along a quantifiable dimension.

26. The _____ refers to the tendency to think that you and your thoughts and feelings are unique.

27. Infants in the _____ substage repeat actions involving something in their environment.

28. A cognitive operation that allows children to recognize the relationship among elements in a series is _____.

29. Understanding that certain properties of a substance or object remain the same despite superficial changes in appearance is called _____.

30. The tendency to focus on a single aspect of problem when more aspects are relevant is called _____.

31. Understanding that knowledge depends on the subjective perspective of the person with the knowledge is associated with _____.

32. Understanding that subclasses are included in a whole class is _____.

33. The ability to focus on two or more dimensions of a problem at one time is called _____.

34. Providing a structure to support children's learning occurs with _____.

35. The term _____ represents Piaget's recognition that different cognitive skills related to the same stage of cognitive development may emerge at different times.

36. The activity of knowing and the processes through which knowledge is acquired is called _____.

37. The ability to separate prior knowledge and beliefs from the demands of the current task is called _____.

38. Some children in the preoperational stage may invent an _____ using their capacity for symbolic thought.

39. Infants in the substage of _____ combine secondary actions to achieve simple goals.

40. The ability to detect inconsistencies among ideas and try to reconcile these develops with _____.

MULTIPLE-CHOICE SELF-TEST

For each multiple choice question, read all alternatives and then select the best answer.

1. An example of accommodation is
   a. believing that all four-legged animals with fur are dogs.
   b. realizing that a cat fits into a different category than a dog.
   c. the confusion that a child experiences when new events challenge old schemas.
   d. a child who sees a cat and refers to it as a dog.

2. Which of the following statements best characterizes Piaget's position on the nature-nurture issue?
   a. The environment is responsible for providing children with cognitive skills.
   b. Innate mechanisms are primarily responsible for determining intelligence.
   c. Ideas are not innate or imposed by others, but are constructed from experiences.
   d. Some cognitive skills result from innate characteristics while others are influenced only by environmental experiences.

3. Throughout the sensorimotor stage, infants' knowledge of the world shifts from
   a. focusing on symbols to using simple mental operations.
   b. an egocentric perspective to one that considers other viewpoints.
   c. relying on reflexes to mentally planning how to solve simple problems.
   d. focusing on sensory information to focusing on motoric information.

4. Which of the following is an example of object permanence?
   a. Visually tracking a moving object
   b. Searching for a shoe under the bed because this seems like a likely hiding place
   c. Searching for a toy where the child just watched it being hidden
   d. Using goal-directed behavior to systematically check all possible hiding locations for a toy

5.   Which of the following responses to a conservation problem indicates that the child has reversibility of thought?
       a.   The amount of water in the two cups is the same because even though one is taller, the other one is wider.
       b.   The amount of water in the two cups looks about the same, so I'd say they were equal.
       c.   I didn't see you spill any water, so the amounts are the same.
       d.   If you'd pour the water back into the original container, you'd see it has the same amount of water as the other container.

6.   Research on Piaget's description of preoperational thought has found that
       a.   when task demands are reduced, young children can successfully solve some problems at a more sophisticated level.
       b.   when task demands are reduced, it has little impact on performance because children do not yet have the cognitive capabilities to solve the problem.
       c.   Piaget was correct in his description of when certain abilities emerged, but was not always accurate in his description of what underlying thought was required for these abilities.
       d.   Piaget overestimated what most preschool-aged children can do.

7.   Formal operational children are different from concrete operational children in that
       a.   formal operational children can deal with possibilities.
       b.   formal operational children focus on realities.
       c.   concrete operational children systematically test all possible solutions to a problem.
       d.   concrete operational children are more likely to be egocentric.

8.   Longitudinal research (the LOGIC study) on acquisition of scientific reasoning has revealed that
       a.   even children can apply scientific reasoning to most tasks presented to them.
       b.   children and adolescents are very similar in their recognition and use of scientific reasoning principles.
       c.   adolescents are far more advanced in their scientific reasoning than Piaget believed.
       d.   recognizing scientific reasoning principles occurs earlier than producing scientific reasoning principles.

9.   Research with older adults solving Piagetian tasks shows that the older adults
       a.   are all reasoning at the formal operational level.
       b.   perform worse than younger adults on many concrete operational tasks.
       c.   perform similarly to younger adults on all Piagetian tasks.
       d.   are more egocentric than younger adults and tend to use transductive reasoning.

10. Piaget has been criticized by modern developmentalists who suggest that
    a. Piaget was pessimistic concerning the timing of cognitive abilities in adolescents.
    b. Piaget was overly optimistic concerning the abilities of infants and toddlers.
    c. development is a gradual process rather than a stagelike process.
    d. development follows a different pattern of stages than what Piaget suggested.

11. Which of the following is NOT a valid criticism of Piaget's theory?
    a. He underestimated what infants and young children understand.
    b. He claimed that development progressed through a few universal stages.
    c. He did not give as much attention to social influences as he should have.
    d. He did not do a very good job of describing development.

12. Vygotsky used the term *zone of proximal development* to refer to the
    a. influence that thought and language have on one another.
    b. child's approximate level of cognitive skill on a particular task.
    c. difference between what someone can do independently and what he/she can do with another person's help.
    d. point at which the child progresses from one level of understanding to another.

13. Vygotsky would be MOST likely to agree with which one of the following statements?
    a. Knowledge depends on one's culture and social experiences.
    b. Interaction with the physical environment is critically important to development.
    c. Cognitive development precedes language development.
    d. Children's cognitive development progresses in a universal fashion.

14. Which of the following is the best example of Vygotsky's idea of *guided participation*?
    a. A child asks a friend to participate in a new game.
    b. A child works through a new puzzle with the help of a parent.
    c. A child uses a new word to request something from a parent.
    d. A child volunteers to help set the dinner table.

15. In comparing Piaget's view to Vygotsky's view, which of the following is TRUE?
    a. Piaget emphasized independent exploration of the world, while Vygotsky believed that social interactions were needed for development of more advanced thinking.
    b. Both believed language development was independent of cognitive development.
    c. Vygotsky believed that private speech was not a developmentally important phenomenon, while Piaget used it as evidence of egocentrism.
    d. Piaget and Vygotsky both proposed that children progress through major stages in reaching mature cognitive understanding of the world.

COMPARE THE MAIN IDEAS OF PIAGET AND VYGOTSKY

This exercise will help you compare Piaget's views on cognitive development with those of Vygotsky. Use Table 7.3 on page 237 in the text to check your answers.

	PIAGET	VYGOTSKY
1. Is cognitive development universal or context-specific?		
2. What sorts of activities lead to cognitive growth?		
3. Is knowledge best constructed individually or with others?		
4. How do cognitive development and language relate to one another?		
5. Are peers or adults more important in the development of cognition?		
6. What is the relationship between learning and development?		

CRITICAL THINKING QUESTIONS

By answering the following questions, you will strengthen your understanding of the material in this chapter. These questions require higher-level thinking skills such as integration and application of concepts. Sample answers are provided for three of the questions. These illustrate one possibility, but there are other answers you could provide that might be just as good. For the other questions, you can check yourself by referring to the text (a hint is provided), or by asking a peer or your instructor to review your answer.

1. Apply Piaget's description of cognitive development to a social issue such as divorce, birth of a new sibling, or adoption. What would a child's understanding of one these events be in each of Piaget's four stages of cognitive development?
    [*Sample answer provided.*]

2. When you consider the preschool-aged child in light of Piaget's description of the preoperational stage and modern research findings, how would you characterize the cognitive abilities of the preschool-aged child?
[*Sample answer provided.*]

3. Suppose you need to design a program to teach 6-year-old children a new academic skill. How would you approach this from Piaget's perspective? How would you approach this from Vygotsky's perspective? How would the two programs be similar or different?
[*Sample answer provided.*]

4. Piaget's theory has stimulated a tremendous amount of research on cognitive development over the past 30 years. Considering what we have learned from this research, how would Piaget's theory need to be updated to account for the findings that have emerged since the theory was developed?
[*Hint: Read the "Challenges to Piaget" section in the text, as well as the research on Piaget's theory that was discussed in sections on "The Infant," "The Child," "The Adolescent," and "The Adult."*]

5. Some researchers have demonstrated that Piagetian skills such as conservation can be taught. What are the implications of this for the principles of Piaget's theory?
[*Hint: Read "Did Piaget underestimate the preschool child?" and "Challenges to Piaget."*]

ANSWERS

Chapter Summary and Guided Review (fill in the blank)

1. cognition
2. stages
3. clinical method
4. adapt
5. schemes
6. symbolic
7. organization
8. adaptation
9. assimilation
10. accommodation
11. disequilibrium
12. constructivism
13. invariant
14. rate
15. sensorimotor
16. reflexes
17. primary circular reactions
18. secondary circular reactions
19. coordination of secondary schemes

20. tertiary circular reactions
21. beginning of thought
22. object permanence
23. A-not-B error
24. symbolic capacity
25. imaginary companions
26. perceptual salience
27. conservation
28. decentration
29. centration
30. transformations
31. egocentric
32. class inclusion
33. logical
34. horizontal decalage
35. seriation
36. transitivity
37. class inclusion
38. abstract

39. hypothetical
40. hypothetical-deductive
41. decontextualize
42. moral
43. adolescent egocentrism
44. imaginary audience
45. personal fable
46. expertise
47. postformal
48. relativistic
49. contradictions
50. underestimated
51. performance

52. stages
53. explaining
54. social
55. proximal
56. independently
57. guided participation
58. scaffolding
59. language
60. private speech
61. social
62. inner
63. social interaction
64. peers (other children)

Review of Key Terms

1. egocentrism
2. guided participation
3. organization
4. object permanence
5. imaginary audience
6. adaptation
7. A-not-B error
8. postformal thought
9. assimilation
10. primary circular reaction
11. transformational thought
12. zone of proximal development
13. perceptual salience
14. reversibility
15. private
16. static thought
17. accommodation
18. clinical method
19. hypothetical-deductive
20. tertiary circular reactions

21. equilibration
22. scheme
23. adolescent egocentrism
24. symbolic capacity
25. seriation
26. personal fable
27. secondary circular reaction
28. transitivity
29. conservation
30. centration
31. relativistic thinking
32. class inclusion
33. decentration
34. scaffolding
35. horizontal décalage
36. cognition
37. decontextualize
38. imaginary companion
39. coordination of secondary schemes
40. dialectical thinking

Multiple-Choice Self-Test

1. B (p. 212)
2. C (p. 212)
3. C (p. 213-216)
4. C (p. 214)
5. D (p. 217)

6. A (p. 220)
7. A (p. 222)
8. D (p. 224; 226)
9. B (p. 229)
10. C (p. 232)

11. D (p. 233)
12. C (p. 234)
13. A (p. 234)
14. B (p. 235)
15. A (p. 236-237)

<u>Critical Thinking Questions</u>

1.   *Considering adoption, children in the sensorimotor stage most likely would not understand the concept because they are just experiencing the beginning of thought at the end of this stage.*

A preoperational child might be able to tell people, "I'm adopted," but he/she wouldn't really understand what this meant. For one thing, the child might have static thought and focus on end results. He/she would only know that he/she ended up with the people he/she calls Mom and Dad, but not really grasp the process that led to this. In addition, preoperational children exhibit centration, which allows them to focus on only a single aspect of a problem. They might be able to focus on where babies come from, but not integrate this with other concepts that occur with adoption. Another difficulty for the preoperational child is class inclusion. This child would have trouble understanding that adoption is one "classification" of ways a parent can "get" a child, but that most children are not gotten this way. Also, children in preoperations are egocentric, so they would have trouble understanding the perspective of other people involved (e.g., the mother who gave them up for adoption). Finally, preoperational children can't understand that they are the children of their biological mother <u>and</u> their adoptive mother; they center on one or the other.

The concrete operational child would be better able to comprehend adoption because of his/her increased powers of logical reasoning. For instance, concrete operational children can decenter, so they can focus on more than one aspect of the problem. They would also understand that adoption is one of several ways that children end up in a particular family. Not until formal operations, though, would adolescents gain a better understanding of <u>why</u> they were adopted. They could consider all the abstract issues that go into adoption decisions and reason about possibilities (e.g., what might have happened if they had not been adopted). On the negative side, formal operational children could devise hypothetical reasons for why their biological parents did not want to raise them, and this might create some anguish. They may also be interested in knowing more about their biological parents, as this information might allow them to systematically test various theories they have constructed about their circumstances.

2.   *Preschool-aged children are able to use the symbolic capacity that they achieved at the end of the sensorimotor period to expand their language as well as their play. They can, for example, engage in pretend play by using one thing to represent something else. They begin to internalize more of their cognition—i.e., they no longer have to act motorically on sensory information in order to learn about the world around them.*

Preschoolers are limited in their ability to think logically. Young children are often fooled by the surface appearance of something and aren't advanced enough cognitively to delve beneath the surface. When tested with the original tasks used by Piaget, preschoolers often appear far less capable than concrete operational older children. But when tasks are simplified, or training is provided, preschoolers demonstrate a greater understanding. There is a difference between preschool-aged children and elementary school-aged children, but the gap is not as wide as Piaget claimed. Preschool-aged children do tend to be egocentric, as Piaget claimed, but there are times and situations when this is not the case. Similarly, there are times and situations when older children (and even adults) <u>are</u> egocentric.

In sum, preschoolers have some accurate intuitions about the world, but lack the ability to systematically test these intuitions. They are more bound by their perceptions than older children.

Cognition   Page 115

3.   *Piaget's program would be organized to encourage children to interact with their physical environment. He believed that children needed opportunities to explore objects in order to discover properties of these objects as well as elementary principles about the world in general. Thus, interactions between the individual and physical objects would be a key feature of the Piagetian program. The individual has to construct her own understanding of the world; it can't come from someone else. Piaget would expect that all the children in the program would proceed through his four universal stages of cognitive development. He would also argue that children can't be rushed to learn something before they are cognitively ready. They can only assimilate and accommodate information at their own pace. Development can't be sped up.*

     Vygotsky's program would be organized to encourage social interactions among children and especially between a child and a more knowledgeable peer. He believed that children learned a great deal through interactions with others. Vygotsky used the term zone of proximal development to highlight the gap between what a learner can do independently and what she can do or understand with the guidance and support of a more skilled partner. This suggests that children can be led to learn something earlier than they might otherwise have learned on their own. Vygotsky would not believe that all the children would progress through the same stages. Depending on their cultural background and the sorts of social interactions they had, they might follow quite different paths of cognitive development.

CHAPTER EIGHT

MEMORY AND INFORMATION PROCESSING

OVERVIEW

This chapter focuses on memory processes and uses the information-processing model to describe how information is moved in and out of the memory stores. You will learn that young children and older adults have trouble with some learning and memory tasks. To understand these difficulties with memory, four hypotheses are explored. These involve changes in 1) basic capacities, 2) memory strategies, 3) metamemory, and 4) knowledge base. These provide a useful way to organize much of the research on developmental changes in memory and information processing.

The chapter also considers the intriguing question of why we cannot remember much, if anything, from our infancy and early childhood years. You will learn when autobiographical memories begin and how such memories are stored. You will also learn how time and experience can alter our memories, something that has significant implications for eyewitness testimony.

LEARNING OBJECTIVES

After reading and studying the material in this chapter, you should be able to answer the following questions.

8.1   THE INFORMATION-PROCESSING APPROACH
1.   What is the general orientation of the information-processing model to cognition? What are the specific components of the model, and how does information "flow" through the system?

2.   What are the different forms or types of memory?

8.2   THE INFANT
3.   How do researchers assess infant memory? What information can infants typically remember? What are the limitations of infants' memory?

8.3   THE CHILD
4.   What are four major hypotheses about why memory improves with age? Is there evidence to support each hypothesis?

5.   When do autobiographical memories begin, and what possible explanations can account for childhood amnesia?

6.   How do scripts, or general event representations, influence memory?

7.   How do problem-solving capacities change during childhood? What explanation does Siegler propose for changes in problem solving?

8.4   THE ADOLESCENT
8.   What developments occur in the information-processing abilities of adolescents?

8.5   THE ADULT
9.   In what ways do memory and cognition change during adulthood? What are the strengths and weaknesses of older adults' abilities?

10.   What factors help explain the declines in abilities during older adulthood? And what can be done to minimize losses with age?

11.   How are problem-solving skills affected by aging?

CHAPTER SUMMARY AND GUIDED REVIEW

The following summary provides an overview of the main points contained in this chapter of the text. Fill in the blanks with terms that appropriately complete the sentence. Scattered throughout the summary are questions in parentheses. These are meant to encourage you to think actively as you read and connect this summary to the more detailed information provided in the text.

8.1   THE INFORMATION-PROCESSING APPROACH
Information-processing theorists attempt to understand human learning and remembering by comparing these processes to the workings of a (1) _____.

The Memory Systems
A popular information-processing model proposes that information coming into the information-processing system (i.e., the person) is held very briefly in a (2) _____. If the person pays attention to this information, it will be moved into (3) _____, also called working memory. Information to be remembered for any length of time must somehow be moved into (4) _____ memory.
In order to remember something, it must first get into the system by being (5) _____. Second, it must be processed and organized through (6) _____ so that it is ready to go into (7) _____, which is when it is held in long-term memory. When the information is needed, it must be taken out or (8) _____ from long-term memory. Retrieval of information by reproducing it without cues uses (9) _____, which is more difficult than indicating whether or not the information has been previously experienced, which uses (10) _____ memory. Between these two forms of retrieval is (11) _____ recall where some sort of hint is given.

Implicit and Explicit Memory
Some tasks involve (12) _____ memory, which occurs automatically and without conscious effort. In contrast, other tasks require deliberate attempts to remember something; they involve memory that is (13) _____. More specifically, remembering general facts about the world involves (14) _____ memory, whereas remembering specific experiences involves (15) _____ memory. Implicit and explicit memory stores operate (16) _____ and are stored in different areas of the brain.

Problem Solving

Using the information-processing system to achieve a goal or make a decision is problem solving. To be able to do this, the information-processing system includes a number of executive (17) _____ to monitor, plan, and interpret information.

8.2   THE INFANT
Memory

Researchers use a variety of techniques to assess infant memory. Infants show memory when they repeat an action performed by a model, called (18) _____. Or assessment might be done by repeatedly presenting them with a stimulus until they no longer respond to it, a process called (19) _____. To test long-term memory, some researchers have used (20) _____ to train an infant to respond to a stimulus. (*Can you explain how this can be used to demonstrate infant memory?*) Infants will likely have trouble with retrieval of information unless they are provided with sufficient (21) _____ to aid retrieval. Evidence of pure recall memory comes when infants show (22) _____ imitation and also when they can solve object permanence tasks.

Problem Solving

By 9 months, there is some evidence of simple problem-solving skills. Infants increasingly seek cues from adults to help them solve problems.

8.3   THE CHILD
Explaining Memory Development

Although the basic memory and information-processing skills are present during infancy, memory clearly improves during childhood. There are four main hypotheses about why this improvement occurs.

Do basic capacities change? One possibility is that basic capacities change. For example, some neo-Piagetian theorists propose that working memory space increases during childhood. Research shows that total capacity increases somewhat, but more importantly, children become more efficient and faster at using the space they have as many processes become (23) _____ and require little effort. These improvements correspond to maturational changes in the brain, particularly the (24) _____ of the brain.

Do memory strategies change? Another possibility for the improvement in learning and memory is that memory strategies improve with age. Although young children can deliberately remember when they are highly motivated, their memory strategies are not always very effective. They often continue to use the same strategy that might have been successful in the past but is not currently successful, an error referred to as (25) _____. When they begin to use strategies, children may use (26) _____, or repeating the items to be remembered. Another strategy is (27) _____, or classifying items to be remembered into meaningful groups. A third strategy is to use (28) _____, or creating meaningful links between the items to be remembered. Rehearsal typically develops first, followed by use of organization and finally by spontaneous use of elaboration in adolescence.

Strategies emerge gradually. At first, children cannot use or benefit from a strategy even if taught to use one, called a (29) _____. In the next phase of strategy use, children show (30) _____ when they use strategies they are taught but do not produce them on their own. In a phase called (31) _____, children can produce the strategy, but their performance does not benefit from it. Effective strategy use occurs when children can produce and benefit from a strategy. Even when effective memory strategies are used, appropriate (32) _____ strategies must also be employed for successful recall.

Does knowledge about memory change? A third explanation for the improvement in learning and memory is that knowledge about memory and other cognitive processes changes with age. Knowledge of memory and memory processes is called (33) _____ and does improve with age. (*Can you provide evidence that shows growth in this skill?*) These improvements are associated with increases in memory, although the relationship depends on the nature of the task. This knowledge is part of a broader understanding of the human mind called (34) _____.

Does knowledge of the world change? A fourth possibility is that increased knowledge of the world in general, or (35) _____, leads to improvements in memory. There is research evidence that children who have extensive knowledge bases in a particular area can outperform adults who are novices in the same area.

Autobiographical Memory

Memories for events that have happened to you personally constitute your autobiographical memory. Although infants and toddlers show evidence of memory, older children and adults exhibit (36) _____ for events that occurred during the first few years of life. Research shows that we have few, if any, memories of events prior to age (37) _____. Prior to this, there may not be enough space in working memory to hold multiple pieces of information about an event, and lack of (38) _____ may also reduce what can be stored. Infants and toddlers may also lack a sense of self that they can use to organize memories of things that happened to them. Another possibility comes from (39) _____ theory, which predicts that verbatim and general accounts of an event are stored separately.

Children construct general event representations or (40) _____ of routine daily activities and use these when retelling events. Memories for an event change over time and change with the introduction of new information, indicating that memory is a (41) _____ and not an exact replication. Reporting events that you have witnessed is a form of (42) _____. (*What factors affect the accuracy of this recall?*)

Problem Solving

Problem-solving capacities also change during childhood. Cognitive researcher Robert Siegler uses an approach he calls (43) _____ to determine what information children take in and what rules they generate to solve a problem. Siegler's research shows that 3-year-olds use no strategies; instead, they (44) _____. By age 4 or 5, most children are rule governed, but the type of rule used changes with age, and children have trouble integrating multiple pieces of information. Siegler believes that problem-solving skills develop, not as a series of stages, but as (45) _____ where children have a variety of strategies available at any given time and gradually choose the ones most effective for the task at hand.

8.4   THE ADOLESCENT

Strategies

During adolescence, some new learning and memory strategies, such as elaboration, emerge. Adolescents' use of strategies is more deliberate, selective, and spontaneous than younger children's.

Basic Capacities

Adolescents perform many mental operations (46) _____ than children. Their working memory also functions more efficiently.

Metamemory and Knowledge Base

Adolescents know more in general, so their (47) _____ expand. They also show improvements in their understanding of their learning and memory processes, or their (48) _____.

8.5   THE ADULT

Developing Expertise

During adulthood, developing expertise in a field facilitates memory and problem solving in this field. (***How can this affect memory and problem solving?***) Experts have more extensive and organized knowledge bases than novices. Expertise, though, is (49) _____ because expertise in one area does not improve memory in other areas.

Autobiographical Memory

Autobiographical memory is influenced by several factors. For one, events that have greater (50) _____ will likely be recalled better than less important events. Second, the uniqueness or (51) _____ of an event affects its recall. Third, events with greater (52) _____ intensity will be better recalled. Finally, the time of (53) _____ when the event occurs affects the likelihood of its later recall. In general, people remember more events from their (54) _____ than from other periods of their life. (***Can you provide an explanation of why this is the case?***)

Memory and Aging

Self-reports suggest that memory declines with age. Declines in memory are slight and usually do not occur until one's 60s or 70s. Also, since much of the research in this area has used (55) _____ designs, the apparent declines could be due to other factors related to cohort differences. Not all adults experience memory problems and not all tasks create memory difficulties for older adults. Older adults tend to have trouble with (56) _____ tasks because they are slower than younger adults to learn and retrieve information. They also have trouble on tasks that are (57) _____ or have little relevance to them. Tasks requiring rarely used skills and tasks requiring (58) _____ memory rather than recognition memory are also problematic for older adults. Finally, older adults show more trouble with (59) _____ memory tasks that require effortful learning.

Possible explanations for the learning and memory declines observed in older adults are the same as those considered for young children's performance. Unlike young children, older adults know much about the world, so they do not have deficient (60) _____. Metamemory problems also do not seem to contribute greatly to memory declines in older

---

adults. Older adults do not always spontaneously use effective strategies. They also need to devote more space than younger adults to short-term or (61) _____ memory, which leaves less space to devote to other purposes. (*What might account for declines in short-term memory capacity?*)

Sensory losses experienced by many older adults can also impede memory performance. In addition, there are many (62) _____ factors associated with the specific learner and task that influence memory. For instance, the declines in memory observed for older adults compared to younger adults may be due to generational or (63) _____ differences. Older adults tend to be less educated and may not be as motivated to perform as younger adults.

Problem Solving and Aging

Older adults also seem to perform more poorly than young adults on problem-solving tasks. On a 20-questions task, being able to rule out multiple items by asking (64) _____ questions is most efficient. Older children and young adults use this strategy, but older adults do not unless the task is altered to make it more familiar to them. Older adults perform better on problems involving everyday challenges than on unfamiliar or laboratory tasks.

Older adults may cope with declines in their cognitive functioning by being selective in what they choose to do. They (65) _____ their strengths and find ways to (66) _____ for weaknesses.

REVIEW OF KEY TERMS

Below is a list of terms and concepts from this chapter. Use these to complete the following sentence definitions. You might also want to try writing definitions in your own words and then checking your definitions with those in the text.

autobiographical memories

childhood amnesia

consolidation

constraint-seeking questions

cued recall memory

deferred imitation

elaboration

encoding

episodic memory

executive control processes

explicit memory

eyewitness memory

fuzzy-trace theory

general event representation

implicit memory

information-processing approach

knowledge base

long-term memory

mediation deficiency

memory

metacognition

metamemory

mild cognitive impairment (MCI)

organization (as memory strategy)

overlapping waves theory

perseveration errors

problem solving

production deficiency

recall memory

recognition memory

rehearsal

retrieval

rule assessment approach

script

semantic memory

sensory register

short-term memory

storage

utilization deficiency

working memory

1.   Reporting events that you have seen is the essence of _____.

2.   The memory strategy of _____ involves repeating items to be remembered.

3.   According to _____, verbatim and general accounts of an event are stored separately in memory.

4.   Memory that occurs unintentionally is _____.

5.   An older adult with _____ has some memory loss, but it is not the pathological memory loss associated with disease.

6.   Getting information out of long-term memory when it is needed is _____.

7.   The memory strategy of _____ involves classifying items to be remembered into meaningful groups.

8.   Memory that requires individuals to indicate whether they have previously experienced a stimulus is _____.

9.   We often construct a _____ of familiar events and then use this mental representation to guide future behavior in similar settings.

10. Sometimes, children can produce a strategy but do not benefit from it because of task demands; this is known as _____.

11. A memory store that temporarily stores a limited amount of information and allows active use of this information is _____.

12. Our _____ consists of everyday events that we have experienced.

13. The memory strategy of _____ involves creating meaningful links between the items to be remembered.

14. A relatively permanent memory store that holds our knowledge of the world and our past experiences is the _____.

15. Knowledge of our own memory and memory processes is called _____.

16. Young children often exhibit _____ when they continue to use a strategy that may have been successful in the past but is not successful in the current context.

17. The process of getting information into the information-processing system and processing it is _____

18. A type of memory that requires individuals to reproduce a previously encountered stimulus without cues is _____.

19. Our lack of memory for the first few years of life is called _____.

20. Holding information in long-term memory is referred to as _____.

21. Using the information-processing system to achieve a goal or make a decision is known as _____.

22. A person's _____ is their knowledge of a content area.

23. The information processing tools that plan and monitor problem solving and decision making are called _____.

24. Memory that is intentional and deliberate is termed _____.

25. The _____ approach to cognition uses a computer analogy and emphasizes mental processes involved in attention, perception, memory, and decision making.

26. Knowledge about the mind and cognitive processes that might be used constitutes a person's _____.

27. A type of episodic memory that stores specific experiences from one's life is _____.

28. Children exhibit a _____ when they use strategies they are taught, but do not produce the strategies on their own.

29. A problem-solving strategy that rules out several possible solutions rather than just one is called _____.

30. The _____ holds a very brief but literal image or record of stimuli.

31. The _____ is an analysis of problem-solving ability that determines what information is encoded and what rules are generated by the problem solver.

32. Providing a hint to facilitate retrieval is _____.

33. Short-term memory is also referred to as _____.

34. Infants show _____ when they can reproduce an action they have previously seen at some later time.

35. Children who do not use or benefit from a strategy even when they are taught to use it show a _____.

36. During the process of _____, information is processed and organized to make it suitable for long-term storage.

37. According to Siegler's _____, development of problem-solving skills involves knowing a variety of strategies and becoming increasingly selective over time in choosing the best one for a given task.

38. Our ability to store and later retrieve information about the past constitutes our _____.

39. A type of episodic memory that consists of general facts is called _____.

40. Another term for the scripts that are created to represent the typical sequence of actions related to an event is _____.

MULTIPLE-CHOICE SELF-TEST

For each multiple choice question, read all alternatives and then select the best answer.

1. In the information-processing model, the "hardware" would be the _____ and the "software" would be the _____.
   a.   short- and long-term memory stores; strategies for storing or recalling information
   b.   memory knowledge; short-term and long-term memory stores
   c.   sensory receptors; central nervous system
   d.   central nervous system; sensory receptors

2. Tim is introduced to a professional colleague at a meeting, but has no idea what the person's name is immediately after it was spoken! It is most likely that the name
   a.   never made it past Tim's sensory register.
   b.   is stuck in Tim's short-term memory.
   c.   is lost in Tim's long-term memory.
   d.   could be cued to recall later on if Tim would relax a bit.

3. Taking an essay exam is an example of _____, while taking a multiple choice exam uses _____ memory.
   a.   long-term memory; short-term
   b.   recall; reconstruction
   c.   recall; recognition
   d.   recognition; long-term

4. Memory that is deliberate and effortful is _____, and memory that is unconscious or effortless is _____.
   a.   implicit; explicit
   b.   recall; recognition
   c.   explicit; implicit
   d.   cued recall; automatized

5. Habituation is sometimes used to assess infant's memory. Habituation occurs when an infant
   a. stops responding to a repeatedly presented stimulus.
   b. is conditioned to respond to a familiar stimulus.
   c. learns to respond to a desired stimulus.
   d. turns in the direction of a novel stimulus.

6. At age 8, Jill can remember more than her 3-year-old brother, Harry. This is MOST likely because
   a. Jill is smarter than Harry.
   b. Jill has a larger sensory register than Harry.
   c. Jill has a much better understanding of the strengths and weaknesses of her memory system than Harry.
   d. Jill makes more efficient use of her working memory than Harry does.

7. Memory strategies tend to develop in order, with _____ appearing first, followed by _____, and then _____.
   a. organization; elaboration; rehearsal
   b. organization; rehearsal; elaboration
   c. rehearsal; elaboration; organization
   d. rehearsal; organization; elaboration

8. Bob knows that he remembers the material in biology better when he takes notes from a chapter he is reading, than when he simply highlights passages in the text. His knowledge of this BEST illustrates _____.
   a. chunking   c. metamemory
   b. elaboration   d. organization

9. Most children and adults cannot remember much about their lives prior to about age 3. This is because
   a. early experiences are unimportant.
   b. they store verbatim rather than general accounts of events, leading to greater loss of information.
   c. they are not using adequate retrieval strategies.
   d. they have no ability to store memories prior to age 3.

10. Siegler's research regarding the rule assessment approach to problem solving (with the balance beam problem) shows that
    a. most children master the correct rule by age 8.
    b. even the youngest children, age 3, use logical rules to solve the problem.
    c. children master a single rule, applying it to all tasks, before moving on to another rule.
    d. children progress from guessing to trying several rules to selection of correct rules.

11. One difference between the memory strategy use of preadolescents and adolescents is that adolescents
   a. randomly select a strategy.
   b. use fewer strategies to remember important information.
   c. remember more irrelevant information than younger children.
   d. are better able to distinguish the more relevant points from the irrelevant points.

12. Research on expertise shows that
   a. experts do not know any more than nonexperts but are able to organize their knowledge more effectively.
   b. it depends on domain-specific knowledge and strategies.
   c. experts spend more time thinking through all possible options on a problem before selecting the correct one.
   d. expertise generalizes from one area to another, so experts tend to be good on multiple tasks.

13. Which of the following statements accurately describes memory performance of adults?
   a. Memory systematically declines throughout adulthood.
   b. Memory declines may occur in older adulthood, but they are typically small.
   c. Memory does not change from adolescence through middle adulthood, but after this, memory declines quite rapidly.
   d. Older adults experience no memory declines because they use more memory strategies than younger adults.

14. Some older adults develop a mild cognitive impairment and demonstrate
   a. substantial memory loss and signs of dementia.
   b. an inability to store new memories.
   c. lack of interest in the world around them.
   d. memory loss beyond what is considered normal, but not the pathological loss associated with disease.

15. Among adults, problem-solving skills
   a. tend to improve steadily across the lifespan.
   b. decline rapidly during middle age.
   c. frequently depend on the meaningfulness of the problem at hand.
   d. decline more rapidly in women than in men.

CRITICAL THINKING QUESTIONS

By answering the following questions, you will strengthen your understanding of the material in this chapter. These questions require higher-level thinking skills such as integration and application of concepts. Sample answers are provided for three of the questions. These illustrate one possibility, but there are other answers you could provide that might be just as good. For the other questions, you can check yourself by referring to the text (a hint is provided), or by asking a peer or your instructor to review your answer.

1.	What practical suggestions regarding the memory and problem-solving skills of older adults would be helpful to someone who works with older adults?
	[*Sample answer provided.*]

2.	In what ways are the memory and problem solving-skills of young children and older adults similar?
	[*Sample answer provided.*]

3.	What factors might explain the childhood amnesia that prevents most of us from recalling events of our infancy and early childhood?
	[*Sample answer provided.*]

4.	As children's eyewitness testimony in court proceedings has increased, we have seen more research on children's reliability as witnesses. Based on what you know about memory development from this chapter, what conclusions and suggestions can you make regarding the use of children as witnesses?
	[*Hint: Review the section on "The Child," with attention to strengths and weaknesses of children's memory.*]

5.	What advice would you give elementary and secondary school aged students to improve their memory and learning skills?
	[*Hint: Review the section "The Child" and "The Adolescent."*]

ANSWERS
Chapter Summary and Guided Review (fill in the blank)

1.	computer	21.	cues
2.	sensory register	22.	deferred
3.	short-term	23.	automatized
4.	long-term	24.	hippocampus
5.	encoded	25.	perseveration
6.	consolidation	26.	rehearsal
7.	storage	27.	organization
8.	retrieved	28.	elaboration
9.	recall	29.	mediation deficiency
10.	recognition	30.	production deficiency
11.	cued	31.	utilization deficiency
12.	implicit memory	32.	retrieval
13.	explicit memory	33.	metamemory
14.	semantic	34.	metacognition
15.	episodic	35.	knowledge base
16.	independently	36.	childhood amnesia
17.	control processes	37.	2 to 3
18.	imitate	38.	language
19.	habituation	39.	fuzzy trace
20.	operant conditioning	40.	scripts

Chapter Eight

41. reconstruction
42. eyewitness memory
43. rule assessment
44. guess
45. overlapping waves
46. faster
47. knowledge bases
48. metacognition
49. domain-specific
50. personal significance
51. distinctiveness
52. emotional

53. life
54. teens and 20s
55. cross-sectional
56. timed
57. unfamiliar
58. recall
59. explicit
60. knowledge bases
61. working
62. contextual
63. cohort
64. constraint-seeking

Review of Key Terms
1. eyewitness memory
2. rehearsal
3. fuzzy trace theory
4. implicit memory
5. mild cognitive impairment (MCI)
6. retrieval
7. organization
8. recognition memory
9. script
10. utilization deficiency
11. short-term memory
12. autobiographical memories
13. elaboration
14. long-term memory
15. metamemory
16. perseveration error
17. encoding
18. recall memory
19. childhood amnesia
20. storage

21. problem-solving
22. knowledge base
23. executive control processes
24. explicit
25. information-processing
26. metacognition
27. episodic memory
28. constraint-seeking questions
29. production deficiency
30. sensory register
31. rule assessment approach
32. cued recall memory
33. working memory
34. deferred imitation
35. mediation deficiency
36. consolidation
37. overlapping waves theory
38. memory
39. semantic memory
40. general event representation

Multiple-Choice Self-Test
1. A (p. 245)
2. A (p. 245)
3. C (p. 246)
4. C (p. 246)
5. A (p. 248)
6. D (p. 250-55)
7. D (p. 252)
8. C (p. 253)
9. B (p. 255)
10. D (p. 257-58)
11. D (p. 259)
12. B (p. 262)
13. B (p. 263; 265)
14. D (p. 264)
15. C (p. 270)

Critical Thinking Questions
1. *It's true that older adults have some trouble with memory and problem solving relative to younger adults. Still, like everyone, they have strengths and weaknesses, and the trick is to maximize their strengths and minimize their weaknesses. To help them perform better, avoid*

timed tasks. Older adults are slower to learn and retrieve information and may need more time to accomplish these tasks than their younger counterparts. They also do poorly when given novel words to remember or unfamiliar tasks to solve. But they do just fine if the material and tasks are familiar to them. Indeed, given their life experiences, older adults have a more extensive knowledge base than other age groups. Another disadvantage for older adults is that they are often tested in situations that are common for young adults who are working or going to school, but not for people who have been retired or away from school for many years. By testing older adults in situations that they typically experience, where they can use well-practiced skills, they perform better. Like all age groups, older adults are better on recognition tasks than recall tasks, so we can optimize their performance by testing them with a recognition format. Similarly, we can optimize performance by structuring learning situations as implicit rather than explicit. It's also important to consider sensory changes that older adults might experience—visual and auditory declines can tax the information-processing system leading to memory trouble. Correcting vision and hearing problems can help memory problems in some cases. Fortunately, research shows that older adults can benefit from memory training (you can teach an old dog new tricks), and significant problems with memory and problem solving are unusual.

2.   The memory and problem-solving abilities of young children and older adults have some common features but also some important differences. Like young children, older adults may not spontaneously use strategies. And both young children and older adults need to devote more space in working memory to carrying out basic mental operations such as recognizing stimuli. This leaves less space for other purposes, such as thinking about or rehearsing material. Both young children and older adults do relatively well when learning and remembering can take place automatically (i.e., when mental effort is not required), but struggle when they need to exert more mental effort. The problem with working memory is probably due to slower functioning of the nervous system both early and late in life.

Although the question asks for similarities and not differences between young children and older adults, there are two differences worth noting. Older adults have a much larger knowledge base than younger children, and they also know more about how their memory works (metamemory). These advantages may allow older adults to compensate for their slow working memory and their lack of spontaneous strategy use so that they end up outperforming young children on many memory tasks.

3.   Most people have trouble remembering anything that happened to them before the age of 2 or 3 years. This is called childhood amnesia. One explanation for this is that infants and toddlers may not have enough space in working memory to hold all the pieces of information about an event that would be needed to recall the event. Another possibility is that their language limitations constrain what infants and toddlers can store and later recall about an event. Thus, perhaps language is needed to store memories in some kind of linguistic code that can be retrieved later on. A third explanation is that memories from this early period of life are no longer useful in light of the new developmental tasks that children face. Finally, the fuzzy-trace theory suggests that verbatim and general accounts of an event are stored separately. Verbatim information is problematic and likely to be lost over long periods of time, but general accounts (e.g., remembering the "gist" of an event) remain viable for longer periods of time. Young children seem to store more verbatim information about events and gradually move to storing the more efficient general information as they get a little older.

CHAPTER NINE

INTELLIGENCE AND CREATIVITY

OVERVIEW

The chapter opens by considering the meaning of intelligence: Is it a single ability or many? If it consists of multiple abilities, what are these? The relationship between intelligence and creativity is also discussed. As with other chapters, there are sections devoted to each of the major age groups—infants, children, adolescents, and adults— where developmental changes in intelligence and creativity are discussed. In particular, the stability and continuity of IQ scores are considered, as are the potential uses of IQ scores.

Genetic and environmental factors that influence IQ scores are discussed in this chapter. Recall that genetic influences on intelligence were discussed earlier in the text (Chapter 3), and it might be useful for you to review the evidence for genetic contributions that was presented in the earlier chapter. The section in this chapter focuses on environmental factors, including the home, social class, and culture.

Finally, a discussion of the extremes of intelligence—intellectual disability and giftedness—is also included in this chapter.

LEARNING OBJECTIVES

After reading and studying the material in this chapter, you should be able to answer the following questions.

9.1   DEFINING INTELLIGENCE AND CREATIVITY
1.   What is the psychometric approach to intelligence, and how have different psychometric theorists defined intelligence?

2.   What are the traditional measures of intelligence, and what are some of the advantages and disadvantages of these approaches? What are some alternatives to these traditional measures of intelligence?

3.   What is creativity, and how does it relate to intelligence?

9.2   THE INFANT
4.   What methods have been used to assess infant intelligence, and how successful is each method? To what extent is infant intelligence related to later intelligence?

9.3   THE CHILD

5.   Are IQ scores stable during childhood? What factors contribute to gains and losses in IQ scores?

6.   What are the typical characteristics of creative children?

9.4   THE ADOLESCENT

7.   How well do IQ scores predict school achievement?

8.   How can creativity be fostered?

9.5   THE ADULT

9.   To what extent is IQ related to occupational success and to health?

10.   How do IQ and mental abilities change with age? What factors predict declines in intellectual abilities in older adults?

11.   To what extent does wisdom exist in older adults?

12.   How does creativity change throughout adulthood?

9.6   FACTORS THAT INFLUENCE IQ SCORES

13.   What evidence shows genetic influence on IQ scores? What other factors influence IQ scores?

9.7   THE EXTREMES OF INTELLIGENCE

14.   How are intellectual disability and giftedness defined? What are the outcomes for individuals who have an intellectual disability or giftedness?

9.8   INTEGRATING COGNITIVE PERSPECTIVES

15.   How do the various approaches to understanding cognitive development fit together?

CHAPTER SUMMARY AND GUIDED REVIEW

The following summary provides an overview of the main points contained in this chapter of the text. Fill in the blanks with terms that appropriately complete the sentence. Scattered throughout the summary are questions in parentheses. These are meant to encourage you to think actively as you read and connect this summary to the more detailed information provided in the text.

9.1   DEFINING INTELLIGENCE AND CREATIVITY

There are numerous perspectives on what intelligence is and how it can be measured.

The Psychometric Approach

The psychometric approach views intelligence as a trait, or set of traits, that vary among people and can be measured. Early views of intelligence were influenced by Spearman, who concluded that a (1) _____ factor contributed to performance on many different tasks. Cattell and Horn proposed a still popular idea that intelligence consists of two major dimensions. The ability to solve novel problems is (2) _____ intelligence, and the ability to use knowledge acquired through experiences is (3) _____ intelligence.

One of the earliest measures of intelligence used age-graded problems to determine a child's (4) _____. This test evolved into the Stanford-Binet Intelligence Scale, which calculates a person's (5) _____ by comparing mental age to chronological age. The test now uses standards of normal or average performance, called (6) _____, to estimate an individual's IQ score. Another standardized measure of intelligence is the set of tests called the (7) _____, which each yield subscores of verbal and performance IQ. Scores on these standardized IQ tests form a symmetrical or (8) _____ around the average score. About two-thirds of those taking the test score within one (9) _____ of the average score. *(What are the pros and cons of such standardized tests for assessing intelligence, and what are some alternative approaches?)*

Gardner's Theory of Multiple Intelligences

Howard Gardner proposed that there are multiple intelligences, including at least eight distinct abilities. *(Can you give examples or list the different abilities?)* Evidence that someone can be good in one area but poor in another comes from individuals with (10) _____.

Sternberg's Triarchic Theory

Sternberg's triarchic theory emphasizes three aspects of intelligent behavior. According to the (11) _____ component of the model, intelligent behavior depends on the sociocultural context in which it is displayed and so can be expected to vary from one culture or subculture to another. The (12) _____ component predicts that intelligent behavior will be affected by the experience that one has with a situation or task. The intelligent response to a task the first time it is encountered may differ from what is considered intelligent after many encounters with the same task. The increased efficiency that comes with familiarity and practice with a task reflects (13) _____. Administering an intelligence test to two groups of people that has items familiar to one group but not to the other introduces (14) _____ and makes it unfair to compare performances of the two groups. The third aspect of Sternberg's triarchic model is the (15) _____ component and includes the information-processing strategies used to solve problems. Sternberg has expanded his triarchic theory of intelligence to include the idea that intelligence involves the ability to do well in life, something he calls (16) _____.

Creativity

Creativity is the ability to produce responses to a problem that are (17) _____. Creativity involves (18) _____ thinking, or the ability to come up with a variety of ideas or solutions to a problem. Creativity is often measured by the total number of different ideas that one can generate in response to a problem, or (19) _____. IQ tests typically measure (20) _____ thinking, which involves coming up with the one "correct" answer to a problem.

9.2   THE INFANT
Developmental Quotients

Infant achievement is typically measured with the (21) _____ Scales of Infant Development. This test includes a motor scale and a mental scale, which are used to assign a (22) _____. A third component of the test is an infant behavioral record. Bayley scores can be used to chart developmental progress, and low scores may indicate intellectual disability.

Infant Intelligence and Later Intelligence

Scores on the Bayley do not accurately predict later IQ, possibly because infant tests and IQ tests for children and adults measure qualitatively different abilities. Another possibility is that intelligence during infancy is highly influenced by universal (23) _____ processes. Starting around the age of two, these forces lessen, and individual differences become more apparent. Research suggests that later IQ may be better predicted by performance on some measures of infant (24) _____, such as speed of habituation and preference for novelty. (***Why might this be a better predictor?***)

9.3   THE CHILD
How Stable are IQ Scores during Childhood?

Starting at age 4, there is a fairly strong relationship between IQ scores obtained at different times throughout childhood. However, although group scores are fairly stable, scores of individual children can fluctuate quite substantially. (***What do these findings suggest?***)

Causes of Gain and Loss

One reason for fluctuating IQ scores is an unstable environment. The (25) _____ hypothesis suggests that intellectual development of children from impoverished environments is diminished, and this effect builds over time so that children's intelligence actually seems to decline. (***Is there any research support for this hypothesis?***)

The Emergence of Creativity

Levels of creativity may drop as children enter school, where convergent thinking is typically encouraged. Children who are creative tend to show more freedom, originality, humor, violence, and playfulness and engage in more pretend play than children who are not creative. Creativity seems to be related to a child's (26) _____ but is not affected by race or socioeconomic status.

9.4   THE ADOLESCENT
Continuity between Childhood and Adulthood

Intelligence continues to grow during early adolescence, but levels off in late adolescence. This may be related to basic brain changes. Individual performance on IQ tests tends to be more stable at this age and predicts adult IQ performance quite well.

IQ and School Achievement

IQ scores are often used to predict school achievement, and they are fairly good at doing this. Prediction is more accurate for high school grades than for college grades. (***Why is this true?***)

Fostering Creativity

Creativity often increases during adolescence, but this depends on the type of task. Individuals who have creative talent are likely to achieve accomplishments if they are highly (27) _____ and grow up in a nurturing environment. Scores on creativity tests may predict accomplishments outside the classroom better than in-class performance.

9.5   THE ADULT

IQ and Occupational Success

In adults, there is a relationship between IQ scores and occupational status. Specifically, the more prestigious jobs are filled with people who, overall, have higher IQs than people in less prestigious jobs. IQ scores are also related to measures of actual job performance.

IQ and Health

Correlational research shows that people who score higher on IQ tests are often healthier and live longer than people who score lower. One possible explanation for this connection is   (28) _____ because people who are smarter may have better jobs. In addition, people who are smarter may be better at monitoring health and applying treatments.

Changes in IQ with Age

Cross-sectional research on intelligence across the lifespan indicates that IQ scores rise slowly until age 44 and decline thereafter. Longitudinal research has also shown some decline in IQ in old age. However, sequential studies of changes in intelligence show that some gains in intelligence are made throughout middle adulthood, and declines, if they occur, typically occur only late in life. (***Do you remember how sequential designs eliminate the weaknesses inherent to cross-sectional and longitudinal designs?***) Sequential designs are able to illustrate generational or (29) _____ · effects on intelligence. This research also indicates that (30) _____ intelligence declines earlier and more sharply than   (31) _____ intelligence. On the Wechsler adult test, IQ scores on the (32) _____ scale decline earlier than IQ scores on the (33) _____ scale. In addition, performance on (34) _____ tests declines in old age and may reflect a general slowing of the adult's information-processing ability. However, declines in intellectual performance are not universal.

Predictors of Decline

For individuals who do experience a decline in intellectual performance, poor (35) _____ is often the culprit. People tend to experience a (36) _____ a few years before they die. Another factor contributing to declining intellectual performance is lack of a (37) _____ lifestyle.

Potential for Wisdom

A person who has exceptional insight about life is often considered to have wisdom. In general, wisdom is not common among older adults. Research indicates that (38) _____ is more relevant than age to the development of wisdom. (*What qualities are thought to indicate wisdom?*) Certain cognitive styles seem to foster wisdom, as does a supportive social environment.

Creative Endeavors

Creative output seems to increase throughout early adulthood and declines only in older adulthood. This pattern varies, though, depending on the field of work. According to one theory, people may have a certain limit on their creative potential. Creativity involves generating the ideas, or (39) _____, and executing the ideas to produce creative output, which is (40) _____. Individuals may generate ideas at different rates, accounting for differences in creativity across different fields as well as age differences.

FACTORS THAT INFLUENCE IQ SCORES
Flynn Effect

According to the Flynn effect, average IQ scores have increased around the world in recent decades (*What factors might account for this phenomenon?*)

Genes and Environments

Differences in IQ scores across the lifespan are influenced by genetic factors, as evidenced by the results of twin studies and adoption studies. (*What pattern of results would demonstrate a genetic influence on IQ scores?*)

Research shows that numerous environmental factors influence IQ scores. An instrument for measuring the amount and type of intellectual stimulation in a child's home is the (41) _____. Scores on this inventory predict children's cognitive functioning fairly well. In particular, (42) _____ involvement with the child, provision of appropriate (43) _____ materials, and opportunities for various types of stimulation were strongly related to the child's cognitive functioning. Research suggests that the best predictor of a child's IQ at age two is (44) _____. Later, quality of home environment significantly predicts IQ.

Poverty

IQ scores are affected by the socioeconomic status of the child's family, such that children who experience poverty while growing up score lower than children from middle-class homes. Children from impoverished backgrounds who are adopted into advantaged homes show improvements in IQ.

Race and Ethnicity

A great deal of controversy has surrounded the finding that children of different racial and ethnic backgrounds score lower on IQ tests than Caucasian children. There are several possible reasons for this. One is (45) _____ in testing because the tests are more appropriate for children from white, middle-class backgrounds. In an attempt to eliminate or reduce this possibility, (46) _____IQ tests have been developed. Differences between racial and ethnic groups are still apparent on these tests.

Another possibility is that minority children are not as highly (47) _____ in testing situations as white, middle-class children. Related to this, research shows that African-American children perform poorly when they believe that tests may be measuring qualities associated with negative stereotypes of African Americans, a phenomenon called (48) _____.

A third possibility is that there are (49) _____ differences between ethnic and racial groups that contribute to observed differences on IQ tests. There are, in fact, genetic differences (50) _____ groups, but these differences do not translate into differences (51) _____ groups.

A fourth explanation for average group differences is environmental variation. Support for this explanation comes from the finding that the IQ scores of African-American children increase when these children are adopted into white, middle-class homes. This suggests that children, regardless of their racial background, do better when they grow up in intellectually (52) _____ environments, with responsive parents and exposure to the culture of the test.

9.7 THE EXTREMES OF INTELLIGENCE

Intellectual Disability

Individuals who are diagnosed with an intellectual disability show below average intellectual functioning and impairments in (53) _____. (***What are the different levels of intellectual disability?***)

Giftedness

Individuals who have high IQ scores or show special abilities are considered gifted. Terman's longitudinal of gifted children dispelled a number of myths about gifted individuals. In short, gifted individuals are not the social misfits or weaklings that many people believed them to be. As adults, children from Terman's study were generally healthy, happy, and productive.

9.8 INTEGRATING COGNITIVE APPROACHES

Four major approaches to cognitive development have been presented in Chapters 7, 8, and 9. These include Piaget's theory of (54) _____ in Chapter 7, the information-processing approach in Chapter 8, and the testing or (55) _____ approach presented in Chapter 9. (***What is the essential "take home" message of each approach?***)

REVIEW OF KEY TERMS

Below is a list of terms and concepts from this chapter. Use these to complete the following sentence definitions. You might also want to try writing definitions in your own words and then checking your definitions with those in the text.

analytic component
automatization
Bayley Scales of Infant Development

child poverty
convergent thinking
creative component

creativity
crystallized intelligence
culture bias
cumulative-deficit hypothesis
developmental quotient (DQ)
divergent thinking
fluid intelligence
Flynn effect
giftedness
HOME inventory
intellectual disability
intelligence quotient (IQ)
mental age (MA)
normal distribution

practical component
psychometric approach
savant syndrome
standard deviation
Stanford-Binet Intelligence Scale
stereotype threat
Sternberg's Triarchic Abilities Test
    (STAT)
successful intelligence
terminal drop
test norms
triarchic theory of intelligence
Wechsler Scales
wisdom

1. The increase in average IQ scores that has occurred over the course of the 20th century is termed the _____.

2. The ability to solve novel problems is considered _____.

3. A group of tests that assess intelligence over the lifespan and provide subscores of verbal and performance IQ are collectively called the _____.

4. The _____ provides an index of an infant's performance on developmental tasks relative to other infants the same age.

5. The rapid decline in intellectual abilities that often occurs within a few years before dying is called the _____.

6. The _____ is a theoretical perspective that views intelligence as a trait or set of traits on which people differ and these differences can be measured.

7. Intelligence tests typically measure _____, or thinking that produces a single answer to question or problem.

8. The ability to use knowledge acquired through specific learning and life experiences is _____.

9. The ability to produce novel responses or words is referred to as _____.

10. The _____ proposes that impoverished environments inhibit intellectual growth, and these negative effects accumulate over time.

11. On an intelligence test, the _____ is level of age-graded problems that a child can solve.

12. Sternberg's _____ is an information-processing theory that emphasizes the context, experience, and information-processing components of intelligent behavior.

13. Standards of typical performance on a test as reflected by average scores and the range of scores around the average are referred to as _____.

14. Creativity tests often measure _____, the type of thinking that produces a variety of solutions to a problem when there is no one right answer.

15. Low income and inadequate levels of meeting children's basic needs contribute to _____.

16. The process of _____ refers to the increased efficiency of information-processing that comes with familiarity and practice.

17. People with _____ either have high IQ scores or show special abilities in areas valued by society.

18. A developmental assessment of infant's motor, mental, and behavior milestones is provided by the _____.

19. In Sternberg's triarchic theory of intelligence, the ability to select the appropriate mental process to succeed on a task is the _____.

20. An index of a person's performance on an intelligence test relative to their chronological age is a(n) _____.

21. The idea that IQ tests favor children from certain cultural backgrounds, namely, white middle-class backgrounds, is _____.

22. Some members of minority groups may experience _____ because they fear that others will assume they have the qualities associated with the negative stereotypes of their group.

23. Sternberg argues that people are intelligent to the extent that they have the ability to succeed in the life they choose for themselves, a concept he calls _____.

24. A person who has an extraordinary talent but who is otherwise mentally retarded is diagnosed with _____.

25. Individuals with _____ perform significantly below average on intelligence tests and show deficits in adaptive behavior skills during the developmental period.

26. The _____ is an instrument for measuring the amount and type of intellectual stimulation in a child's home environment.

27. A standardized test comparing a person's mental age to his/her chronological age is
_____.

28. Some older adults are believed to show _____, or sound judgment and advice about important life issues.

29. The _____ is a bell-shaped distribution with most scores falling close to the average score.

30. Sternberg's triarchic theory draws attention to the importance of being able to solve everyday problems, a component he calls _____.

31. Effectively dealing with novel problems and automating your response to familiar problems is Sternberg's _____ of intelligence.

32. The range or spread of scores around an average score is the _____ of the scores.

33. An alternative test of intelligence that assesses practical, creative, and analytic components is _____.

MULTIPLE-CHOICE SELF-TEST

For each multiple choice question, read all alternatives and then select the best answer.

1. Which of the following is an example of crystallized intelligence?
   a. Remembering unrelated word pairs (e.g., dog-couch)
   b. Solving verbal analogies
   c. Realizing the relationship between geometric figures
   d. Solving word comprehension problems (e.g., what does "participate" mean?)

2. Practical intelligence is best indicated by
   a. successfully solving everyday tasks.
   b. automating familiar tasks to deal more effectively with new tasks.
   c. selecting the most appropriate mental process for solving a problem.
   d. thinking critically and being able to compare and contrast ideas.

3. Sternberg's concept of successful intelligence is characterized by
   a. getting a high score on an intelligence test such as the Stanford-Binet.
   b. gaining knowledge at a faster rate than other individuals the same age.
   c. demonstrating the abilities needed to succeed in one's chosen field, within a particular sociocultural context.
   d. doing well in school.

4. Creativity is typically assessed by using measures of _____ thinking, whereas intelligence tests typically measure _____ thinking.
   a. divergent; contextual
   b. experiential; divergent
   c. crystallized; fluid
   d. divergent; convergent

5. The Bayley Scale of Infant Development is a useful indicator of
   a. childhood intelligence.
   b. whether or not the child is gifted.
   c. a child's developmental progress through major milestones.
   d. problem-solving abilities that the child possesses.

6. Correlations between scores on infant intelligence tests and scores on later intelligence tests show that
   a. infants who score high typically score high as children and adolescents.
   b. infant intelligence scores can predict later intelligence for those who score around the mean of 100.
   c. there is little relationship between infant intelligence and later intelligence.
   d. infant intelligence scores predict childhood intelligence but not adult intelligence.

7. Correlations of IQ measured during early and middle childhood with IQ measured during adolescence and young adulthood indicate that for individuals, IQ scores
   a. are quite stable.
   b. can fluctuate quite a bit.
   c. generally increase with age.
   d. generally decrease with age.

8. The cumulative-deficit hypothesis suggests that
   a. lack of intellectual stimulation produces an overall deficit in intelligence that is stable over time.
   b. lack of intellectual stimulation depresses intellectual growth more and more over time.
   c. lack of intellectual stimulation early in life is less damaging than lack of intellectual stimulation later in life.
   d. parents with low IQ scores will have children with low IQ scores.

9. The relationship between IQ and occupational status indicates that
   a. IQ scores are more likely to predict job preference than job performance.
   b. people with high IQ scores do not work in low status occupations.
   c. people with high IQ scores are more likely to work in high status occupations than people with low IQ scores.
   d. there is no relationship between these two factors.

10. Which of the following describes how intellectual abilities change with age?
    a. Overall, intellectual abilities decline significantly with age.
    b. Crystallized intelligence declines with age more than fluid intelligence.
    c. Fluid intelligence declines with age more than crystallized intelligence.
    d. No decline in intelligence occurs with age.

11. Declines in intellectual performance among older adults may occur because of all of the following EXCEPT
    a. unstimulating lifestyles.
    b. slower response times.
    c. poor health.
    d. lack of sufficient knowledge base.

12. With respect to creativity in adulthood,
    a. creative endeavors decrease throughout adulthood.
    b. creative endeavors increase in young adulthood and then usually peak and remain steady in middle adulthood.
    c. creative endeavors are at their peak during college years and early adulthood.
    d. creative endeavors decline significantly for older adults in all fields.

13. A child's home environment
    a. is unrelated to his/her intelligence.
    b. can increase or decrease intelligence depending on whether children have lots of toys and frequent visits from friends.
    c. can increase intelligence when parents are involved and responsive to his/her needs.
    d. can decrease intelligence if parents are overly responsive and spoil their children.

14. Research on ethnic and racial differences in IQ scores shows that differences
    a. do not really exist.
    b. result from genetic differences between racial groups.
    c. can be reduced with the appropriate environmental intervention.
    d. do exist but cannot be reduced or eliminated.

15. Intellectual disability is defined by
    a. deficits in intelligence and difficulties with adaptive behavior, both evidenced during the developmental period.
    b. abnormal brain development.
    c. inability to function at grade level in school.
    d. low scores on standardized intelligence tests that become increasingly poor over time.

COMPARE THEORETICAL VIEWS ON INTELLIGENCE

Answer the three questions on the left for each theory or theorist. Use Table 9.6 on page 306 of the text to check yourself.

	PIAGET	VYGOTSKY	INFORMATION PROCESSING	PSYCHOMETRIC APPROACH
What is intelligence?				
What changes with age?				
What is of most interest?				

CRITICAL THINKING QUESTIONS

By answering the following questions, you will strengthen your understanding of the material in this chapter. These questions require higher-level thinking skills such as integration and application of concepts. Sample answers are provided for three of the questions. These illustrate one possibility, but there are other answers you could provide that might be just as good. For the other questions, you can check yourself by referring to the text (a hint is provided), or by asking a peer or your instructor to review your answer.

1. In order to make the most accurate prediction about later IQ based on <u>infant</u> measures, what information or test would you want to have access to? Justify your answer.
   [*Sample answer provided.*]

2. How would you describe a smart infant, a smart child, a smart adolescent, and a smart adult?
   [*Sample answer provided.*]

3. How can we best define and identify a child who has an intellectual disability?
   [*Sample answer provided.*]

4. How do schools foster or discourage creative thinking? What are the advantages of encouraging creative thought?
   [*Hint: Review subsection on "Fostering creativity" within The Adolescent.*]

5. It has been noted that there may be culture bias in intelligence testing, resulting in certain groups of people scoring lower or higher than other groups of people. Another finding

---

Intelligence and Creativity

Page 143

© 2012 Cengage Learning. All Rights Reserved. May not be scanned, copied or duplicated, or posted to a publicly accessible website, in whole or in part.

regarding intelligence tests is that they are relatively accurate at predicting academic success, job performance, and even health. What conclusions can be logically drawn from these two seemingly disparate findings?

[*Hint: You need to integrate your understanding of these two pieces of information. Review the sections of the chapter on "IQ and school achievement," "IQ and occupational success," and "Culture bias." Then consider how you could synthesize these findings to arrive at a logical conclusion.*]

ANSWERS

Chapter Summary and Guided Review (fill in the blank)

1. general
2. fluid
3. crystallized
4. mental age
5. intelligence quotient (IQ)
6. test norms
7. Wechsler Scales
8. normal distribution
9. standard deviation
10. savant syndrome
11. practical
12. creative
13. automatization
14. culture bias
15. analytic
16. successful intelligence
17. novel or original
18. divergent
19. ideational fluency
20. convergent
21. Bayley
22. developmental quotient
23. maturational
24. attention
25. cumulative-deficit
26. home environment
27. motivated
28. socioeconomic
29. cohort
30. fluid
31. crystallized
32. performance
33. verbal
34. timed
35. health
36. terminal drop
37. stimulating
38. expertise
39. ideation
40. elaboration
41. HOME inventory
42. parental
43. play
44. mother's IQ
45. culture bias
46. culture fair
47. motivated
48. stereotype threat
49. genetic
50. within
51. between
52. stimulating
53. adaptive behavior
54. cognitive development
55. psychometric

Review of Key Terms

1. Flynn effect
2. fluid intelligence
3. Wechsler Scales
4. developmental quotient (DQ)
5. terminal drop
6. psychometric approach
7. convergent thinking
8. crystallized intelligence
9. creativity
10. cumulative-deficit hypothesis

11. mental age (MA)
12. triarchic theory of intelligence
13. test norms
14. divergent thinking
15. child poverty
16. automatization
17. giftedness
18. Bayley Scales of Infant Development
19. analytic component
20. intelligence quotient (IQ)
21. culture bias
22. stereotype threat
23. successful intelligence
24. savant syndrome
25. intellectual disability
26. HOME inventory
27. Stanford-Binet Intelligence Scale
28. wisdom
29. normal distribution
30. practical component
31. creative component
32. standard deviation
33. Sternberg Triarchic Abilities Test (STAT)

Multiple-Choice Self-Test
1. D (p. 277)
2. A (p. 280-81)
3. C (p. 281)
4. D (p. 282)
5. C (p. 283-84)
6. C (p. 284)
7. B (p. 285)
8. B (p. 285)
9. C (p. 290)
10. C (p. 291-92)
11. D (p. 293)
12. B (p. 295-96)
13. C (p. 298-99)
14. C (p. 300-302)
15. A (p. 303)

Critical Thinking Questions
1.   *I would want to have access to a measure of infant attention, such as how quickly an infant becomes bored with a stimulus (speed of habituation) or the extent to which an infant prefers a novel stimulus rather than a familiar one (preference for novelty). These sorts of measures show how quickly an infant processes information. The faster infants process information, the more quickly they learn, and the brighter they will be later on.*

The Bayley DQ scores don't correlate very well with later IQ scores, probably because the Bayley measures motor skills and behaviors. While these may be important measures during infancy of whether an infant is "on track," they are not important components of later intelligence. Intelligence tests focus on verbal and quantitative reasoning, not motor skills.

Another useful measure to collect during infancy might be scores on the HOME Inventory. This provides an estimate of how stimulating the home is, and correlates to later performance on IQ tests. Infants and young children who grow up in homes that provide stimulation and interaction with parents typically score higher on measures of intelligence.

Finally, it might also help to know the IQ score of the infant's mother. Maternal IQ predicts infant's IQ, although it is less useful as children get older, suggesting that environmental factors begin to influence intelligence.

2.   *The simplest way to answer this question is to note that a smart person of any age is someone who can process lots of information quickly. Efficient information processing allows a person to take in more information than someone who doesn't process the same information as quickly. It also means they can solve problems more efficiently. This is why measures of information processing and attention during infancy correlate with later IQ scores more than scores on traditional infant tests like the Bayley Scales.*

3.	*The American Association on Intellectual and Developmental Disabilities uses three criteria to diagnose intellectual disability:*

- *Significantly below average intellectual functioning on a standard intelligence test such as Stanford-Binet. Significantly below average is normally interpreted as two standard deviations below the mean of 100, which would be a cut-off score of 68-70, depending on which IQ test is used.*
- *Significant deficits in adaptive behaviors such as being able to take care of oneself. Thus, the person has trouble meeting age-appropriate standards of everyday functioning.*
- *Starting before the age of 18. Intellectual disability is thought to be a problem originating during the developmental period. If the first two criteria are first observed after the age of 18, some disorder other than intellectual disability would be diagnosed.*

CHAPTER TEN

LANGUAGE AND EDUCATION

OVERVIEW

This chapter begins by delving into language development, a complex skill learned though an informal educational system of parents and others. You will need to understand the various components of language that children need to master in order to learn language. You will also need to understand the developmental course of language. Finally, how do theorists account for the fact that children learn language with little formal instruction? The textbook covers the three major theoretical views on language development—learning theory, Chomsky's nativist perspective, and the social interactionist perspective—and also considers whether there is support for a critical period for language acquisition.

Next, the chapter addresses the formal educational system and achievement motivation. Even infants show evidence of motivation when they try to control or master their environments. Mastery motivation is enhanced by sensory stimulation and growing up in a responsive environment. Many young children attend some sort of preschool program, which can be beneficial to disadvantaged children. Children exhibit clear differences in levels of achievement motivation and you will learn about some of the factors that contribute to these differences. Children also enter the formal school system and must focus on the complex task of learning to read. You'll need to understand what it takes to master this skill and why some children experience difficulties.

Among adolescents, research reveals the discouraging finding that achievement motivation often declines as children move from elementary school to middle school to high school. Science and math education become higher priorities as children move through school, and cross-cultural research illustrates some differences in this area between U.S. teens and teens in other cultures. Some teens integrate work with school, which seems to interfere with academic success when work hours are long and the job is menial.

Adults' motivation is influenced by their work and family contexts. Some adults struggle with problems associated with illiteracy, and some adults seek continued educational opportunities.

LEARNING OBJECTIVES

After reading and studying the material in this chapter, you should be able to answer the following questions.

10.1   MASTERING LANGUAGE
1.   What skills or knowledge must we develop in order to acquire language?

2.   What is the typical developmental course of language acquisition over the first few years?

3. How does brain activity support and influence language development?

4. How do learning, nativist, and interactionist perspectives explain the acquisition of language? Which explanation is best supported by research?

10.2 THE INFANT

5. What factors influence mastery motivation of infants? How is this related to later achievement?

10.3 THE CHILD

6. What are the pros and cons of early education?

7. What factors contribute to differences in levels of achievement motivation during childhood, and what can be done to foster achievement motivation?

8. What are the components of learning to read? Is there a most effective way of teaching reading? What distinguishes skilled and unskilled readers?

9. How does school affect children? What factors characterize effective schools?

10.4 THE ADOLESCENT

10. What changes in achievement motivation occur during adolescence? What factors contribute to these changes?

11. How does science and math education in the United States compare to science and math education in other countries?

12. What are the pros and cons of integrating work with school during adolescence?

10.5 THE ADULT

13. How does achievement motivation change during adulthood?

14. How do literacy, illiteracy, and continued education affect adult's lives?

CHAPTER SUMMARY AND GUIDED REVIEW

The following summary provides an overview of the main points contained in this chapter of the text. Fill in the blanks with terms that appropriately complete the sentence. Scattered throughout the summary are questions in parentheses. These are meant to encourage you to think actively as you read and connect this summary to the more detailed information provided in the text.

10.1 MASTERING LANGUAGE

Despite its complexity, language is mastered at a young age. Language is a system of symbols that can be combined using agreed-on rules to produce messages.

What Must Be Mastered?

The basic units of sound are called (1) _____, and the basic units of meaning in a word are (2) _____. The rules specifying how to combine words in meaningful ways is the (3)_____ of language, and the meaningful way in which words are combined into sentences is the (4) _____ of language. Finally, the rules specifying how language is to be used in different contexts and with different audiences are the (5) _____ of language. Producing meaningful speech also involves how sounds are produced, referred to as the melody or (6) _____ of speech.

When Does Language Develop?

Infants must be able to detect a target word in a stream of speech, demonstrating (7)_____. They begin making prelinguistic vocalizations soon after birth with several distinct cries. By the end of the first month, infants begin (8) _____, or repeating vowel-like sounds, and by 3 or 4 months of age, infants combine vowel and consonant sounds to produce (9) _____. These early utterances are the same across all cultures until about six months of age, when experience begins to alter them. (***What evidence shows that experience has an impact on babbling?***) Infants demonstrate that their understanding or (10) _____ many words before they can (11)_____ the words. Infants and caregivers often engage in (12) _____ by both looking at and attending to a common item. Infants may use syntax or word placement to help understand the meaning of the word, a process called (13) _____.

At about one year, infants produce their first meaningful words, often called (14)_____ because they can convey the meaning of an entire sentence when combined with gestures or intonation. The pace at which language develops escalates around 18 months of age during a (15) _____. Young children often err in their speech by using fairly specific words to refer to a general class of objects, which is a mistake called an (16) _____. Young children may also err by using a general word too narrowly, which is an (17) _____. (***Can you provide examples of these errors?***)

Around 18 to 24 months, infants typically begin to combine two or more words into simple sentences called (18) _____ speech. These early sentences may be best described in terms of a (19) _____, which focuses on the semantic relations between words. As children acquire an understanding of grammar, they often make mistakes, such as overapplying rules they have learned to cases that are irregular, an error called (20)_____. Chomsky proposed that language be described in terms of (21)_____, which consists of rules of syntax for transforming basic sentences into other forms. (***Can you provide an example of one of these rules?***)

School-age children refine their pronunciation skills and produce longer and more complex sentences. They demonstrate better command of the pragmatics of language and can talk about events that have happened in the past or will happen in the future. They also develop an ability to think about language and use it in ways not possible at younger ages, which shows increased (22) _____.

How Does Language Develop?

In most humans, there is more activity in the brain's (23) _____ hemisphere when listening to speech and more activity in the brain's (24) _____ hemisphere More specifically, an area of the brain associated with language comprehension is called

(25)_____; one associated with speech production is called
(26)_____. In some individuals, the fibers connecting these two parts of the
brain are damaged, resulting in a language disorder called (27) _____.

There are several theoretical explanations of how children come to learn language. Children
may learn language the same way they learn everything else—through observation, imitation,
and reinforcement, a perspective offered by (28) _____. This perspective seems
to best explain how children acquire the phonology and (29) _____ of language.
(*What evidence supports this explanation of language acquisition?*)

Another perspective proposes that humans are born with knowledge of common rules of
language, or (30) _____, that allows them to learn any language. Specifically,
children have an inborn mechanism, called a (31)_____ that allows them to infer
the rules governing the speech they hear and then apply these rules to their own speech. (*What
evidence supports this nativist explanation of language acquisition?*) This theory may explain
grammar or (32) _____ developments but has difficulty with other aspects of
language acquisition. (*What are the two major problems with this perspective?*)

Combining elements of both the learning and nativist perspectives is the
(33)_____ perspective, which argues that innate capacities and the language
environment interact to influence language development. These theorists emphasize how the
social interactions between infants and adults contribute to language and cognitive
developments. Adults typically converse with infants using (34) _____ speech, a
simplified speech that is spoken slowly and in a high-pitched voice. Adults may also respond to a
child's vocalization by using (35)_____, or a more complete expression of
what the child said. (*What other things do adults do to facilitate language development?*)

10.2 THE INFANT
Mastery Motivation
Infants are thought to have mastery motivation, or the desire to successfully control their
environment. Mastery motivation is influenced by the presence of appropriate sensory
stimulation, a secure relationship with a caregiver, and an environment that is
(36)_____ . (*Can you describe how these factors influence mastery
motivation?*)

Early Education
Many children attend preschool prior to entering kindergarten and first grade. Children in
high-quality preschools are often ahead of children who do not attend preschool in
(37)_____ skills, but are not significantly different in terms of intellectual
skills, at least once they enter the formal school system. However, children who come from
disadvantaged homes often show gains in the area of (38) _____ development
compared to similar children who do not participate in an early childhood program. (*What
general conclusions can be made about early education?*)

10.3 THE CHILD
Young children have developed internal standards of performance and can begin to appraise
their performances.

Achievement Motivation

High achievers tend to attribute their successes to internal and stable factors such as (39)_____, and attribute their failures to (40) _____ factors, or to internal factors that they can change. Students with this pattern of attributions have a (41)_____, which means they thrive on challenges and will keep working on a problem because they believe their work will eventually pay off. Low achievers often attribute their failures to internal and stable causes, which may cause them to develop a (42)_____ orientation, or the belief that one cannot control the consequences of certain situations and so fails to act in these situations.

Young children are less likely than older children to have a helpless orientation. In part, this is because younger children tend to adopt (43) _____ in achievement situations so that they can learn new things and improve their abilities. Older children tend to adopt (44) _____ to demonstrate what ability they have, but not really to improve it. Students who continue to focus on (45) _____ tend to do better in school. (***What can parents do to foster their child's achievement and mastery orientation? What can schools do to promote achievement?***)

Learning to Read

Learning to read is a complex perceptual task that begins when children understand that letters in printed words represent the sounds in spoken words—that is, they understand the (46)_____. Learning to read also depends on grasping that words can be broken down into basic units of sound, an understanding called (47) _____. The developmental precursors of reading are referred to as (48) _____ and can be fostered by repetitive storybook reading. Serious problems with reading might indicate (49)_____, which shows up in a variety of ways depending on the child. (***What distinguishes skilled from unskilled readers?***) Research suggests that the best approach to teaching reading is based on (50) _____, or a code-oriented approach that teaches children letter-sound correspondence rules.

Effective Schools

Some elementary and secondary schools are more effective than others. Factors that do <u>not</u> contribute to effective schooling include the amount of monetary support that a school receives, the average size of classes (within a range of 20 to 40 students), and clumping students by skill level, known as (51) _____. Factors that <u>do</u> contribute to the effectiveness of a school include a strong emphasis on (52) _____, well-managed classrooms (both in terms of classroom activities and discipline problems), and teachers who are qualified and experienced. In addition, student characteristics interact with school factors to affect student outcome, something called (53) _____.

10.4   THE ADOLESCENT
Declining Levels of Achievement

Achievement motivation patterns change over the course of childhood and adolescence. Research suggests that children value academic achievement more as they progress through school, but their expectations for (54) _____ drop, and they become more focused on (55)_____ rewards such as grades and less concerned about the intrinsic satisfaction associated with achieving greater competence. This trend may occur

---

because of cognitive growth as egocentric thinking decreases. Children who receive (56)_____ at school for their failures may also experience a decline in achievement motivation. In addition, peer pressure and changes related to puberty may also influence the achievement motivation. Finally, declines in achievement motivation are more likely when there is a mismatch or (57)_____ between the adolescent and their school situation.

Science and Mathematics Education

Secondary schools often take reading skills for granted and focus on content areas such as science and math. Cross-cultural research suggests that U.S. students do not do as well in these subjects as students in other countries. There are several possible reasons for this difference. For example, Asian students spend more time on academics and complete more (58)_____ than U.S. teens. In addition, Asian parents seem especially committed to the educational enterprise. *(What other factors might contribute to this pattern of findings?)*

Integrating Work and School

Many adolescents work during their high school years. Most of the research on working students suggests that the consequences are (59)_____, especially when work hours are long and tasks are menial. *(What factors can make the work experience for high school students a positive one?)*

Pathways to Adulthood

As they enter adolescence, the educational paths of many individuals are already determined. Intelligence, school aptitude, and (60)_____ are reasonably stable and influence whether an individual gets good grades. Grades, in turn, influence whether an individual graduates from high school and college, and level of education affects the sorts of occupations a person can hold.

10.5   THE ADULT
Achievement Motivation

Overall, level of achievement motivation remains fairly stable from childhood and adolescence to adulthood. Research with adults shows some changes in need for achievement, but younger and older men are more similar than different on this quality. Achievement motivation of women declines, at least as it pertains to (61)_____ motivation. Changes in motives during adulthood are influenced more by work and family contexts than by a person's (62)_____.

Literacy

Literacy is the ability to use printed information to function in society and achieve goals. Few adults are completely illiterate, but many do not have (63)_____ literacy that would allow them to develop their full potential. Literacy programs have not been very successful. *(What factors contribute to the success/failure of these programs?)*

Continuing Education

An increasing number of adults seek continued educational experiences. These learners represent a very (64) _____ group of adults with various reasons for enrolling in postsecondary course work.

REVIEW OF KEY TERMS

Below is a list of terms and concepts from this chapter. Use these to complete the following sentence definitions. You might also try writing definitions in your own words and then checking your definitions with those in the text.

ability grouping	mastery motivation
alphabetic principle	mastery orientation
aphasia	metalinguistic awareness
babbling	morphemes
child-directed speech	overextension
cooing	overregularization
cooperative learning	performance goal
dyslexia	phonemes
emergent literacy	phonological awareness
expansion	pragmatics
functional grammar	prosody
helpless orientation	semantics
holophrases	syntactic bootstrapping
inclusion	syntax
integration	telegraphic speech
joint attention	transformational grammar
language	underextension
language acquisition device (LAD)	universal grammar
literacy	vocabulary spurt
mastery (learning) goal	word segmentation

1. An important skill in learning to read is _____, or knowing that spoken words can be broken down into basic units.

2. When two people (such as an infant and caregiver) look at the same object at the same time, they are engaged in _____.

3. Some schools use _____ in which students are grouped and taught according to their competence level.

4. The idea that letters in printed words represent the sounds in spoken words is the

    _____.

5. Children who adopt a _____ in achievement settings try to learn new things to improve their abilities.

6. An infant's repetition of vowel-like sounds in association with positive affective states is called _____.

7. Young children sometimes use a general word too narrowly, an error called a(n) _____.

8. The _____ is an inborn mechanism for acquiring language that allows children to infer rules governing others' speech and then use these rules to produce their own speech.

9. The basic units of meaning in a word constitute the _____ of language.

10. During the _____ there is a dramatic increase in language acquisition.

11. Children with _____ have serious trouble learning to read despite normal intellectual ability.

12. A form of simplified speech used by adults when speaking to young children is termed _____.

13. The rules of syntax specifying how to transform basic sentences into other forms are called _____.

14. Children use _____ when they construct two- or three-word sentences that contain only critical content words.

15. The motive to successfully interact with one's environment is called _____.

16. The process of _____ is intended to fully integrate students with disabilities into the regular classroom.

17. The analysis of early language in terms of the semantic relations between words is called the _____ of language.

18. Children who adopt a _____ in achievement settings try to prove their ability rather than improving it.

19. The _____ of language refers to the relationship between words or symbols and what they represent or mean.

20. Developmental precursors of reading skills in young children are called _____.

21.   Knowledge of language as a system is _____.

22.   The system of rules specifying how to combine words to form sentences is the _____ of language.

23.   _____ consists of a system of symbols that can be combined according to agreed-on rules to create messages.

24.   Working together in teams to produce a group effort rather than competing individually is known as _____.

25.   Children are _____ when they repeat consonant-vowel combinations.

26.   Single words that, when combined with gestures or intonation, convey the meaning of an entire sentences are called _____.

27.   The rules specifying how language is to be used appropriately in different social contexts are called the _____ of language.

28.   The basic speech sounds of a language are called _____.

29.   Children sometimes overapply grammatical rules to irregular nouns and verbs, an error known as _____.

30.   A language disorder characterized by an inability to vocally produce or repeat information that has been heard is referred to as _____.

31.   An attribution style called _____ credits successes to internal and stable causes and failures to internal causes that can be changed.

32.   How sounds are produced affects the melody or the _____ of language.

33.   Individuals with a(n) _____ believe they cannot control the consequences of certain situations; as a result, they give up trying to succeed in these situations.

34.   Children may use the placement of a word in a sentence to help determine the word's meaning, a process called _____.

35.   Young children have a tendency to use fairly specific words to refer to a general class of objects or events, an error known as _____.

36.   Parents often use _____ when they provide comments that are more complete follow-up expressions of a thought expressed by a child.

37. The ability to use printed information to function in society and achieve goals is
    _____.

38. The ability to detect a word in a stream of speech is _____.

39. The nativists believe that humans have an inborn system of common rules called a
    _____ that allows them to learn any language.

40. Teaching children of different backgrounds in the same classroom rather than segregating
    them is the premise behind school _____.

MULTIPLE-CHOICE SELF-TEST

For each multiple-choice question, read all alternatives and then select the best answer.

1. Syntax refers to the _____ of language, whereas semantics refers to the
   _____ of language.
   a. rhythm or melody; meaning
   b. rules for forming sentences; meaning
   c. meaning; rules for how to use language
   d. rules for combining sounds; rules for forming sentences

2. Calling all four-legged animals "doggie" is an example of _____.
   a. overregularization   c. overextension
   b. underextension   d. telegraphic speech

3. Johan speaks with simple two- and three-word sentences, such as "Kitty gone." This
   indicates that Johan has developed _____ speech.
   a. overregularized   c. telegraphic
   b. holophrastic   d. organizational

4. When getting ready for bed, Rachel says that she is going to "go brush my tooths." This
   is an example of _____.
   e. overregularization   g. overextension
   f. underextension   h. holophrastic speech

5. Learning theorists argue that language is acquired through
   a. biologically programmed learning capacities.
   b. imitation of others' language and reinforcement for recognizable speech.
   c. cognitive understanding of speech sounds and their relationship to real objects
      and actions.
   d. a device that allows children to sift through language and generate rules that
      govern the language.

6.   Which of the following claims does Chomsky make about language acquisition?
   a.   Infants have an inborn knowledge of all aspects of language and automatically begin using language.
   b.   Infants have an inborn mechanism for sifting through the language they hear and eventually generate rules for that language.
   c.   Infants are able to listen to the language around them and imitate the sounds they hear.
   d.   Infants must be exposed to language in the first two years of life in order for language to develop.

7.   Research indicates that
   a.   infants do not have a sense of motivation.
   b.   from a very early age, infants are motivated to control their environments.
   c.   infants can develop mastery motivation if they are externally rewarded for all their efforts.
   d.   infants who are insecurely attached to their parents will not develop any mastery motivation.

8.   A child with mastery orientation toward learning might say which of the following?
   a.   I did well on that test because it was easy.
   b.   I did well on that test because the teacher likes me.
   c.   I did well on that test because I knew the material.
   d.   I did well on that test because I wanted to earn the money Dad promised me for getting an "A."

9.   Children with a helpless orientation
   a.   have high expectations for success and get upset when they cannot achieve these high standards.
   b.   work hard to achieve only small gains in performance.
   c.   have low expectations for success and give up easily.
   d.   believe that external factors are responsible for their failures.

10.   Young children are often more confident than older children about their chances for success because younger children
   a.   adopt mastery goals.
   b.   adopt performance goals.
   c.   are given easier tasks than older children.
   d.   attribute outcomes to external factors while older children attribute outcomes to internal factors.

11.   Compared to skilled readers, unskilled readers tend to
   a.   emphasize the meaning of a sentence rather than the pronunciation of individual words.
   b.   systematically focus on all syllables in a word.
   c.   skip over words or parts of words.
   d.   be less motivated to learn to read.

12. One factor that contributes significantly to school effectiveness is
    a. a comfortable setting where the emphasis is on academics.
    b. average class size.
    c. level of monetary support that the school receives.
    e. strict guidelines and adherence to rules.

13. Achievement motivation declines during adolescence for all of the following reasons EXCEPT
    a. cognitive advances that allow adolescents to understand their strengths and weaknesses.
    b. pressure from peers to be popular or athletic.
    c. increasingly receiving positive feedback based on quality of accomplishments rather than effort.
    d. having teachers who use cooperative learning styles.

14. Cross-cultural research on science and math education indicates that
    a. United States' teens perform higher than teens in most other nations.
    b. teens in the U.S. spend more time studying science and math subjects in school but do not perform as well on standardized tests compared to teens in other nations.
    c. teens in the U.S. spend less time on academics during school hours than teens in some other nations and score about in the middle compared to other nations.
    d. parents of U.S. teens have high expectations for their children and push them to succeed in science and math more so than parents of teens from other nations.

15. Research on adolescents and work indicates that
    a. working while in high school is beneficial for most adolescents.
    b. there are more potential disadvantages than advantages to working while in high school.
    c. work contributes to improvements in social-emotional development, but does not influence cognitive development.
    d. work is associated with higher levels of achievement and self-esteem.

COMPARE MASTERY AND PERFORMANCE GOALS

Answer the following questions for mastery and performance goals. Use Table 10.3 on page 327 of the text to check your answers.

	MASTERY GOALS	PERFORMANCE GOALS
What is the child's view of ability?		
What is the child's focus in the classroom?		
How does the child explain successes and failures?		
Who regulates the child's learning?		
What is the child's reaction to successes and failures?		

CRITICAL THINKING QUESTIONS

By answering the following questions, you will strengthen your understanding of the material in this chapter. These questions require higher-level thinking skills such as integration and application of concepts. Sample answers are provided for three of the questions. These illustrate one possibility, but there are other answers you could provide that might be just as good. For the other questions, you can check yourself by referring to the text (a hint is provided), or by asking a peer or your instructor to review your answer.

1.   Based on research described in the text, what recommendations would you make regarding adolescents and work?
     [Sample answer provided.]

2. How could you prevent the drop in achievement motivation that often occurs as children move through school?
    [*Sample answer provided.*]

3. Trace the course of language development through infancy and early childhood and note factors that might influence the path of early language development.
    [*Sample answer provided.*]

4. Consider how deafness affects language development of children. Questions to think about: Do you need to hear speech to develop speech? More generally, do you need to be exposed to a language (spoken or unspoken) in order to develop a language? What is the relationship between thought and language? Is language an important basis for thought (Is it a <u>necessary</u> basis for thought)?
    [*Hint: Read the Exploration box, "Language Acquisition among Deaf Children" on page 321 of the text. You might also review the section in Chapter 7 that covers Piaget's and Vygotsky's views on the thought-language connection.*]

5. What factors are likely to increase or decrease our achievement motivation as we move through childhood and adolescence?
    [*Hint: Review the sections in the text on "Achievement motivation" and "Declining achievement motivation."*]

ANSWERS

Chapter Summary and Guided Review (fill in the blank)

1.	phonemes	22.	metalinguistic awareness
2.	morphemes	23.	left
3.	syntax	24.	right
4.	semantics	25.	Wernicke's area
5.	pragmatics	26.	Broca's area
6.	prosocy	27.	aphasia
7.	word segmentation	28.	learning theory
8.	cooing	29.	semantics
9.	babbling	30.	universal grammar
10.	comprehension	31.	language acquisition device
11.	production (or expression)	32.	syntactic
12.	joint attention	33.	interactionist
13.	syntactic bootstrapping	34.	child-directed
14.	holophrases	35.	expansion
15.	vocabulary spurt	36.	responsive
16.	overextension	37.	social
17.	underextension	38.	cognitive
18.	telegraphic	39.	ability
19.	functional grammar	40.	external
20.	overregularization	41.	mastery orientation
21.	transformational grammar	42.	helplessness

43.	learning goals	54.	success
44.	performance goals	55.	external
45.	learning goals	56.	negative feedback
46.	alphabetic principle	57.	poor fit
47.	phonological awareness	58.	homework
48.	emergent literacy	59.	negative
49.	dyslexia	60.	achievement motivation
50.	phonics	61.	career-related
51.	ability grouping	62.	age
52.	academics	63.	functional
53.	goodness of fit	64.	diverse (or heterogeneous)

Review of Key Terms

1.	phonological awareness	21.	metalinguistic awareness
2.	joint attention	22.	syntax
3.	ability grouping	23.	language
4.	alphabetic principle	24.	cooperative learning
5.	mastery (learning) goal	25.	babbling
6.	cooing	26.	holophrases
7.	underextension	27.	pragmatics
8.	language acquisition device	28.	phonemes
9.	morphemes	29.	overregularization
10.	vocabulary spurt	30.	aphasia
11.	dyslexia	31.	mastery orientation
12.	child-directed speech	32.	prosody
13.	transformational grammar	33.	helpless orientation
14.	telegraphic speech	34.	syntactic bootstrapping
15.	mastery motivation	35.	overextension
16.	inclusion	36.	expansion
17.	functional grammar	37.	literacy
18.	performance goal	38.	word segmentation
19.	semantics	39.	universal grammar
20.	emergent literacy	40.	integration

Multiple-Choice Self-Test

1. B (p. 313)	6. B (p. 319)	11. C (p. 330)
2. C (p. 315)	7. B (p. 323)	12. A (p. 333)
3. C (p. 316)	8. C (p. 326)	13. D (p. 336-337)
4. A (p. 317)	9. C (p. 326)	14. C (p. 338-340)
5. B (p. 319)	10. A (p. 326)	15. B (p. 340)

Critical Thinking Questions

1.   *Overall, I would have to recommend NOT working, or working a limited number of hours. Research shows that adolescents who work 20 or more hours a week while going to high school get lower grades than those who do not work at all or work less than 10 hours. The ones who work a lot also tend to be disengaged in school; they cut class and do not spend as much*

time on homework. Further, the more teenagers work, the less control their parents have in their lives, which may contribute to higher rates of delinquency and alcohol and drug use. Some of the problems with school and parents started before the teens started working, but increased once they started working.

Not all work experiences for teenagers are negative. Work that teaches teenagers valuable skills and allows for some advancement can be valuable. Unfortunately, most teenagers get jobs that are menial and repetitive and provide little opportunity for decision-making.

2.　　Research shows that achievement motivation is high throughout elementary school, but then declines, usually starting with the entry to middle or junior high school. Several factors contribute to the decrease in achievement motivation including family characteristics, cognitive growth, negative feedback, and peer pressures. Some of the variables that contribute to lowered levels of achievement motivation cannot be changed, nor would we want to change all of them. For example, advances in cognitive development may bring the realization that you are not very good at something, leading to a decline in motivation. There is also not a lot we can do to change the family characteristics of children. Children who come from a small, caring family with a stable parent who uses consistent discipline will be advantaged when it comes to school achievement, whereas children who come from unstable families will be at risk academically.

But several factors can be addressed. When children are in the early grades of school, teachers often praise them for effort and not for the end product. Thus, if a child spends a lot of time drawing a picture, he may receive praise for his effort even if the picture looks terrible. As children get into the later grades, effort is no longer rewarded. Grades are awarded on the basis of measurable end products. Students end up moving from learning goals in elementary school (i.e., working on something because they want to try to improve their understanding of it) to performance goals when they move to middle school (i.e., working on something in order earn an external reward such as a good grade). Students can benefit if teachers and schools can keep the focus on learning goals throughout middle and high school.

The peer group that a student belongs to can also make a difference in achievement motivation. Peers become increasingly influential as children enter middle and high school. Most children want to feel accepted and liked by their peers. They might downplay their intelligence if they believe that being smart will detract from how their peers perceive them. This may be especially true for students from minority groups.

Finally, there is also evidence that experiencing puberty during the transition from elementary to middle or junior high school might affect achievement motivation more than if puberty is experienced either earlier or later than the school transition. This could have implications for when schools have children switch from the smaller, friendlier elementary school to the larger and often stricter middle school.

3.   *Infants can communicate even before they begin to use a language system. Their earliest form of communication is crying, which can be used to convey hunger, pain, fatigue, and other basic states. Around 6 weeks of age, infants begin to coo or repeat vowel-like sounds. They add consonant sounds at around 3-4 months of age and are babbling between 4 and 6 months. Up until about 6 months, the babbling from babies all over the world sounds about the same. But from this point on, experience begins to show as babbling begins to more closely resemble the language that infants are hearing around them. During the second half of the first year, infants can understand many words that they hear even though they can't yet produce the words. At around 1 year, infants begin to produce recognizable words and often use these to convey fairly complex ideas (holophrases). At around 18 months, they experience a vocabulary spurt when their vocabulary increases substantially. The next stage in language acquisition is combining words into simple sentences called telegraphic speech. Children often make mistakes as they are acquiring language, but these mistakes are often "smart" because they show that children are mastering the rules of language but have just not learned all the exceptions to the rules. For example, they might say, "the dog goed out" because they know the rule of adding "-ed" to the end of verbs but haven't learned that "go" is an exception requiring "went." By the age of 5 and with no formal instruction, children have acquired adult-like speech.*

CHAPTER ELEVEN

SELF AND PERSONALITY

OVERVIEW

How do perceptions of ourselves develop and change over the lifespan? How do personalities emerge and change? This chapter addresses these sorts of questions about self-conceptions and personality. A sense of self emerges during infancy and becomes more established during childhood. Children think of themselves and others in fairly concrete terms, whereas adolescents and adults think more abstractly.

The beginnings of personality are evident in an infant's temperament. You will learn that some aspects of personality are fairly stable from childhood on, but other aspects change in response to changes in a person's social environment. This chapter elaborates on Erikson's theory of psychosocial development, introduced in Chapter 2. Erikson believed that personality evolved over the entire lifespan as people are confronted with different crises that can be resolved in positive or negative ways. The chapter ends by discussing factors that contribute to successful aging, including issues related to retirement.

LEARNING OBJECTIVES

After reading and studying the material in this chapter, you should be able to answer the following questions.

11.1 CONCEPTUALIZING THE SELF AND PERSONALITY
1. How is personality typically defined, and what are the five principles of defining personality?

2. How do psychoanalytic, trait, and social learning theories explain personality development?

11.2 THE INFANT
3. How does self-concept emerge during infancy, and how does it change across the lifespan?

4. How has infant temperament been categorized? How do these temperament styles interact with caregiver characteristics? How does temperament relate to later personality?

11.3 THE CHILD
5. What changes occur in the development of children's self-esteem? What factors influence self-esteem?

6. How does personality evolve over childhood, and what do children understand of their personality?

11.4   THE ADOLESCENT

7.   How do adolescents conceptualize their selves, including self-esteem and personality?

8.   What factors influence the development of identity during adolescence? How do adolescents make vocational choices, and how does work affect adolescents' identities?

11.5   THE ADULT

9.   How does personality change during adulthood? Why do people change or remain the same? How does culture influence personality?

10.   What is the focus of each of Erikson's psychosocial stages? What factors can influence how each crisis is resolved?

11.   How do career paths change during adulthood? How do adults cope with age-related changes that affect their working selves? How are older adults influenced by retirement?

12.   How can we characterize successful aging?

CHAPTER SUMMARY AND GUIDED REVIEW

The following summary provides an overview of the main points contained in this chapter of the text. Fill in the blanks with terms that appropriately complete the sentence. Scattered throughout the summary are questions in parentheses. These are meant to encourage you to think actively as you read and connect this summary to the more detailed information provided in the text.

11.1   CONCEPTUALIZING THE SELF AND PERSONALITY
Basic Concepts
    An organized set of attributes, motives, values, and behaviors unique to an individual is that person's (1) _____ . Personalities are often described in terms of (2)_____ that are thought to be relatively consistent across situations and times. People differ in situation-specific and changeable ways known as (3)_____, and differ as well in our unique life stories, or (4) _____. Your perception of your traits and attributes is your (5) _____ and your overall evaluation of the characteristics of your self-concept is (6) _____.

Theories of Personality
    According to Freud, personality forms in infancy and early childhood and changes very little after this. Erikson believed that personality continued to grow and change across the lifespan. Erikson also stressed (7) _____ influences more so than Freud did. (***In what other ways are Freud and Erikson different?***)
    According to trait theory, personality is a set of traits that can be measured. Statistical procedures have been used to identify distinct groups of personality traits. Research suggests that personality can be described in terms of dimensions of neuroticism, extraversion, openness to experience, agreeableness, and conscientiousness, collectively referred to as the

(8)_____. All of these traits are influenced to some extent by (9)_____ factors, although culture also has some influence.

Social learning theories propose that personality is strongly influenced by (10)_____ factors and can change when these factors change. (***How are stage theory views of personality different from non-stage theory views of personality?***)

11.2   THE INFANT
The Emerging Self

Infants begin to differentiate themselves from the world around them when they realize they can make things happen. They demonstrate an understanding of different views starting around 9 months when they engage in (11) _____ with caregivers. One of the first signs that infants recognize themselves as distinct individuals is when they recognize themselves in a mirror. (***When does this understanding emerge?***) Infants begin to form a (12)_____ self and classify themselves along dimensions such as age and gender. The ability to recognize self depends on social experiences as well as (13)_____ development. Our understanding of self is also influenced by social interactions and reflects how others people respond to us, a concept known as the (14)_____ self. (***Can you describe how other people might affect our self-concept and self-esteem?***)

Temperament

Temperament is the tendency to respond in predictable ways to events. Thomas and Chess classified infant temperament using categories that are based on behavioral dimensions such as mood, regularity of habits, and adaptability. In their original research, about 40% of the infants had regular habits, were typically happy and content, and were adaptable to new experiences, earning them the classification of (15) _____ temperament. About 10% of the infants were active, irritable, did not have regular habits, and responded negatively to new experiences, classified as a (16) _____ temperament because they were. About 15% of the infants were inactive, somewhat moody, and had somewhat regular habits, characteristic of a (17) _____ temperament.

Jerome Kagan has studied (18) _____, or the tendency to be shy and restrained with unfamiliar people or situations. There seems to be a genetic influence on this characteristic as well as stability across time. (***What is the evidence showing a genetic influence?***)

Another classification of temperament uses emotion reactions and how infants regulate these reactions. Based on this, infants who approach new situations with positive emotions are classified as having (19) _____. Those who are sad, fearful, easily frustrated, and irritable express a (20) _____ temperament. Developing somewhat later is the temperament of (21) _____, or the ability to control your behavior and regular your emotions. These dimensions of infant temperament are related to the Big 5 personality characteristics.

Whether or not infant temperament persists into childhood and adulthood may depend on (22) _____ between the individual and environment. (***Can you describe how this might lead to change or to consistency of temperamental characteristics?***)

11.3   THE CHILD

Elaborating on a Sense of Self

Preschool children's self-concepts tend to be physical and (23) _____.
School-age children can describe their inner traits and begin to compare their abilities to those of companions. This leads to (24) _____ where children evaluate themselves relative to others.

Self-Esteem

Self-esteem is also developing during childhood. Preschoolers can distinguish between their competencies and their inadequacies. By the middle of elementary school, children have well-defined feelings about themselves and are able to distinguish between their competencies in different areas, indicating that self-esteem is (25) _____. Evaluations of self become more realistic around age 8, when children begin to organize their self-esteem into different levels, demonstrating that self-esteem is (26) _____. Finally, children develop an (27) _____ based on what they think they *should* be like.

Influences on Self-Esteem

In general, some children have higher self-esteem than others because they are more competent and they receive more positive feedback from others. High self-esteem is fostered by parents who are warm and democratic. (***How does feedback from others contribute to the development of high or low self-esteem?***)

The Developing Personality

A number of important personality dimensions do not stabilize until childhood, although some aspects of early temperament do carry over to later personality. By age 3, some predictions about later personality can be made based on observations of temperament.

11.4   THE ADOLESCENT

Self-Conceptions

The self-concepts of adolescents become less physical and more psychological as well as less concrete and more (28) _____. They are also more self-aware than younger children. Adolescents' descriptions of themselves are more differentiated and more coherent or (29) _____ than those of younger children.

Self-Esteem

For a small group of adolescents, there is a drop in self-esteem, particularly among girls with multiple stressors. Most adolescents, though, leave adolescence with self-esteem that is about the same as when they entered adolescence. Social context and social comparisons can influence adolescents' self-esteem. In general, adolescents feel better about themselves when the average academic achievement of peers is lower, a phenomenon known as the (30) _____ effect.

Forging a Sense of Identity

Erikson believed that adolescents are faced with the important psychosocial task of identity versus (31) _____. Some cultures support an extended

(32)_____ period to allow adolescents to experiment with various identities. There are several developmental trends in achieving a sense of identity. Adolescents who have not experienced a crisis of identity and have not made a commitment to an identity are in the (33)_____ status, while adolescents who have not experienced a crisis but have made a commitment fall into the (34) _____ status. Adolescents who have faced a crisis (or are currently facing one) but have not yet made a commitment fall into the (35)_____ status. Adolescents who have faced a crisis about who they are and what they believe in, and who have made a commitment, have achieved (36)_____ status. (*What gender differences exist in identity formation?*)

Identity formation is a lengthy process and occurs at different rates for different domains. Forming an identity includes developing an (37) _____ or sense of belonging to an ethnic group. This begins in infancy with detection of racial-ethnic differences and then classification of self into a racial/ethnic group. Adolescents go through the same stages in forming an ethnic identity as they do in forming their overall identity.

Another important part of identity formation is choosing a career. Adolescents consider their interests, abilities, and values when thinking of careers. They become increasingly more (38)_____ about possible careers and narrow their choices based on available opportunities. Vocational choice is really a matter of finding a good fit between your personality and an occupation.

Identity development is influenced by cognitive development, relationships with parents, and (39) _____. (*What kinds of parent-adolescent relationships are associated with each of the identity statuses?*) It's also important for adolescents to have opportunities to (40) _____.

11.5   THE ADULT
Self-Conceptions
Self-esteem and descriptions of self are fairly stable throughout adulthood, and self-esteem may even increase in mid-adulthood but then decreases somewhat in old age. Older adults' evaluations of their ideal selves are closer to their evaluation of their real selves than those of younger adults. Individuals also change their (41) _____ of evaluation over time, as well as their comparison group. By resisting negative stereotypes of old people, older adults seem to be able to avoid or delay some of the declines predicted by the stereotypes.

Culture influences self-concept. In (42) _____ cultures, individuals put their personal goals ahead of group goals. In (43) _____ cultures, individuals give greater priority to personal goals. (*What does cross-cultural research show about how these different orientations affect self-concept and self-esteem?*)

Continuity and Discontinuity in Personality
In addressing whether personality is stable across adulthood, two questions arise. One question is whether an individual's (44) _____ within a group on some personality trait remains the same, which is the stability of individual differences. A second question is whether there is stability in the (45) _____ levels of some personality trait within a group. With respect to the first question, individual rankings on the Big 5 dimensions of personality are fairly stable across time. (*Can you provide a concrete example of what this means for a specific individual?*) With respect to the second question, cross-sectional research suggests that older adults have different personalities than younger adults. However,

these results may reflect (46) _____ or generational effects, suggesting that the (47) _____ context in which people develop affects their personalities.

   Personality shows some growth from adolescence to middle adulthood, but there is little systematic change from middle adulthood to later adulthood. The personalities of some people remain stable, whereas those of other people change across the lifespan. Personalities may remain stable because of the influence of (48) _____ factors or because childhood experiences continue their influence throughout adulthood. In addition, personalities may remain stable because (49) _____ remain stable. Changes in the environment might explain why some personalities change, and maturation and aging might also contribute to change. Change may also occur when there is a poor fit between the person and his/her environment.

Eriksonian Psychosocial Growth

   According to Erikson, infants confront the conflict of (50) _____. Toddlers must achieve a sense of (51) _____ or risk feeling shame and doubt. Preschool children and kindergartners struggle with the conflict of (52) _____, and school-aged children must master (53) _____ or possibly develop feelings of inferiority. As already noted, adolescents face the task of developing an identity. Young adults face the psychosocial task of (54) _____ versus isolation. Research supports Erikson's claim that individuals must achieve a sense of (55) _____ before being able to develop true intimacy. (**How might the relationship between identity and intimacy differ for men and women?**) Middle-aged adults are concerned with the psychosocial crisis of (56) _____ as they work to produce something lasting and important for future generations. Finally, older adults face the psychosocial conflict of (57) _____ versus despair. Elderly adults may engage in a process of (58) _____ where they reflect on unresolved issues in order to come to terms with their lives.

Midlife Crisis?

   According to Levinson's theory, adults continually work on crafting their (59) _____, which describes the pattern of their life. During middle age, many adults experience a (60) _____, when they question their entire life structure. Research suggests that this is more a self-evaluation than a crisis.

Vocational Development and Adjustment

   Young adults explore a number of careers before settling into one that is a good fit. As they or the job changes, they reevaluate the fit. Vocational development is influenced by personality as well as one's (61) _____. (**Explain how these variables influence vocational development.**) In turn, vocational experiences influence our personality and adjustment.

   Despite age-related physical and cognitive declines, older adults remain good workers because they use a strategy of (62) _____. (**How do the three processes that make-up this strategy help older adults cope?**)

   Workers go through several phases as they adjust to retirement. Initially, the freedom of retirement creates a (63) _____ phase, which may then give way to the (64) _____ phase as the novelty of being retired wears off. Eventually, they move on to the (65) _____ of constructing a satisfying lifestyle post-retirement.

Personality and Successful Aging

The text presents two general theories about successful aging. One is the (66)_____ theory, which suggests that adults will be satisfied with their lives if they can continue to maintain their preexisting activity levels. The other theory of aging holds that successful aging requires (67)_____ of the aging individual from society and vice versa. (***Does one of these theories more accurately portray successful aging? Why?***)

REVIEW OF KEY TERMS

Below is a list of terms and concepts from this chapter. Use these to complete the following sentence definitions. You might also want to try writing definitions in your own words and then checking your definitions with those in the text.

activity theory
autonomy versus shame and doubt
behavioral inhibition
Big-fish-little-pond effect
Big Five
categorical self
characteristic adaptations
collectivist culture
difficult temperament
diffusion status
disengagement theory
dispositional traits
easy temperament
effortful control
ethnic identity
foreclosure status
generativity versus stagnation
goodness of fit
ideal self
identity
identity achievement status
identity versus role confusion

individualistic culture
industry versus inferiority
initiative versus guilt
integrity versus despair
intimacy versus isolation
life review
midlife crisis
moratorium period
moratorium status
narrative identities
negative affectivity
personality
selective optimization with
   compensation
self-concept
self-recognition
self-esteem
slow-to-warm-up temperament
social comparison
surgency/extraversion
temperament
trust versus mistrust

1. The process of _____ takes into account how one compares to others, and uses that information to judge one's self.

2. An identity status called _____ is when a person has not experienced a crisis and has not reached a commitment.

3. Having a clear sense of who you are, where you are heading, and where you fit into society refers to having a(n) _____.

4. The psychosocial conflict of _____ occurs when a young child tries to accept more grown-up responsibilities that she/he may not be able to handle.

5. A(n) _____ is achieved when a person has experienced a crisis and has made a commitment to certain goals.

6. The psychosocial conflict of _____ usually occurs during elementary school when children need to acquire important academic and social skills.

7. Classification of one's self along dimensions such as age and sex shows development of a(n) _____ .

8. A person's _____ is reflected in his/her tendency to respond in predictable ways to events.

9. An identity status in which a person has not experienced a crisis but has made a commitment is _____.

10. Your understanding of yourself, including unique attributes or traits, is your _____.

11. A _____ is the process of reflecting on unresolved conflicts of the past in order to come to terms with yourself and derive new meaning from the past.

12. The psychosocial conflict of _____ faces young adults who must develop strong friendships and intimate relationships.

13. Erikson's first psychosocial conflict in which infants must develop a basic sense of trust is labeled _____.

14. Your feelings about the characteristics that make up your self constitute your _____.

15. Adolescents experience the psychosocial conflict of _____ when they must develop a sense of who they are socially, sexually, and professionally.

16. Older adults face the psychosocial conflict of _____ during which they must assess their life and find it meaningful.

17. The identity status in which a person is currently experiencing a crisis or actively addressing identity issues and has not yet made a commitment is _____.

18. An organized combination of attributes, motives, values, and behaviors that is unique to each individual is terms _____.

19. The psychosocial conflict of _____ involves being productive in one's work and with one's family.

20. The major dimensions of personality are collectively referred to as the _____.

21. During the psychosocial conflict of _____, toddlers must learn some independence.

22. Aspects of personality that are more situation-specific and changeable than traits are referred to as _____.

23. The degree to which a child's temperament is compatible with the expectations and demands of his/her environment is reflected in the _____ between child and environment.

24. Adults experience a _____ when they question their life structure and raise concerns about the direction of their lives.

25. Infants who are generally content, adaptable to new experiences, keep regular habits, and tolerate frustrations/discomforts are classified with a(n) _____.

26. Someone whose temperament is characterized with _____ is sad, fearful, irritable, and easily frustrated

27. Infants who are inactive, moody, moderately regular in their habits, and take some time to adapt to new situations are classified with a(n) _____.

28. The tendency to be very shy or restrained in unfamiliar settings is called _____.

29. A person's _____ are their relatively enduring dimensions of personality.

30. _____ refers to a sense of personal identification with the values and traditions of a particular ethnic group.

31. Infants who are active, irritable, irregular in their habits, not very adaptable to new situations, and easily frustrated are classified with a(n) _____.

32. Society provides a _____ for most adolescents so that they can experiment with different roles in order to find their identity.

33. The ability to recognize one's self in a mirror or photo is _____.

34. The degree to which one is interested in and responsive to people is reflected in the personality trait of _____.

35. According to _____, aging adults will find their lives satisfying to the extent that they are able to maintain their existing levels of activity.

36. In a(n) _____, people place greater emphasis on group identity and goals than on personal identity and goals.

37. A strategy called _____ involves focusing on important skills, practicing these skills, and finding ways to get around the need for other skills.

38. According to _____, successful aging involves a mutual withdrawal of the aging person from society and society from the aging individual.

39. In a(n) _____, people emphasize personal goals rather than group goals, and socialize children to be independent.

40. The tendency to approach new situations actively and energetically is a temperament dimension called _____.

41. Our _____ is composed of expectations of what we think we "should" be like.

42. Self-concept is likely to be higher when students are in smaller groups of similar-ability students than larger groups or groups with higher-achieving students, a phenomenon known as the _____.

43. The unique life stories that we construct to give meaning and identity to our lives are _____.

44. The _____ dimension of temperament refers to the ability to sustain attention, control one's behavior, and regulate one's emotions.

MULTIPLE-CHOICE SELF-TEST

For each multiple-choice question, read all alternatives and then select the best answer.

1. Self-esteem refers to a person's
    a. cognitive understanding of self.
    b. perception of his/her abilities and traits.
    c. overall evaluation of his/her worth as a person.
    d. knowledge of who he/she is.

2. According to Erik Erikson, personality
    a. develops in the first five or six years after birth and changes little after this.
    b. develops and changes throughout the lifespan.
    c. development is complete in adolescence once a sense of identity has been achieved.
    d. is formed in childhood and only changes later in life under extreme environmental conditions.

3. Someone who adheres to social learning theory would believe that
    a. personality develops through a series of systematic stages that are similar for all people.
    b. personality is shaped by the environment during childhood, but once it is formed, changes very little in response to environmental changes.
    c. some aspects of personality are determined only by genetic factors while others are determined only by environmental factors.
    d. personality traits are only consistent across the lifespan if the person's environment remains the same.

4. Infants with a spot of rouge on their noses who recognize themselves in a mirror will
    a. reach for the nose of their mirror image.
    b. reach for their own nose.
    c. look behind the mirror.
    d. begin to cry indicating that they are confused.

5. Research on behavioral inhibition suggests that
    a. whether one is inhibited as a toddler determines whether one will be shy as an adult.
    b. inhibited toddlers are more likely to turn out to be shy children than uninhibited toddlers.
    c. inhibited toddlers were securely attached as infants.
    d. inhibited children show the same patterns of physiological arousal to events as uninhibited children.

6. An infant who is classified as "slow-to-warm-up"
   a. follows a somewhat regular schedule, is inactive, and somewhat moody.
   b. follows a somewhat regular schedule, is active, and tolerates frustrations fairly well.
   c. follows a regular schedule, appears content, and is adaptable to new experiences.
   d. does not follow a regular schedule, is inactive, and reacts very negatively to new experiences.

7. When Harter's self-perception scale was administered to children in the third through ninth grades, it was found that
   a. only the oldest children had well-defined self-concepts.
   b. children typically did not distinguish between their competencies in different areas.
   c. children showed a "halo effect" by evaluating themselves high in all areas.
   d. children's ratings of themselves were consistent with how others rated them.

8. Adolescents who have experienced a crisis involving identity but have not resolved the crisis or made a commitment are classified in Marcia's _____ status.
   a. diffusion   c. foreclosure
   b. moratorium   d. identity achievement

9. An adolescent says, "My parents taught me that abortion is wrong, and so I just would not consider having an abortion or voting for someone who supports abortion." This statement reflects which identity status?
   a. Diffusion   c. Foreclosure
   b. Moratorium   d. Identity achievement

10. Vocational choices
    a. are stable across an individual's lifespan.
    b. become increasingly realistic across adolescence.
    c. are usually not related to one's ability.
    d. are influenced very little by environmental opportunities.

11. Longitudinal research on the major dimensions of personality suggests that they
    a. are relatively consistent over time in adults.
    b. change considerably over time in adults.
    c. are strongly correlated with infant temperament.
    d. cannot be reliably measured in adults.

12. Findings from cross-sectional research that, as a group, adult personalities change systematically over time, may reflect
    a. the fact that personality is affected by the historical context in which it develops.
    b. changes in the way personality has been measured over the years.
    c. the fact that personality begins to disintegrate as we age.
    d. the fact that people grow more similar as they get older.

13. Compared to adults who do not achieve a firm sense of identity, those adults who <u>do</u> achieve a sense of identity are
    a. equally likely to form genuine intimacy with another person.
    b. more likely to form genuine intimacy with another person.
    c. less likely to form intimate relationships because they feel very good about themselves as individuals.
    d. more likely to form many pseudo intimate relationships but no intimate relationships.

14. Research suggests that older adults in the workforce
    a. slow down and perform less well than their younger counterparts, leading to poorer evaluations and lower pay.
    b. are bored with repetitive tasks and seek new challenges.
    c. are more motivated and confident than younger workers.
    d. maintain their performance by compensating for weaknesses and strengthening select skills.

15. The theory that successful aging requires a gradual withdrawal from society is
    a. selective optimization with compensation.
    b. disengagement theory.
    c. withdrawal theory.
    d. activity adjustment theory.

REVIEW THE FOUR IDENTITY STATUSES

For this exercise, consider the area of career identity. For each of the four identity statuses, note whether or not a crisis has been experienced (Yes or No) and whether or not a commitment has been made (Yes or No). Also provide an example related to career identity for each type of status. Check your answers by referring to Figure 11.2 on page 359 of the text.

TYPE OF IDENTITY STATUS	CRISIS?	COMMITMENT?	EXAMPLE
Diffusion			
Moratorium			
Foreclosure			
Identity Achievement			

Chapter Eleven

CRITICAL THINKING QUESTIONS

By answering the following questions, you will strengthen your understanding of the material in this chapter. These questions require higher-level thinking skills such as integration and application of concepts. Sample answers are provided for three of the questions. These illustrate one possibility, but there are other answers you could provide that might be just as good. For the other questions, you can check yourself by referring to the text (a hint is provided), or by asking a peer or your instructor to review your answer.

1. Taking into consideration everything you have read about personality, how would you summarize the findings on stability of personality characteristics across the lifespan? [*Sample answer provided.*]

2. Discuss evidence on the genetic and environmental influences on personality. [*Sample answer provided.*]

3. How does self-esteem change across the lifespan, and what factors influence self-esteem in positive or negative directions? [*Sample answer provided.*]

4. To what extent is personality continuous and/or discontinuous in adulthood? [*Hint: Review the section on "Continuity and discontinuity in personality."*]

5. Based on research, what could you tell parents who are concerned about their infant's or toddler's temperament (perhaps it is a difficult temperament, or the infant is inhibited)? [*Hint: Review the section on "Temperament," especially the part on "Goodness of fit."*]

ANSWERS

Chapter Summary and Guided Review (fill in the blank)

1. personality
2. dispositional traits
3. characteristic adaptations
4. narrative identities
5. self-concept
6. self-esteem
7. social
8. Big Five
9. genetic
10. environmental
11. joint attention
12. categorical
13. cognitive
14. looking-glass
15. easy
16. difficult
17. slow-to-warm-up
18. behavioral inhibition
19. surgency/extraversion
20. negative affectivity
21. effortful control
22. goodness of fit
23. concrete
24. social comparison
25. multidimensional
26. hierarchical
27. ideal self
28. abstract
29. integrated
30. big-fish-little-pond
31. role confusion
32. moratorium

33. diffusion
34. foreclosure
35. moratorium
36. identity achievement
37. ethnic identity
38. realistic
39. personality
40. explore
41. standards
42. individualistic
43. collectivist
44. ranking
45. average
46. cohort
47. historical
48. hereditary (or genetic)
49. environments
50. trust vs. mistrust

51. autonomy
52. initiative versus guilt
53. industry
54. intimacy
55. identity
56. generativity versus stagnation
57. integrity
58. life review
59. life structure
60. midlife crisis
61. gender
62. selective optimization with compensation
63. honeymoon
64. disenchantment
65. reorientation
66. activity
67. disengagement

Review of Key Terms
1. social comparison
2. diffusion status
3. identity
4. initiative versus guilt
5. identity achievement status
6. industry versus inferiority
7. categorical self
8. temperament
9. foreclosure status
10. self-concept
11. life review
12. intimacy versus isolation
13. trust versus mistrust
14. self-esteem
15. identity versus role confusion
16. integrity versus despair
17. moratorium status
18. personality
19. generativity versus stagnation
20. Big Five
21. autonomy versus shame and doubt
22. characteristic adaptations
23. goodness of fit

24. midlife crisis
25. easy temperament
26. negative affectivity
27. slow-to-warm-up temperament
28. behavioral inhibition
29. dispositional traits
30. ethnic identity
31. difficult temperament
32. moratorium period
33. self-recognition
34. sociability
35. activity theory
36. collectivist culture
37. selection optimization with compensation
38. disengagement theory
39. individualistic culture
40. surgency/extraversion
41. ideal self
42. big-fish-little-pond effect
43. narrative identities
44. effortful control

Multiple-Choice Self-Test
1. C (p. 348)   6. A (p. 352)   11. A (p. 367-368)
2. B (p. 349)   7. D (p. 355)   12. A (p. 368)
3. D (p. 349)   8. B (p. 358-59)   13. B (p. 370)
4. B (p. 351)   9. C (p. 358-59)   14. D (p. 373-374)
5. B (p. 352)   10. B (p. 362)   15. B (p. 377)

Critical Thinking Questions

1. *Personality begins to emerge during infancy with temperament characteristics. Some of these characteristics persist beyond infancy if there is "goodness of fit" between the child's characteristics and the demands of the environment. Social experiences shape temperament into what we think of as a child's personality. Components of this personality tend to persist over time if the traits are valued by society and consistent with gender-role expectations. In terms of the "Big Five" personality traits, there is a good deal of stability throughout adulthood. Thus, an extraverted young adult is likely to be extraverted as an older adult. Correlations, though, between scores on personality measures are not perfect, indicating that there is some change over time. In particular, research shows that personalities are still forming throughout adolescence and early adulthood, and become more established sometime during one's 30s.*

2. *Personality is often conceptualized in terms of the Big Five characteristics of openness, conscientiousness, extraversion, agreeableness, and neuroticism. All five characteristics seem to be influenced by genetic factors; identical twins score more similarly to one another on these traits than do other less genetically related pairs of individuals. These traits are also consistent over a person's lifespan, which suggests either a genetic basis or a consistent environment. The Big Five traits appear to be universal; they characterize personality differences across cultures that differ in terms of parenting, values, and language. Some personality characteristics seem more influenced by genetic factors; others are more open to influence from the environment.*

3. *Self-esteem emerges during childhood when children begin to compare themselves to others and evaluate their worth. By age 9 or 10, children can distinguish between at least five dimensions of self-worth and have well-defined feelings about whether they are good or bad on these dimensions. Accuracy of their evaluations increases throughout elementary school. Self-esteem is influenced by how competent children are; those who are more competent usually recognize this and feel better about themselves. Self-esteem is also influenced by the kind of feedback children receive from others; those who receive more positive feedback feel better about themselves than children who receive negative feedback. Self-esteem tends to drop as children enter adolescence, partly because they have a more realistic understanding of their abilities and where they fit with others. Adolescents who are the "big fish in a little pond" tend to feel better about themselves than adolescents who are the little fish in a big pond. After the drop in adolescence, self-esteem gradually increases throughout adulthood, reaching a peak about the time that adults retire. There is a slight decline in self-esteem in old age, but most adults retain their level of self-esteem in old age. They tend to be more realistic than when they were young. They also change their standards as they age so that what might have been a failure at age 30 is not perceived as a failure at age 75. Finally, they compare themselves to other old people rather than to younger adults, which helps preserve their self-esteem.*

CHAPTER TWELVE

GENDER ROLES AND SEXUALITY

OVERVIEW

Most students find this chapter particularly interesting, perhaps because gender issues are so central to our lives. The first and larger part of this chapter is devoted to discussion of gender roles across the lifespan. This includes a description of several theoretical explanations of how gender role behaviors are acquired: Money and Ehrhardt's biosocial theory, Freud's psychoanalytic theory, social-learning theory, and the cognitive theories. Pay particular attention to how these theories can be integrated to best explain gender typing and to the evidence that supports the theories.

The second part of the chapter covers developmental issues related to sexuality. This includes expressions of sexuality during infancy and childhood, with discussions of children's knowledge about sex, their sexual behavior, and the sexual abuse of children. This section also covers the sexual orientation, behavior and morality of adolescents, and changes in sexuality during adulthood.

LEARNING OBJECTIVES

After reading and studying the material in this chapter, you should be able to answer the following questions.

12.1   SEX AND GENDER
1.   What is the difference between one's biological sex and one's gender, and why is it important to make this distinction?

2.   What are gender roles and stereotypes? How do they play out in the behaviors of men and women?

3.   What actual psychological differences and behaviors exist between males and females?

12.2   THE INFANT
4   How do gender-role stereotypes influence infants' behavior and treatment?

12.3   THE CHILD
5.   How do children acquire gender-role stereotypes? In what ways do children exhibit gender-typed behavior?

12.4   THE ADOLESCENT
6.   What theoretical explanations account for gender-typed behaviors? How well supported are these theories?

12.5 THE ADULT

7. How do gender roles change throughout adulthood?

8. What is androgyny? To what extent is it useful?

12.6 SEXUALITY OVER THE LIFESPAN

9. How are infants affected by their sex? What do we know about infant sexuality?

10. What do children know about sex and reproduction? How does sexual behavior change during childhood?

11. What factors contribute to the development of sexual orientation?

12. What are adolescents' sexual attitudes today? How would you characterize the sexual behaviors of today's teens?

13. What changes occur in sexual activity during adulthood?

CHAPTER SUMMARY AND GUIDED REVIEW

The following summary provides an overview of the main points contained in this chapter of the text. Fill in the blanks with terms that appropriately complete the sentence. Scattered throughout the summary are questions in parentheses. These are meant to encourage you to think actively as you read and connect this summary to the more detailed information provided in the text.

12.1 SEX AND GENDER

Physical characteristics that distinguish males and females comprise our (1)_____, whereas differences between men and women that are imposed by society make up our (2) _____. Males and females differ genetically because they have inherited different (3)_____, which trigger release of different levels of (4) _____. Males and females also differ because societies expect them to adopt different patterns of behavior, or (5) _____, specifying how they should act as males or females. Society's expectations of what males and females should be like are called gender-role norms and these create gender-role (6) _____, or overgeneralizations about what males and females are like.

Gender Norms and Stereotypes

Some generalizations arise because women are able to bear and nurse children, pushing them into the role of nurturer, with its emphasis on traits of (7)_____. In contrast, men have been encouraged to adopt traits such as dominance, independence, assertiveness, and competitiveness that are indicative of the masculine gender role or (8) _____.

Some researchers suggest that men focus on work, achievement, and independence because of their brain's tendency to (9) _____ or analyze how things work. Stereotypes about women's and men's roles continue to exist, although women describe themselves as having more (10) _____ traits than they did in the past.

Gender Differences or Similarities?

Research reveals some differences between males and females, although these are often small and inconsistent. Some experts believe that it is most accurate to adopt a (11) _____ hypothesis, which states that males and females are similar on most but not all psychological variables. One difference is that, on average, females have somewhat greater (12) _____ ability than males. Beginning in adolescence, males outperform females on measures of (13) _____ reasoning such as the mental rotation task. As early as age 2, males tend to behave more (14) _____ than females, both physically and verbally. (*What other gender differences have been supported by more recent research?*) Findings of psychological sex differences are based on averages for males and females and do not apply to all individuals. Many differences that we think exist between males and females are based on (15) _____. In addition, Eagly's (16) _____ hypothesis suggests that the roles played by men and women in society help create our stereotypes about gender.

12.2   THE INFANT
Differential Treatment

Our society begins to treat males and females differently at birth. Adults interact differently and interpret reactions differently when they believe they are interacting with a male infant rather than a female infant.

Early Learning

By age 2 1/2 to 3, children show that they have acquired an awareness of themselves as males or females, or (17) _____. Even before this time, children are beginning to act in ways that society finds gender-appropriate.

12.3   THE CHILD

At about the same time that young children acquire gender identity, they begin to learn gender (18) _____, or society's ideas about what males and females are like. They also acquire gender-typed behaviors.

Acquiring Gender Stereotypes

Children as young as 2½ years hold stereotypical beliefs about boys' and girls' activities. Children around 6 or 7 years believe that these stereotypes are absolute whereas older children tend to be more (19) _____ in their thinking about gender-role stereotypes. (*Why might there be this age difference in gender-role stereotypes?*) Young children also express positive feelings about gender-stereotypic occupations and negative feelings about gender counter-stereotypic ones.

Gender-Typed Behavior

Young children prefer toys that society deems gender-appropriate, and they develop a preference for same-sex playmates, with increased (20) _____ into separate groups of boys and girls during elementary school. Boys are under more pressure than girls to behave in gender-appropriate ways. (*Can you explain why this is the case?*)

12.4 THE ADOLESCENT

<u>Adhering to Gender Roles</u>

Adolescents tend to adhere more strictly to gender roles than do younger children. (***Why does this occur?***) In the process of gender (21) _____, increased pressure among adolescents to conform to gender roles magnifies differences between males and females.

<u>Explaining Gender-Role Development</u>

There are several theories that try to explain the development of gender roles. Money and Ehrhardt proposed a (22) _____ theory that focuses on the interaction of biological and social influences. According to this theory, several critical events contribute to gender-role development. One is receiving an X or Y chromosome, and the second event is the release of (23) _____, which stimulates the development of a male internal reproductive system. A third event occurs at 3 to 4 months after conception, when testosterone triggers development of male external genitals or, in its absence, development of female external genitalia. This hormone also affects development of the (24) _____ and nervous system. Hormones released during (25) _____ will stimulate the growth of the reproductive system and secondary sex characteristics. These biological events trigger several (26) _____ reactions that will further differentiate males and females.

Evidence from several sources indicates that biological factors do influence the development of males and females. Children who are chromosomally XX but who were exposed to male hormones prenatally are called (27) _____. (***How are these girls behaviorally different from other girls?***) The level of male hormones may also relate to (28)_____ in animals and humans. Social labeling also has an impact on gender development. Evidence suggests that there may be a sensitive or (29) _____ period between 18 months and 3 years of age when gender identity is established. (***Can you explain the evidence that suggests this?***)

Social-learning theorists believe that gender-role development occurs through (30) _____, where children are reinforced for sex-appropriate behaviors and punished for behaviors considered appropriate for members of the other sex. In addition, gender-role development also occurs through (31) _____,where children adopt attitudes and behaviors of same-sex models. (***What are some likely sources of gender-stereotyped behavior that children observe?***)

Cognitive-developmental theorists argue that gender-role development depends on a child's level of cognitive development. Children must first acquire a recognition of being male or female, called gender (32)_____. They must also acquire the understanding that gender identity is constant across time, or gender (33) _____, and knowledge that gender is constant across situations, called (34) _____. (***What level of cognitive development is needed for these understandings?***) According to this view, once children understand that biological sex is unchanging, they actively socialize themselves by seeking out same-sex models. (***What are criticisms of this view of gender-role development?***)

An information-processing model proposed by Martin and Halverson suggests that children acquire (35) _____, which are organized sets of expectations and beliefs about males and females, and that these beliefs influence the things that children pay attention to and remember. According to this theory, children classify people and things as belonging to a simple in-group or out-group. Children then construct an (36) _____ by collecting more elaborate information about the role of their own sex. (***What evidence supports this perspective?***)

Together, the biosocial, social-learning, and cognitive theories help explain how gender-typed behaviors develop. Biological factors guide development, people react to a child's gender, and children actively socialize themselves to act in ways consistent with their understandings of their gender.

12.5   THE ADULT
Changes in Gender Roles
In adulthood, male and female roles are often similar until marriage and parenthood begin to differentiate the roles. The roles become more similar again during middle age when childcare responsibilities decline.

Androgyny?
Someone who has both agentic and communal traits is characterized by psychological (37)_____. Some research suggests that these individuals are able to behave with greater (38) _____ than individuals with traditional traits. Although this might be regarded as a strength, the benefits of androgyny seem to come primarily from the (39)_____ traits.

Gutmann refers to demands placed on a person by parenthood as the (40) _____. The demands often mean that men emphasize their masculine qualities and women emphasize their feminine qualities. Gutmann proposes that when no longer constrained by the parental imperative, psychologically masculine men adopt more (41) _____ qualities and psychologically feminine women adopt more (42) _____ qualities. A related hypothesis is that a midlife (43) _____ occurs, and adults retain their gender-typed qualities but add qualities associated with the other gender. Gutmann's hypothesis is partially supported. Parenthood does tend to make people more traditionally sex-typed, but they tend to become (44) _____ in the post-parental phases of life, rather than replacing sex-typed traits with other-sex traits.

12.6   SEXUALITY OVER THE LIFESPAN
Are Infants Sexual Beings?
Not really. Although the genitals of infants are sensitive to stimulation, and both male and female infants have been observed to engage in masturbation-like activities, there is no evidence that infants interpret these activities sexually.

Childhood Sexuality
Children's understanding of sex and reproduction is related to their level of cognitive development. They often interpret information about sex and reproduction in terms of what they already know, a process Piaget called (45)_____. According to Freud, preschoolers are in the (46) _____ stage, making them interested in their genitals, and school-aged children are in a phase of (47) _____ in which sexuality is repressed. But contrary to what Freud believed, sexual interest and experimentation do not decrease during childhood. Some research indicates that an important milestone occurs around the age of (48) _____, when children experience their first sexual attraction. Children's sexual behaviors are influenced by parental and societal attitudes.

Children who are sexually abused exhibit a variety of problems common to emotionally disturbed individuals, such as anxiety and depression. In particular, lack of self-worth and distrust of others affect victims' abilities to build successful relationships. One problem among victims of sexual abuse is their tendency to act out sexually, called (49) _____. A second problem is (50) _____, a clinical disorder involving flashbacks and nightmares about the event.

Adolescent Sexuality

As part of establishing their sexual identity, adolescents must become aware of their sexual (51) _____, or preference for sexual partners of the same or other sex or both. Many establish a heterosexual orientation without much thought. Others may experiment with homosexual activities, but do not necessarily end up with an enduring homosexual orientation. Sexual orientation is influenced by both genetic and environmental factors.

Sexual morality of adolescents has changed during the past century. Most adolescents believe that sex with (52) _____ in the context of a relationship is acceptable. Different rules regarding sexual behavior of males and females, or what is called the (53) _____, has declined but has not disappeared. There is increased confusion about sexual (54) _____ because individuals must now decide for themselves what is right or wrong, rather than adhering to general rules.

Sexual behaviors have also changed during the last century. Adolescents engage in sexual behaviors at earlier ages and more adolescents are having sexual intercourse. An increasing number of adolescents engage in (55) _____, perhaps because this does not technically fit their definition of "having sex." Since many sexually active adolescents fail to use (56) _____, there are a number of unplanned pregnancies. (***What factors influence the sexual behaviors of teens?***)

Adult Sexuality

People continue to be sexual beings throughout middle and late adulthood. Frequency of sexual intercourse declines with age for both single and married individuals. In part, this decline results from (57) _____ changes in men and women as they get older. Sexual capacity can also be affected by diseases and use of prescribed drugs, which both increase as a person gets older. Societal attitudes and lack of a (58) _____ also contribute to the decline of sexual activity of older adults.

REVIEW OF KEY TERMS

Below is a list of terms and concepts from this chapter. Use these to complete the following sentence definitions. You might also want to try writing definitions in your own words and then checking your definitions with those in the text.

agency	double standard
androgenized females	gender
androgyny	gender consistency
androgyny shift	gender constancy
biological sex	gender identity
biosocial theory	gender intensification
communality	gender role

gender-role stereotypes
gender schema
gender segregation
gender similarities hypothesis
gender stability
gender typing

oral sex
parental imperative
posttraumatic stress disorder
sexual orientation
social-role hypothesis
systemize

1.   Understanding that gender identity is stable over time is _____.

2.   A behavior pattern or trait that defines how to act as female or male in a particular
      society is called a _____.

3.   The _____ refers to the belief that sexual behaviors that are acceptable for
      males are not acceptable for females.

4.   A _____ is an organized set of beliefs and expectations about males and
      females that influence the type of information that is attended to and remembered.

5.   Generalizations about what males and females are like are called _____.

6.   The understanding that gender is constant despite changes in appearance or activities is
      called _____.

7.   The process by which children learn their biological sex and acquire the motives, values,
      and behaviors considered appropriate for members of that sex is _____.

8.   The masculine gender role revolves around _____, which is an orientation
      toward dominance, independence, assertiveness, and competitiveness.

9.   Physical characteristics that define male and female comprise a person's
      _____.

10.   The requirements or demands imposed on a person by parenthood are referred to as the
      _____.

11.   The awareness of one's self as male or female is called _____.

12.   The possession of both masculine-stereotyped traits and feminine-stereotyped traits is
      called _____.

13.   Gender-role norms that encourage connectedness to others are the major focus of
      _____.

14.   A female who was exposed prenatally to male hormones and has external genitals that
      appear masculine is labeled a(n) _____.

15. Features that society associates with being male or females constitute _____.

16. One's preference for sexual partners of the same or other sex is a person's _____.

17. An understanding of what it means to be a boy or girl in society is _____.

18. A cluster of symptoms, including nightmares and flashbacks, associated with an extremely traumatic experience is termed _____.

19. The concept of _____ refers to the addition of characteristics typically associated with the other sex to traditionally gender-typed characteristics already held by an individual.

20. The idea that biological events trigger social reactions and together these establish gender-role identity is termed _____.

21. The separation of people into groups of males and females occurs with _____.

22. In the process of _____, there is an increase in sex differences as a result of pressure to conform to gender roles.

23. According to the _____, differences in the societal roles of men and women help create and maintain gender-role stereotypes.

24. Men's focus on work, achievement, and independence may stem from their brain's tendency to _____ or analyze how things work.

25. Sexual contact involving one partner's mouth and another partner's genitals constitutes _____.

26. The idea that males and females are similar on most, although not all, psychological traits is known as the _____.

MULTIPLE-CHOICE SELF-TEST

For each multiple-choice question, read all alternatives and then select the best answer.

1. Females in our society have historically been encouraged to adopt traits that emphasize _____.

    a.   sexuality   c.   communality

    b.   agency   d.   androgyny

2.   Which one the following is TRUE regarding psychological differences between males and females?
    a.   Males and females do not actually differ on any psychological traits or abilities.
    b.   When there are differences, males always outperform females.
    c.   There are no differences between males and females throughout childhood, but beginning in adolescence, males outperform females in most areas.
    d.   Females tend to outperform males on verbal tasks, and males tend to outperform females on tests of spatial ability, but most differences are small.

3.   The process by which children learn their biological sex and acquire the motives, values, and behaviors considered appropriate for the members of that sex is called
    a.   gender typing.   c.   gender differences.
    b.   gender-role norms.   d.   gender consistency.

4.   Which of the following accurately characterizes developmental changes in thinking about gender roles?
    a.   Preschoolers are the most rigid in their thinking about gender roles.
    b.   The period of young adulthood is when people hold the most rigid beliefs about gender roles.
    c.   Children in early elementary school and adolescence hold the most rigid beliefs about gender roles.
    d.   Children in middle childhood hold the most rigid beliefs about gender roles.

5.   Money and Ehrhardt's biosocial theory of gender-role development suggests that
    a.   there are real biological differences between boys and girls, and these differences influence how people react to the children.
    b.   biological differences cause males and females to behave differently and to have different levels of expertise in areas such as math and verbal skills.
    c.   biological differences males and females may exist, but these differences have no impact on psychological differences between males and females.
    d.   biological factors affect males' behavior but not females' behavior.

6.   A woman who receives male hormones while she is pregnant may deliver a child who is
    a.   genetically XY and has external genitals that appear feminine.
    b.   genetically XX and has external genitals that appear masculine.
    c.   genetically XX and becomes very masculine appearing following puberty.
    d.   mentally retarded.

7.   Social-learning theorists explain sex-typing as the result of
    a.   the child's understanding of gender identity and gender constancy.
    b.   the child's desire to be like his or her parents.
    c.   the parents differentially reinforcing behaviors and the child's observation of same-sex models.
    d.   chromosomal and hormonal differences between males and females.

8. According to cognitive-developmental theorists, gender-role development
   a. begins with children's understanding that they are girls or boys.
   b. begins with children imitating same-sex models.
   c. begins when parents differentially reinforce boys and girls.
   d. depends on observational learning.

9. Most children can correctly label themselves as males or females by age _____ and begin to understand that one's sex does not change around age _____.
   a. 5 years; 11 years
   b. 3 years; 6 years
   c. 18 months; 3 years
   d. 2 years; 3 years

10. When children realize that their gender is stable over time, they have achieved _____, and when they realize that their gender is stable over situations, they have achieved _____.
   a. gender stability; gender identity
   b. gender identity; gender consistency
   c. gender consistency; gender stability
   d. gender stability; gender consistency

11. Gender schemas
   a. determine a child's behavior in ambiguous situations.
   b. influence the kinds of information that children attend to.
   c. refer to the child's understanding that their gender is stable over time.
   d. reflect the fact that children have difficulty understanding their appropriate gender roles.

12. With respect to androgyny, research indicates that
   a. androgynous people are less flexible in their behavior than sex-typed people.
   b. children of androgynous parents are more socially responsible and assertive than children of sex-typed people.
   c. the possession of masculine traits leads to higher self-esteem and good adjustment.
   d. the possession of feminine traits by men leads to better adjustment.

13. Which of the following is TRUE regarding changes in sexual attitudes?
   a. Regardless of how they may act, most adolescents believe that premarital sex is wrong.
   b. Most adolescents are quite knowledgeable about sex and clearly understand today's sexual norms.
   c. The "double standard" for males and females sexual behavior no longer exists.
   d. Most adolescents believe that sex with affection is OK.

14. Compared to their parent's generation, today's adolescents are
    a. more likely to engage in oral sex, but less likely to consider this as "having sex."
    b. likely to exhibit a large gender gap in their sexual behaviors and attitudes.
    c. more likely to wait until they are older to engage in sexual activity.
    d. less likely to discuss their sexuality with others.

15. As adults get older, research suggests that sexual behavior
    a. remains at the same level for males but declines for females.
    b. declines for both females and males.
    c. remains the same among married couples but increases among adults who find themselves single after a relationship ends.
    d. remains stable across the lifespan regardless of changes in relationship status or gender.

COMPARE THEORIES OF GENDER TYPING

For each theory of gender typing listed below, note the contribution that it has made to our understanding of the development of gender typing. Use the description of the theories in the text and Table 12.1 to check your answers.

THEORY	CONTRIBUTION
Biosocial	
Social Learning	
Cognitive Developmental	
Gender Schema	

CRITICAL THINKING QUESTIONS

By answering the following questions, you will strengthen your understanding of the material in this chapter. These questions require higher-level thinking skills such as integration and application of concepts. Sample answers are provided for three of the questions. These illustrate one possibility, but there are other answers you could provide that might be just as good. For the other questions, you can check yourself by referring to the text (a hint is provided), or by asking a peer or your instructor to review your answer.

1. One issue debated by scholars in the field of gender roles is the existence of actual differences between males and females. Are there "real" gender differences? Discuss all sides of this issue and provide evidence to support each position.
   [Sample answer provided.]

2.   Use the research on gender-role development to illustrate the nature/nurture issue.
      [*Sample answer provided*.]

3.   What are the most significant developments or changes in our sexual selves across the
      lifespan?
      [*Sample answer provided*.]

4.   Outline the theories that attempt to explain the acquisition of gender-typed behavior.
      Which of these theories has the best empirical support and what is this evidence?
      [*Hint: Review the section on "Explaining gender-role development*."]

5.   What happens to gender roles and gender differences during adulthood?
      [*Hint: Review the section on "The Adult."]*

ANSWERS

Chapter Summary and Guided Review (fill in the blank)

1. biological sex	30. differential reinforcement
2. gender	31. observational learning
3. chromosomes	32. identity
4. hormones	33. stability
5. gender roles	34. consistency
6. stereotypes	35. gender schemata
7. communality	36. own-sex schema
8. agency	37. androgyny
9. systemize	38. flexibility
10. masculine	39. agentic or masculine
11. gender similarities	40. parental imperative
12. verbal	41. feminine
13. spatial	42. masculine
14. aggressively	43. androgyny shift
15. stereotypes	44. androgynous
16. social role	45. assimilation
17. gender identity	46. phallic
18. stereotypes	47. latency
19. flexible	48. ten
20. segregation	49. sexualized behavior
21. intensification	50. posttraumatic stress disorder
22. biosocial	51. orientation
23. testosterone	52. affection
24. brain	53. double standard
25. puberty	54. norms
26. social	55. oral sex
27. androgenized females	56. contraception
28. aggression	57. physiological or health
29. critical	58. partner

Review of Key Terms
1. gender stability
2. gender role
3. double standard
4. gender schema
5. gender-role stereotypes
6. gender consistency
7. gender typing
8. agency
9. biological sex
10. parental imperative
11. gender identity
12. androgyny
13. communality
14. androgenized females
15. gender
16. sexual orientation
17. gender constancy
18. posttraumatic stress disorder
19. androgyny shift
20. biosocial theory
21. gender segregation
22. gender intensification
23. social-role hypothesis
24. systemize
25. oral sex
26. gender similarities hypothesis

Multiple-Choice Self-Test
1. C (p. 383)
2. D (p. 384-385)
3. A (p. 387)
4. C (p. 388)
5. A (p. 391-392)
6. B (p. 392)
7. C (p. 393)
8. A (p. 396)
9. B (p. 396)
10. D (p. 396)
11. B (p. 396-397)
12. C (p. 399)
13. D (p. 405-406)
14. A (p. 406)
15. B (p. 409-410)

Critical Thinking Questions

1. *Some people would argue that there are no "real" differences between men and women other than their different reproductive systems and genitals. People on this side of the issue insist that there are no meaningful psychological, intellectual, or behavioral differences between men and women. They argue that what may appear to be gender differences are actually the result of socialization differences, not inherent differences. Consequently, they believe that if society treated men and women similarly, they would behave similarly.*

   Other people believe that there <u>are</u> some real differences between males and females. They may note that males often perform higher on tests of spatial ability, especially mental rotation tasks, whereas females score higher on some verbal tasks. In addition, on multiple measures of aggression, males score higher than females. These differences in aggression show up very early in life and are observed cross-culturally, which suggests there may be a biological or genetic component to sex differences in aggression.

   Finally, there are still others who believe that there are additional differences between men and women, including activity level, compliance, cooperativeness, nurturance, and others. Again, some of these people believe these differences result from socialization but others think that men and women are different because of physiological differences.

2. *There are biological differences between males and females, starting prenatally with different chromosomes (XX for girls and XY for boys) and different levels of hormones. These lead to differences in internal organs and external genitals. Studies of individuals who have been exposed prenatally to unusually high or low levels of hormones exhibit some differences from individuals who were exposed to normal levels of hormones. For example, androgenized females*

were exposed to excess levels of the male hormone androgen. Even when their genitals were corrected to appear feminine and they were raised as girls, they behaved more tomboyish than other girls and were more likely to describe themselves as homosexual or bisexual.

In addition, some research shows that there are small differences between the behavior of male and female infants. Male infants, for example, are more active and seem to focus more on physical objects. These differences show up very early in life, before the environment would be able to socialize them into different behaviors.

On the nurture side of the issue, it is clear that society treats boys and girls differently— reinforcing them for behaving in ways that are consistent with their gender and discouraging or even punishing them for behaving in gender-inconsistent ways. Boys are allowed to get away with more aggressive behavior than girls because stereotypes "allow" boys to be more aggressive. Children are also exposed to many gender-stereotypic messages in the world around them. In their homes, parents' activities usually fall into gender-stereotypic patterns, with dads doing the outside chores and moms doing the inside chores and more of the childrearing.

3.   The biggest changes in our sexual selves occur during adolescence as we go through puberty. There are dramatic changes in boys' and girls' bodies as they develop secondary sex characteristics and become sexually mature. These changes have psychological implications, depending on whether the timing of maturity is early, late, or on time. For boys, being early or on time is better than being late. For girls, being on time or late has more advantages (or fewer disadvantages) than maturing early. Adolescents spend a great deal of timing thinking about and worrying about their sexual selves. Some come to the realization that they are homosexual, which is a dramatic insight at any age.

Another significant change in the sexual selves of women would be going through menopause, the cessation of menstruation. This is likely to trigger a reevaluation of what it means to be a sexual being. Men may go through a similar process during andropause, but it much more gradual and doesn't have the same conclusion. Men can continue to father children well into old age, whereas women are unable to bear children once they go through menopause (unless they turn to one of the new assisted reproductive technologies).

CHAPTER THIRTEEN

SOCIAL COGNITION AND MORAL DEVELOPMENT

OVERVIEW

Whether you realize it or not, you use social cognitive skills every day when you think about your own or another person's thoughts, behaviors, motivations, or emotions. This chapter discusses what these skills are, how they change across the lifespan, factors that can foster these skills, and the importance of these skills to other areas of development.

A large portion of this chapter is devoted to moral development, including the theoretical explanations of moral affect (Freud's psychoanalytic theory), moral reasoning (Kohlberg's and Piaget's cognitive-developmental theories), moral behavior (social-learning theory), and moral function or purpose (evolutionary theory). Each theory is evaluated in light of research findings. Particularly interesting in this chapter are the discussions of how to foster moral maturity and increase social cognitive skills and how these skills relate to antisocial behavior.

LEARNING OBJECTIVES

After reading and studying the material in this chapter, you should be able to answer the following questions.

13.1   SOCIAL COGNITION
1.   What is a theory of mind? What developmental changes occur in the acquiring a theory of mind, and what factors affect its emergence?

2.   What is involved in developing social perspective-taking skills? Why are these skills important? How do they change over the lifespan?

13.2   PERSPECTIVES ON MORAL DEVELOPMENT
3.   What is morality? What are the three basic components of morality?

4.   What is Freud's explanation for the development of morality?

5.   How did Kohlberg assess moral reasoning? What are the important characteristics of each level and stage of Kohlberg's theory? What are examples of responses at each stage of reasoning?

6.   How do social-learning theorists explain moral behavior?

7.   According to evolutionary theory, what are the functions of morality?

13.3   THE INFANT
8.   What do infants understand about morality and prosocial behavior?

13.4 THE CHILD

9.   What changes in moral reasoning and behavior occur during childhood? What factors influence children's moral thinking?

10. What parenting characteristics contribute to the development of morality? Which parenting style is "best"?

13.5 THE ADOLESCENT

11. What changes in moral reasoning occur during adolescence? How is moral development related to antisocial behavior of adolescents? What other factors influence antisocial behavior?

13.6 THE ADULT

12. What changes in moral reasoning and behavior occur during adulthood?

13. How does Kohlberg's theory of moral reasoning fare in light of research findings? In what ways might the theory be biased or incomplete?

14. What is the difference between religiosity and spirituality, and what paths does each of these follow across adulthood?

CHAPTER SUMMARY AND GUIDED REVIEW

The following summary provides an overview of the main points contained in this chapter of the text. Fill in the blanks with terms that appropriately complete the sentence. Scattered throughout the summary are questions in parentheses. These are meant to encourage you to think actively as you read and connect this summary to the more detailed information provided in the text.

13.1 SOCIAL COGNITION

Social cognition involves the ability to think about thoughts, emotions, motives, and behaviors of one's self and others.

Developing a Theory of Mind

Researchers use an assessment called the (1) _____ task to assess children's understanding that people can have incorrect beliefs and be influenced by these beliefs. *(Can you explain how this task works?)* This task has been used to determine whether children have an understanding of mental states and the role of mental states on behavior, an understanding called (2) _____. Research shows that many children with the condition (3)_____ lack this understanding, which may limit their abilities to have successful social interactions.

Precursors of a theory of mind can be seen as young as 9 months, when infants and caregivers look at the same object together, showing (4) _____. Other research shows that 2-year-olds develop a (5) _____ psychology based on what they want. By age 4, they normally progress to a (6) _____ psychology, which incorporates an understanding of beliefs. The development of a theory of mind seems to involve biological/maturational factors as well as normal interactions with other people. Brain imaging studies show activity in different parts of the brain depending on whether the task involves theory of mind or not. Neurons that are activated both when we perform a task and when we observe someone else perform the task comprise the (7) _____ system. This system may also be involved in theory of mind. (*What evidence supports the nature and nurture components of theory of mind?*)

Describing and Evaluating Other People

Young children tend to perceive people in terms of observable or (8) _____ characteristics. By age 7 or 8, children go beyond the observable and can use (9)_____ traits to describe others, and by 11 or 12 years, they can integrate these characteristics to make sense of seemingly inconsistent traits.

Social Perspective-Taking

Social perspective-taking is the ability to assume another person's perspective. Research by Robert Selman suggests that social perspective-taking skills develop in stages. Preschool children have trouble assuming another person's perspective and are (10)_____. With concrete operational thought, children can understand that there are different perspectives even if people have received the same information. With the development of formal operational thought, adolescents can simultaneously consider two different perspectives and how they fit with the perspective of the broader social group. (*What are the implications of good social cognition skills such as role-taking?*)

Social Cognition in Adulthood

Social cognitive skills of adults are advanced in some ways, although older adults may experience some losses. Losses may result from declines in processing speed and in (11)_____ that affect many older adults. Elderly adults who continue to use their social cognition skills show no decline in these abilities.

13.2   PERSPECTIVES ON MORAL DEVELOPMENT

The ability to distinguish right from wrong, act on this distinction, and experience the accompanying emotion implies morality. Morality includes an emotional or (12)_____ component, a behavioral component, and a (13)_____ component that focuses on how a person reasons and makes decisions about moral dilemmas.

Moral Affect: Psychoanalytic Theory and Beyond

Moral affect refers to the emotions associated with right and wrong behaviors. A child who has done something wrong typically feels some negative emotion such as guilt or shame. Being able to experience another person's feelings, or (14) _____, can lead to positive social acts or (15) _____ behaviors. Freud believed that morality was not present until development of the (16) _____ during the phallic stage of psychosexual development. At this time, children (17) _____ the moral standards of the same-sex parent. The specifics of Freud's theory are not well supported. (*List some of the problems with Freud's explanation of morality.*)

Chapter Thirteen

Moral Reasoning: Cognitive-Developmental Theory

Cognitive-developmental theorists such as Piaget and Kohlberg focused on moral reasoning or the thoughts about what is right or wrong. Social perspective skills allow us to understand the idea of give and take, or (18) _____ between people in a relationship.

According to Piaget, preschool children are (19) _____ and show little awareness of rules. Elementary school-aged children take rules very seriously and believe that consequences are more important than (20) _____. They are in Piaget's stage of (21) _____ morality. Older children view rules as agreements between individuals and believe intentions are more important than consequences. This is Piaget's stage of (22)_____ morality.

Kohlberg developed a theory of moral reasoning that consists of three levels, each with two stages. Progress through these stages follows a fixed, or (23) _____, order. The first level of (24) _____ reasoning consists of stage 1, the punishment-and-obedience orientation, where the emphasis is on the (25) _____ of an act, and stage 2, called (26) _____, where an act is judged by whether it satisfies personal needs or results in personal gain. The (27) _____ level consists of stage 3, the "good boy" or "good girl" morality, where actions are right if they please others or are approved by others, and stage 4, the authority and social-order-maintaining morality with its focus on conforming to (28) _____. The last level of moral reasoning is (29)_____ morality, which includes stages 5 and 6. Stage 5 is the morality of contract, individual rights, and democratically accepted law, and stage 6 is the morality of individual principles of conscience. (***Can you provide responses that portray these six different stages?***) Kohlberg believed that advancement through the stages depended on cognitive growth as well as social interaction with peers.

Moral Behavior: Social-Learning Theory

Social-learning theorists focus mainly on moral behaviors: actions to moral problems. Social-learning theorists believe that moral behavior is learned the same way everything else is learned—through reinforcement (or punishment) and through (30) _____. According to Bandura's social-cognitive theory, moral thinking is connected to moral action through cognitive (31) _____ mechanisms. Normally, such monitoring and evaluation keeps our behavior in line with our internalized standards. But sometimes, we exercise moral (32) _____ in which we ignore or distance ourselves from moral standards, opening the door to immoral behavior.

The Functions of Morality: Evolutionary Theory

Evolutionary theorists examine whether some aspects of morality may be universal and if they have helped humans (33) _____ to their environments. According to this view, altruism may have evolved to aid survival.

13.3   THE INFANT

Infants in our society are often viewed as lacking any sense of morality, or as being (34)_____.

Early Moral Training

Although infants are not held morally responsible for their actions, they are learning lessons about what is right and wrong. Children must learn to experience negative emotions when they do something wrong and to exert self-control when tempted to violate rules. Research suggests that moral development is fostered by a close, warm, cooperative relationship between child and parent, known as a (35) _____ orientation. In addition, emotion-centered discussion is an important component of moral learning.

Empathy and Prosocial Behavior

Infants display some rudimentary signs that they understand another person's feelings, known as (36) _____. During their second year of life, toddlers begin to share or help another person, evidence of (37) _____ behavior.

13.4   THE CHILD

Thinking through Kohlberg's Dilemmas

School-aged children typically reason at the (38) _____ level when tested with Kohlberg's moral dilemmas. As such, they exhibit an (39) _____ perspective of morality reflecting their focus on reward and punishment to themselves.

Weighing Intentions

Research on Piaget's theory of moral reasoning indicates that he underestimated young children. When Piaget's moral reasoning tasks are simplified, even young children can consider a person's (40) _____ when making moral judgments.

Understanding Rules

Contrary to Piaget's claim, young children may not view rules as sacred or absolute. Turiel reports that young children distinguish between two kinds of rules in daily life. Those standards that focus on basic rights and welfare of individuals are (41) _____ rules and those that focus on what social consensus deems right or wrong are (42) _____ rules. Even young children understand the difference between these two types of rules and understand that violating a (43) _____ rule is the more serious transgression.

Applying Theory of Mind

The emergence of a theory of mind helps children better understand how their actions influence other people. Children must continue to develop an understanding of how behaviors and emotions are connected.

Moral Socialization

Research has linked moral development to parental discipline styles. Disciplining by withholding attention, love, or approval is called the (44) _____. Use of physical power to gain compliance to rules is the (45) _____ discipline style. Explaining to a child why a behavior is wrong and pointing out how it affects other people is (46) _____. Higher levels of moral maturity are associated with the use of (47) _____ than use of the other two discipline styles. (*Can you explain why this is true?*) The use of (48) _____ is often associated with immature moral responses, although it may be useful if used sparingly. Use of (49) _____ has been found to have mixed effects. It also helps if parents try to prevent misbehavior from happening at all by using (50)_____ strategies. The way children respond to moral training may depend on their individual (51) _____ style. The interaction of children's enduring style with their social environments illustrates the concept of (52)_____.

13.5   THE ADOLESCENT
Changes in Moral Reasoning
Most adolescents reason at the (53) _____ level of Kohlberg's model, and they begin to view morality as an important part of their identity.

Antisocial Behavior
Some adolescents engage in antisocial behaviors, which may lead to (54)_____, or breaking the law as a minor. There is a weak connection between these behaviors and level of moral reasoning. According to Kenneth Dodge, the way that social cues are processed may provide a better explanation of these behaviors. There are six steps in processing information, starting with encoding and then (55) _____ of the information. Clarifying goals, searching for possible responses, and evaluating these options are followed by the last step, which is behavioral (56) _____. Aggressive adolescents are likely to have problems with every step of processing information. (*Can you provide some examples of faulty information processing that might lead to aggressive behavior?*)

This model helps us to understand the behavior but does not fully explain why someone processes information in this maladaptive way. According to Gerald Patterson, antisocial children often experience (57) _____ family environments, where members try to control one another through negative means. Aggression is likely determined by a combination of genetic and environmental influences. (*Can you explain how genes and environments interact or correlate to determine aggression?*) Within some environments or subcultures, there may be higher levels of peers picking on, or (58)_____, weaker peers. Antisocial behavior is more likely to emerge among adolescents with multiple risk factors. (*What methods have been attempted to reduce or reverse antisocial behavior and to what extent have they been successful?*)

13.6   THE ADULT
Changes in Moral Reasoning
Some adults move into Kohlberg's (59) _____ level of moral reasoning. Moral reasoning does not deteriorate in old age, and indeed it may improve.

Kohlberg's Theory in Perspective
There is support for Kohlberg's claim that moral development is stage-like. However, Kohlberg has been criticized for several reasons. One important criticism is that his theory is biased in several ways. It may be biased against people from different cultures, people with conservative values, and women. Carol Gilligan argues that women reason using a morality of (60) _____ and men reason using a morality of (61) _____. (*Can you explain what these perspectives mean?*) Gilligan claims that neither focus is "right;" they are simply different ways to reason, and reflect differences in how boys and girls are traditionally raised in our society. Gilligan's theory is not well supported by research.

Another criticism of Kohlberg's theory is that it is incomplete because it ignores moral affect and behavior. Kohlberg would predict that moral behavior is related to level of moral reasoning. Overall, however, this relationship is weak.

<u>New Approaches to Morality</u>

Experts in the field are looking more fully at the role of emotions in morality. Some are also exploring how "gut reactions" and intuitions influence morality. This may lead to a (62)_____ model of morality that incorporates both thought and emotion.

<u>Religion and Spirituality</u>

Sharing beliefs and practicing with an organized religious group is the basic definition of (63)_____. Searching for greater meaning and connecting with something larger than oneself is involved in (64)_____. Religiosity decreases somewhat over early and middle adulthood, but then rises in late adulthood. Spirituality is relatively low and flat throughout adulthood, rising only during late adulthood.

REVIEW OF KEY TERMS

Below is a list of terms and concepts from this chapter. Use these to complete the following sentence definitions. You might also want to try writing definitions in your own words and then checking your definitions with those in the text.

amoral	morality of care
autonomous morality	morality of justice
belief-desire psychology	moral reasoning
bullying	moral rules
coercive family environment	mutually responsive orientation
conduct disorder	postconventional morality
conventional morality	power assertion
desire psychology	preconventional morality
dual-process of morality	premoral period
empathy	proactive parenting strategies
false belief task	prosocial behavior
heteronomous morality	reciprocity
induction	religiosity
juvenile delinquency	social cognition
love withdrawal	social conventional rules
mirror neurons	social perspective-taking skills
moral affect	spirituality
moral disengagement	theory of mind
morality	

1.   The _____ is used to assess the understanding that people can have incorrect beliefs that influence their behavior.

2.   Standards of what behaviors are right or wrong based on rights and privileges of individuals are termed _____.

Chapter Thirteen

3.   Kohlberg's fifth and sixth stages are part of the _____ in which judgments are based on broad principles of justice that have validity separate from the views of any particular person or group.

4.   The cognitive process of deciding whether an act is right or wrong is _____.

5.   A discipline style based on physical power of an adult over a child is _____.

6.   Kohlberg's first two stages of moral reasoning are part of the _____ in which the personal consequences of a person's actions are used as the basis for judgments.

7.   Neurons that are activated when we perform an action and when we observe someone else perform the same action are _____.

8.   A moral perspective that emphasizes one's responsibility for the welfare of others is called _____.

9.   Thinking about the thoughts, behaviors, motives, and emotions of oneself and others is called _____.

10.   A type of discipline style based on explanations that focus on how the misbehavior affects other people is _____.

11.   A set of principles that allow a person to distinguish right from wrong, and act on this distinction, is termed _____.

12.   Understanding that people have mental states that influence behavior shows the presence of a _____.

13.   Kohlberg's third and fourth stages are part of the _____ in which actions are judged by whether they conform to the rules set forth by others.

14.   Experiencing another person's feelings is _____.

15.   Sharing beliefs and participating in activities with an organized religion is _____.

16.   The emotional component of morality is called _____ and consists of feelings about right and wrong actions.

17.   The lack of any sense of morality is referred to as being _____.

18.   A discipline style that is based on threatened or actual loss of love or attention is _____.

19.   Adolescents who break the law are engaging in _____.

20. An understanding that a person's beliefs do not always accurately reflect reality is called _____.

21. Positive social acts that show a concern for the welfare of others are known as _____.

22. Standards for defining what behaviors are right or wrong based on social consensus are called _____.

23. A moral perspective emphasizing the laws defining individual rights is _____.

24. Family interactions that are characterized by power struggles where members try to control each other exist in _____.

25. According to _____, young children understand what they want and often use wants to explain behavior.

26. The view that rules are unalterable and handed down by authority figures is part of Piaget's stage of _____.

27. The search for ultimate meaning in life is a significant component of _____.

28. According to Piaget, preschool-aged children have little understanding of rules and are in a _____.

29. Early moral socialization can be enhanced by a close, warm, and cooperative relationship between parent and child, known as a _____.

30. Employing mechanisms of _____ allows people to avoid feeling bad when they engage in immoral behavior.

31. Piaget's final stage of moral development in which children understand that rules can be changed by consensus and pay attention to intentions is called _____.

32. A sense of give and take by both partners in relationships demonstrates _____.

33. The ability to adopt another person's view and understand his/her thoughts and feelings is the major component of _____.

34. Some parents use _____, or techniques to prevent bad behavior from occurring.

35. Peers who pick on or torment their weaker peers are engaging in _____.

36. Incorporating both deliberate thought and emotion into an explanation of morality has been done by those proposing a _____.

37.   A diagnosis of _____ may be warranted if someone exhibits a pattern of behavior that violates the rights of others or age-appropriate societal norms.

MULTIPLE-CHOICE SELF-TEST

For each multiple-choice question, read all alternatives and then select the best answer.

1.   Having a theory of mind shows an understanding that
     a.   people's behavior is guided by a set of internalized rules about right and wrong.
     b.   more than one person is looking at an object at a particular time.
     c.   people have mental states that influence their behavior.
     d.   other people experience different emotions.

2.   Children who are popular and have close friends
     a.   reason at the "good boy"/"good girl" stage of moral reasoning.
     b.   tend to use more reactive aggression than proactive aggression.
     c.   are more likely to have an intuitive theory of emotions.
     d.   tend to have more advanced role-taking skills than other children.

3.   Social cognitive skills
     a.   reach a peak as adolescents finish their formal schooling and then slowly decline.
     b.   remain high in socially active older adults.
     c.   relate specifically to a person's educational level.
     d.   decline from young to older adulthood for most adults.

4.   Research on Freud's explanation of morality shows that all of the following are problems with the explanation EXCEPT
     a.   males do not have stronger superegos than females.
     b.   children do not achieve moral maturity by resolving conflicts of the phallic stage.
     c.   children do not develop greater moral maturity by interacting with cold, punitive parents.
     d.   children do not experience feelings in conjunction with moral transgressions.

5.   Piaget argued that elementary school children
     a.   are largely unaware of moral rules and so do not always act appropriately.
     b.   base decisions on both consequences of an action and intentions of the actor.
     c.   believe that rules can be changed at any time.
     d.   believe that the consequences of an action are more important than intentions of the actor.

6. A child who says that it is wrong to cheat because he or she might get caught would be in Kohlberg's _____ stage.
   a. punishment-and-obedience orientation (stage 1)
   b. instrumental hedonism (stage 2)
   c. "good boy" or "good girl" morality (stage 3)
   d. authority and social-order-maintaining morality (stage 4)

7. A teenager who begins smoking because all his friends are doing it is probably in Kohlberg's _____ stage.
   a. instrumental hedonism (stage 2)
   b. "good boy" or "good girl" morality (stage 3)
   c. authority and social-order-maintaining morality (stage 4)
   d. morality of contract, individual rights, and democratically accepted law (stage 5)

8. Social learning theorists argue that morality is
   a. a generalized trait inherent to the person and subject to little change.
   b. a situation-specific trait that is subject to change.
   c. an emotional reaction and cannot be directly observed.
   d. established in early childhood and changes little after this.

9. Standards of what behaviors are right or wrong based on rights and privileges of individuals are termed _____ rules.
   a. postconventional
   b. social-conventional
   c. moral
   d. altruistic

10. Recent studies of Kohlberg's and Piaget's theories of moral reasoning suggest that
    a. there is no relationship between level of cognitive development and moral reasoning.
    b. they underestimated children's moral reasoning capabilities.
    c. they overestimated children's moral reasoning capabilities.
    d. they focused too much attention on children's actions in a moral situation.

11. Parents who use an induction style of discipline
    a. indoctrinate their child with their own values and beliefs.
    b. withhold attention until their child complies with rules.
    c. use their power to get their child to comply with rules.
    d. explain to their child why the behavior is wrong and emphasize how it affects other people.

12. Moral maturity can be fostered by
    a. using an induction style of discipline.
    b. using love withdrawal as the major disciplinary method.
    c. using power assertion as the major disciplinary method.
    d. harsh discipline that leaves the child in no doubt about whether a behavior is acceptable or not.

13. According to Dodge's social information-processing model, aggressive behavior results from
    a.   growing up in an unresponsive home environment.
    b.   the way that information is processed and interpreted.
    c.   a person's reward and punishment history.
    d.   events of puberty that are largely beyond the individual's control.

14. Carol Gilligan claims that men and women score at different levels on Kohlberg's moral dilemmas because
    a.   males operate on the basis of a morality of justice and women do not.
    b.   Freud was right—females are less morally mature.
    c.   males are more concerned about the needs of others.
    d.   males reason about real life dilemmas and women reason about hypothetical moral issues.

15. According to dual-process models of morality,
    a.   mature levels of morality lead to spirituality.
    b.   morality involves both social-conventional rules and moral rules.
    c.   moral decisions are made on the basis of deliberate thought and emotions or intuition.
    d.   moral decisions combine theory of mind with reciprocity of actions.

COMPARE THE THEORETICAL PERSPECTIVES ON MORAL DEVELOPMENT

For this exercise, review the theoretical perspectives on moral development by completing the table below with the name of the theorist primarily associated with the theory, indicate the focus of the theory (e.g., emotions, reasoning, behavior), and the main message of the theory. Check yourself by referring to Table 13.2 on page 429 of the text.

Perspective	Focus	Essential Message
Psychoanalytic theory (Freud)		
Cognitive-developmental theory (Piaget & Kohlberg)		
Social-learning theory (Bandura)		
Evolutionary theory (Krebs)		

CRITICAL THINKING QUESTIONS

By answering the following questions, you will strengthen your understanding of the material in this chapter. These questions require higher-level thinking skills such as integration and application of concepts. Sample answers are provided for three of the questions. These illustrate one possibility, but there are other answers you could provide that might be just as good. For the other questions, you can check yourself by referring to the text (a hint is provided), or by asking a peer or your instructor to review your answer.

1. What is it about raising a child using an induction approach to discipline that leads to greater moral maturity in comparison to children raised with power assertion or love withdrawal?
    [*Sample answer provided.*]

2. On Halloween night, several of your friends try to talk you into going out with them to pull some pranks in the neighborhood (e.g., soaping the neighbor's windows, scaring young children, and knocking over gravestones). You are considering it. What preconventional, conventional, and postconventional answers might you give (either to join in or to abstain)?
    [*Sample answer provided.*]

3. What factors lead some adolescents to engage in antisocial behaviors while many other adolescents do not? What are some protective factors against antisocial behaviors, and what are some of the risk factors?
    [*Sample answer provided.*]

4. What can parents do to increase a child's social cognitive skills and foster moral maturity?
    [*Hint: There is information on this issue in several places throughout the chapter, including within the discussion of "Theory of mind," "Role-taking skills," "Early moral training," and "How does one raise moral children?" In addition, the Application box on page 396, "Combating youth violence," provides useful information.*]

5. Considering the research that has been conducted on moral reasoning, how has Kohlberg's theory fared?
    [*Hint: Review the section on "Kohlberg's theory and beyond," starting on page 400.*]

ANSWERS

Chapter Summary and Guided Review (fill in the blank)

1. false belief
2. theory of mind
3. autism
4. joint attention
5. desire
6. belief-desire
7. mirror neuron
8. physical
9. psychological
10. egocentric
11. working memory
12. affective
13. cognitive
14. empathy

15. prosocial
16. superego
17. internalize
18. reciprocity
19. premoral
20. intentions
21. heteronomous
22. autonomous
23. invariant
24. preconventional
25. consequences
26. instrumental hedonism
27. conventional
28. laws or rules
29. postconventional
30. observation
31. self-regulatory
32. disengagement
33. adapt
34. amoral
35. mutually responsive
36. empathy
37. prosocial
38. preconventional
39. egocentric

40. intentions
41. moral
42. social conventional
43. moral
44. love withdrawal
45. power assertion
46. induction
47. induction
48. power assertion
49. love withdrawal
50. proactive parenting
51. temperament
52. goodness of fit
53. conventional
54. juvenile delinquency
55. interpretation
56. enactment
57. coercive
58. bullying
59. postconventional
60. care
61. justice
62. dual process
63. religiosity
64. spirituality

Review of Key Terms
1. false belief task
2. moral rules
3. postconventional morality
4. moral reasoning
5. power assertion
6. preconventional morality
7. mirror neurons
8. morality of care
9. social cognition
10. induction
11. morality
12. theory of mind
13. conventional morality
14. empathy
15. religiosity
16. moral affect
17. amoral
18. love withdrawal
19. juvenile delinquency

20. belief-desire psychology
21. prosocial behavior
22. social conventional rules
23. morality of justice
24. coercive family environments
25. desire psychology
26. heteronomous morality
27. spirituality
28. premoral period
29. mutually responsive orientation
30. moral disengagement
31. autonomous morality
32. reciprocity
33. social perspective-taking skills
34. proactive parenting strategies
35. bullying
36. dual-process of morality
37. conduct disorder

Multiple-Choice Self-Test
1. C (p. 417)
2. D (p. 422)
3. B (p. 422-423)
4. D (p. 424)
5. D (p. 425)

6. A (p. 426-427)
7. B (p. 426-427)
8. B (p. 428)
9. C (p. 430)
10. B (p. 432-433)

11. D (p. 433)
12. A (p. 433-434)
13. B (p. 437)
14. A (p. 442)
15. C (p. 443)

Critical Thinking Questions

1. *Induction encourages children to think about how their actions affect other people. This gets them away from thinking egocentrically and focusing solely on how things benefit or harm themselves. This also fosters empathy. By pointing out why a child's behavior was wrong, parents can communicate standards of behavior that children can incorporate into their future actions. All these things help advance morality, particularly in children with temperaments that are high in emotionality and low in impulsivity.*

2. *The answers of preconventional thinkers would reflect their concerns about avoiding punishment (stage 1) or gaining something for themselves (stage 2). In this example, an individual might say that they are not going to participate in pranks because they could get caught and punished. Or they might decide to participate because they think their status among their friends will increase (a personal benefit) following their daring acts.*

   A conventional thinker's answers would focus on acting in ways that are approved by others (stage 3) or acting in ways that conform to the rules of the group (stage 4). An individual might decide to go along with his/her friends because he/she believes he/she would receive approval from these peers for doing so. He/she might decide to not participate because it would be breaking the law to deface another person's property.

   Postconventional thinkers would concentrate on actions that are morally right, not just legally right. They might argue that pulling Halloween pranks violates other individual's rights, even if there is not a specific law prohibiting what they plan on doing.

3. *According to Dodge's social information-processing model, people who engage in antisocial acts process information differently than people who do not engage in these acts. They don't always encode all the relevant information or they encode it in ways that highlight the disadvantages to them. They are also likely to think that others hold hostile intentions toward them and want to hurt them. In response, they lash out. They often act impulsively, without thinking through all the consequences. When they do think of consequences, they are more likely to believe that aggressive acts are a positive solution to their problem.*

   In addition to how they process information, aggressive youth often come from coercive family environments. These are families in which family members threaten, yell, and hit each other in order to control one another. Children learn this way of interaction, which makes them unpopular with the regular peer group, so they drift toward a peer group that is similar. Once they are in the habit of hanging out with other antisocial, rejected youth, it reinforces their aggressive tendencies, making it more likely that they will engage in antisocial acts.

   It's also possible that some people are more genetically predisposed to aggression and antisocial behaviors than others. This might be mediated through temperament and personality characteristics. Certain personality traits may provoke more coercive parenting, which in turn, leads to peer rejection and drifting toward a delinquent peer group.

Chapter Thirteen

CHAPTER FOURTEEN

ATTACHMENT AND SOCIAL RELATIONSHIPS

OVERVIEW

Relationships with others have a tremendous influence on our lives. As noted in the text, close relationships provide learning opportunities that affect all areas of development. They also provide social support that helps us celebrate positive events and protects us from negative ones.

This chapter discusses the first major relationship—the one that develops between infants and their caregivers—and how the quality of this relationship influences later development. Also covered are peer relations and friendships, including how they evolve and change over the lifespan and factors that contribute to the quality of social relationships (for instance, why are some children more popular than others?). For children, play is particularly important because it provides opportunities to interact with others and learn skills for successful social relationships. In particular, pretend play is associated with better performance on some tests of cognitive development, language, and creativity.

The section on adolescents provides an interesting look at attachment relationships between adolescents and their parents. It also covers the transition from platonic, largely same-sex social interactions to romantic, opposite-sex interactions. The discussion of romantic relationships is continued in the section on adults, with an examination of factors that contribute to mate selection.

LEARNING OBJECTIVES

After reading and studying the material in this chapter, you should be able to answer the following questions.

14.1 PERSPECTIVES ON RELATIONSHIPS
1. How do relationships with others contribute to development?

2. How does Bowlby's attachment theory explain attachment? In this model, how do nature and nurture contribute to the development of attachment?

14.2 THE INFANT
3. In what ways are infants emotional beings? How are emotions socialized and regulated?

4. How do infants become attached to a caregiver? What are some observable signs of infant attachment?

5. What types of attachment relationships can develop between infants and caregivers? What infant, caregiver, and contextual factors determine the quality of early attachments?

6. How do early relationships relate to later development? What are the consequences of early social deprivation?

14.3   THE CHILD
7. What features characterize peer relations and friendships at different points of the lifespan?

8. What different types of play evolve during the first few years of life? What are the developmental benefits of play?

9. What factors contribute to peer acceptance and popularity, or to peer rejection, during childhood?

14.4   THE ADOLESCENT
10. How do relationships with peers and parents change during adolescence? How do peers and parents influence adolescents' lives?

14.5   THE ADULT
11. How do social networks and friendships change during adulthood? How do these connections affect adult development?

12. How do early attachment styles relate to romantic relationships?

CHAPTER SUMMARY AND GUIDED REVIEW

The following summary provides an overview of the main points contained in this chapter of the text. Fill in the blanks with terms that appropriately complete the sentence. Scattered throughout the summary are questions in parentheses. These are meant to encourage you to think actively as you read and connect this summary to the more detailed information provided in the text.

14.1   PERSPECTIVES ON RELATIONSHIPS
Two of the most important relationships are those between parents and infants and those among peers.

Attachment Theory

John Bowlby developed an influential theory of parent-child attachment. According to Bowlby, attachment is a strong affection that binds one person to another. Infants express attachment by trying to maintain (1) _____ to the figure of their attachment and by showing a preference for this person. Bowlby claims that infants are biologically predisposed to form attachments. Some species experience an innate form of learning called (2)_____, where the young will follow and become attached to the first moving object they encounter during a (3) _____ early in life. Bowlby believes that early attachments between parent and infant affect later development because infants develop (4) _____ models, or representations, of what relationships should be like.

<u>Peers and the Two Worlds of Childhood</u>

Relationships with members of one's social group, or (5) _____, are also important and are quite different from relationships with parents, forming two distinct social worlds during childhood.

14.2   THE INFANT

Infants are social creatures right from the start, although the nature of social relationships changes substantially throughout infancy. Attachments are emotional connections.

<u>Early Emotional Development</u>

Research confirms that infants show a wide range of emotions, which emerge in a predictable order starting with (6) _____ emotions of contentment, interest, and distress. Secondary or (7) _____ emotions emerge around 18 months of age when infants have acquired a sense of self. These earliest emotions emerge in all infants at about the same time, suggesting that they may be (8) _____ predisposed. Environment and culture influence expression of emotions, as illustrated by the finding that infants learn that (9)_____ emotions are more accepted than (10)_____ ones. Infants also monitor the emotional reactions of other people in ambiguous situations to regulate their own reactions, which is called (11) _____. To manage their own emotions, infants must develop strategies for initiating, maintaining, and altering emotional responses, referred to as (12) _____. (***What are some of these early strategies?***)

<u>An Attachment Forms</u>

Just as infants become attached to caregivers, caregivers become attached to infants. Infants have a number of features that seem to facilitate the development of attachment. (***What are some of these features?***) Infants and caregivers learn to take turns responding to each other's leads by developing (13) _____ routines or interactions.

Infants progress through several phases as they develop a relationship with their caregivers. In the first phase, called (14) _____ social responsiveness, infants are responsive to social stimuli but show no preference for one person over another. In the second phase, (15)_____ social responsiveness, infants begin to show preferences for familiar companions. In the third phase, active (16) _____, or true attachment, infants actively pursue the object of their attachment. The final phase is evident when children can consider a parent's plans and participate in a (17) _____ partnership with the parent.

One sign that an attachment has formed occurs when infants show distress when separated from the object of their attachment, displaying (18) _____. Infants may also show a wary response to the approach of an unfamiliar person, called (19)_____. (***What factors can affect this response?***) Once infants have formed an attachment, they often use that attachment figure as a (20) _____ for exploration. Thus, attachment facilitates exploratory behavior.

<u>Quality of Attachment</u>

To measure the quality of an infant's attachment, Mary Ainsworth created the (21)_____ in which an infant's reactions to a series of mildly stressful events are observed. Infants who are classified with a (22) _____ attachment show distress when separated from their caregiver, joy when reunited, and use of the caregiver as a secure base. Infants who show (23) _____ attachment show distress when separated from their caregiver, but are ambivalent about being reunited, and do not really use the caregiver as a secure base. Infants characterized by (24) _____ attachment show little distress at separation from caregiver, avoid the caregiver when reunited, and do not use the caregiver as a secure base. Infants who have been abused often show a fourth pattern of attachment called (25) _____, which is a combination of elements from the resistant and avoidant styles of attachment.

What factors influence the quality of early attachment? Freud claimed that feeding is critical for the development of attachment because of the oral pleasure it provides. However, early research with monkeys does not support this. Harlow used the term (26) _____ to describe the pleasurable sensations provided by clinging to something soft and warm. Research indicates that the availability of contact comfort contributes more to attachment than feeding. Also, infants develop secure attachments to caregivers who are generally responsive to their needs. (*Which theories are supported by these findings? Explain how they are supported*.) Inconsistent parenting is associated with (27) _____ attachment, and inappropriate amounts (too much or too little) stimulation are associated with (28)_____ attachment. In addition to the way parents interact with their infants, an infant's level of cognitive development and their (29) _____ influence the quality of infant-caregiver attachments. Secure attachment can occur with any temperament style as long as there is a good fit with the caregiver's behavior. Finally, the broader social context influences attachment behaviors. (*Can you explain how culture influences attachment?*)

Implications of Early Attachment

Research with infants who have been raised in deprived environments shows that social isolation early in life has an adverse effect on development. The negative effects persist into childhood and adolescence, especially among those who were deprived for 6 months or more. Early deprivation often led to an unhealthy style of behavior called (30)_____. Normal development seems to require sustained interactions with caregivers who are (31)_____.

Infants who are separated from a beloved caregiver can recover if they can maintain another existing significant attachment or can form a new attachment, but multiple disruptions can be problematic. Children in daycare situations are largely indistinguishable from children who do not experience care outside the home. Participating in a high-quality program can lead to cognitive and language advances.

Having a secure or insecure attachment affects later development. Children who had formed secure attachments during infancy are more socially competent, more curious and eager to learn, and more emotionally healthy than children without secure attachments. In addition, a secure attachment during infancy is related to quality of relationships in childhood and adolescence. Finally, research shows that children who had secure attachments as infants process information differently than children who had insecure attachments. This supports Bowlby's idea that infants form (32) _____ of attachment relationships.

First Peer Relations

Infants are interested in other infants and begin to interact socially with them around 6 months of age through smiles, vocalizations, and gestures. Some infants show a preference for a specific playmate.

14.3 THE CHILD

Parent-Child Attachments

Children's attachments to their parents change throughout childhood, with interactions becoming more like a (33) _____ partnership where children take the plans of another person into consideration before taking action. Children are better able to handle separations when they are predictable and controllable.

Peer Networks

Children increasingly spend more time with their peers and in these interactions, children spend more and more time in (34) _____ groups playing with same-sex peers.

Play

Children between the ages of 2 and 5 play quite a bit, which provides opportunities to interact with others and sharpen their social skills. Their play becomes more (35)_____ and more imaginative. According to Parten's scale for classifying children's play, children progress from individual and solitary forms of play to play that is associative and cooperative.

Play of preschool-aged children also becomes more imaginative. When they use one thing to symbolize something else, they are engaging in (36) _____ play. They increasingly engage in (37) _____ play, combining their capacity for imaginary play with their social play.

Elementary school children engage in less symbolic play and more in organized games with (38) _____. According to Piaget, children must be in the (39) _____ stage of cognitive development to play games with rules.

Play is important for a number of reasons. It contributes to cognitive and social development because children get an opportunity to role-play, cooperate with others, and resolve conflicts. Play enhances (40) _____ development because children can express feelings that they might otherwise keep to themselves.

Peer Acceptance and Popularity

Peer acceptance is often studied through (41) _____ techniques where likes and dislikes among the members of a group are examined. Based on this, children can be classified into five district categories of social status. Children well liked by others are (42)_____, whereas children who are rarely liked are (43) _____. Children who are not really liked or disliked but are largely ignored by classmates are considered to be (44) _____. Children who are both liked by many and disliked by many are (45) _____. Children classified as (46) _____ are in the middle on both the liked and disliked scales.

Several factors influence popularity, including some personal characteristics that the child has little control of (e.g. physical appearance and names.) A child's competencies are also important. (*Can you describe specific factors that have been found to be related to whether a child is popular or rejected, neglected, or controversial?*)

Friendships

Popular children are more likely than unpopular ones to have friends. Children with friends are better off than those without friends. Peer interactions contribute to social and emotional development.

14.4   THE ADOLESCENT

Adolescents spend even more time with peers than children do, and the quality of peer interactions changes.

Attachments to Parents

Adolescents remain attached to their parents and may experience anxiety when separated. Those who are securely attached to their parents show better adjustment to transitions such as going to college. (*What are other benefits of a secure attachment between adolescents and parents?*)

Friendships

Friendships during adolescence focus on intimacy and (47) _____ between the partners. Adolescents tend to choose friends who are similar in (48) _____ traits. There are some differences between friendships among males and those among females. Among girls, there may be lots of rehashing of personal problems, or (49) _____.

Changing Social Networks

In late childhood, children are often members of a small, same-sex friendship group of (50) _____ and interact little with the other sex. Collections of several of these friendship groups constitute a (51) _____, which serves mainly as a vehicle for structured social activities. Peers generally foster positive behaviors, but this depends on the type of group that adolescents belong to.

Dating

After interacting with other-sex peers in a group setting, adolescents often begin to form couples and the existence of crowds begins to dissolve. Adolescents begin to move from same-sex peer groups to dating relationships and about half report having been in a special romantic relationship by age 15. Adolescent romantic relationships progress through four phases, starting with initiation and moving to the (52) _____ phase, then to affection, and finally, progressing to the (53) _____ phase. (*How does dating affect same-sex friendships and personal adjustment?*)

14.5   THE ADULT
Social Networks

People who provide support are said to be part of a (54) _____ that changes across the lifespan.

Friendships continue to be important during adulthood, although the nature of the social network changes somewhat over time. Young adults spend a great deal of time interacting with members of the other sex. They also have more friends than middle-aged or older adults. The social network of most adults seems to shrink as they marry and as they get older. The (55) _____ theory suggests that we narrow our social network to include

---

people who are most important to us, which may result in an increase in the
(56)_____ of the relationship. Adults experience fairly positive emotional
lives, perhaps because they focus on more positive information than negative information,
dubbed the (57) _____ in information processing.

Romantic Attachments

An important task of adulthood is forming a romantic relationship. Evolutionary theorists
believe that mate selection is influenced by characteristics that will aid in passing along genes to
future generations. The process may include a series of (58) _____ for sifting
through the pool of all available partners. The greatest influence on mate selection seems to be
similarity, or (59) _____, of partners.

Robert Sternberg has attempted to explain the concept of love with his
(60)_____ theory. Based on this, there are three components of love that can vary
in degree or quality. Feelings of sexual attraction and romantic feelings for another are captured
by the component of (61) _____. Feelings of warmth, caring, and closeness
contribute to the component of (62) _____. The third component involves the
decision that one loves the other person and then forming a (63) _____ to the
relationship. Having high levels of all three components can lead to (64) _____
love. Over time, the intensity of the passion component may decline, leading to
(65)_____ love.

Attachment Styles

There may be some similarities between infants who are attached to a parent and adults who
are in love with a romantic partner. As infants, we constructed internal working models for
attachment relationships that later influence our adult relationships. Adults with a
(66)_____ working model of attachment feel good about themselves and
others and feel comfortable entering into relationships. Adults with a (67) _____
working model feel positive about others but not about themselves. They desperately want a
relationship but fear abandonment. Adults with a (68) _____ working model feel
positive about themselves but not about others. They deny any need for relationships and are
very self-reliant. Adults with a (69) _____ working model of attachment hold
negative views of themselves and others, and while they express a need for relationships, they
also have a fear of closeness. (*Can you describe the implications of these attachment styles for
adults?*) There is some continuity in attachment styles across the lifespan. The internal working
models developed during infancy influence the quality of later relationships.

Friendships

Friendships continue to be important to adults. Men and women continue to show different
styles of interacting with friends. (*What are these differences?*) Adults especially value
friendships that have lasted many years, even if the friends live geographically distant from one
another. Adults typically perceive friendships as most satisfying when the contributions of both
members are balanced, demonstrating (70) _____ in the relationship.

Adult Relationships and Adult Development

Just as attachment is critical for normal infant and child development, friendships are
important for normal adult development. However, it is the (71) _____ of

friendships that is important, not the quantity of friendships. It seems important that adults have a (72) _____or person to whom they are particularly close and to whom they express their feelings and thoughts.

REVIEW OF KEY TERMS

Below is a list of terms and concepts from this chapter. Use these to complete the following sentence definitions. You might also want to try writing definitions in your own words and then checking your definitions with those in the text.

attachment
attachment theory
avoidant attachment
bonding
chumship
clique
companionate love
confidant
consummate love
contact comfort
co-rumination
crowd
disinhibited attachment
disorganized-disoriented attachment
emotion regulation
equity
goal-corrected partnership
homogamy
imprinting
internal working model

oxytocin
peer
positivity effect
pretend play
reactive attachment disorder
resistant attachment
secure attachment
secure base
self-conscious emotion
separation anxiety
social convoy
social pretend play
social referencing
socioemotional selectivity theory
sociometric techniques
stranger anxiety
Strange Situation
synchronized routines
triangular theory of love

1. As innate form of learning in which the young of a species will follow and become attached to a moving object (usually the mother) during a critical period early in life is termed _____.

2. A caregiver-infant relationship characterized by distress at separation, ambivalence at being reunited, and little use of the caregiver as a secure base is called a(n) _____.

3. When separated from a caregiver to whom they are attached, many infants show wariness or fear called _____.

4. A _____ is a small, same-sex friendship group.

5. The sense that there is a balance of contributions and benefits in relationships between spouses, friends, and other intimates is _____.

6.   A close friendship with peers of the same age that emerges at about age 9 to 12 is a
       _____.

7.   A collection of several heterosexual cliques constitutes a _____.

8.   Harlow used the term _____ for the pleasure derived from clinging to
       something soft and warm.

9.   A caregiver-infant relationship characterized by little distress at separation, avoidance of
       the caregiver when reunited, and little exploration is a(n) _____.

10.   A _____ is a member of one's social group and is usually of similar age and
       behavioral functioning.

11.   A _____ is someone to whom an individual feels an especially close
       attachment and with whom thoughts and feelings can be shared.

12.   The _____ consists of a series of mildly stressful events designed to measure
       the quality of an infant's attachment to a caregiver.

13.   Infants may exhibit wariness or _____ when approached by an unfamiliar
       person.

14.   _____ attempts to explain the bond that develops between parent and child as
       well as the emotional ties between other people.

15.   In Bowlby's theory, the most mature phase of attachment is _____ when
       parent and child accommodate to each other's needs and the child becomes more
       independent.

16.   Mate selection is strongly influenced by similarity to ourselves, or _____.

17.   The integrated interactions between partners who take turns responding to each other's
       leads are called _____.

18.   Infants must learn strategies for _____ in order to successfully initiate,
       maintain, and alter their emotional responses.

19.   An attachment figure who serves as a safe place from which an infant can explore the
       environment is considered to be a _____.

20.   Love that is high in intimacy and commitment, but not so high on passion is termed
       _____.

21.   A strong affectionate tie that binds a person to an intimate companion is termed
       _____.

22.   A caregiver-infant relationship characterized by distress at separation, joy at being reunited, and use of the caregiver as a secure base indicates the presence of a _____.

23.   Using one thing to represent something else in a playful context is _____.

24.   Methods of studying social groups by determining likes and dislikes among the members of the group are known as _____.

25.   The changing composition of one's social support system over the lifespan is reflected in one's _____.

26.   A combination of resistant and avoidant styles of attachment in which infants are confused about whether to approach or avoid a parent is a _____.

27.   According to the _____, we narrow our social contact to the people who are most important to us.

28.   A(n) _____ is a cognitive representation about social interactions, which shapes expectations for future relationships.

29.   Social play and symbolic play are combined in _____.

30.   A secondary emotion such as embarrassment is a _____.

31.   Infants engage in _____ when they monitor the reactions of their companion in order to help them decide how to act or feel.

32.   The hormone _____ may facilitate formation of parent-infant attachments.

33.   Children who have been raised in impoverished settings without normal attachment relationships may exhibit a disturbed pattern of behavior called _____.

34.   We may achieve a more positive emotional self by placing greater emphasis on positive information and downplaying the negative information, a process called the _____.

35.   Sternberg has focused our attention on three aspects of love with his _____.

36.   Love that encompasses high levels of passion, intimacy, and decision/commitment is called _____.

37.   Excessive discussion and rehashing of personal problems with friends is the core of _____.

38.   A biologically based connection between parent and infant is termed _____.

39. A clinical diagnosis of _____ may be warranted for individuals who have been socially deprived or maltreated and exhibit disturbed attachment patterns.

MULTIPLE-CHOICE SELF-TEST

For each multiple-choice question, read all alternatives and then select the best answer.

1. According to Bowlby's attachment theory,
   a. infants must develop an attachment during a critical period early in life or they will not form later attachments.
   b. infants become attached to the caregiver who feeds them.
   c. infants are biologically predisposed to form attachments.
   d. through reinforcement, infants learn to form attachments.

2. Self-conscious emotions such as embarrassment
   a. emerge when infants are capable of recognizing themselves.
   b. develop when children enter formal schooling and interact with others.
   c. are determined by a genetic blueprint that dictates when various emotions emerge.
   d. are present soon after birth.

3. In the discriminating social responsiveness phase of developing attachment, infants
   a. respond to many different social stimuli such as voices and faces.
   b. respond differently depending on the social situation.
   c. show preferences for familiar companions.
   d. follow the object of their attachment and protest when this person leaves.

4. Stranger anxiety would be GREATEST if an infant were seated
   a. on mother's lap at the doctor's office as mom warmly greets the doctor.
   b. on mother's lap at home as mom warmly greets the next-door neighbor.
   c. on mother's lap at home as mom neutrally greets a salesperson.
   d. across from mother at the doctor's office as mom neutrally greets the doctor.

5. Infants who have a resistant attachment style
   a. use their mother as a secure base, are upset when she leaves, and express pleasure when she returns.
   b. are upset when their mother leaves them and ambivalent when she returns.
   c. are not upset when their mother leaves and do not welcome her back.
   d. are not distressed when their mother leaves them and express joy when reunite.

6. According to Freud, infants become attached to their mothers because
   a. mothers become associated with pleasurable sensations.
   b. mothers are generally responsive to their needs.
   c. they are innately predisposed to form attachments.
   d. mothers provide oral pleasure.

7.	The finding that infant monkeys in Harlow's research preferred the cloth surrogate over the wire surrogate regardless of which one provided food is consistent with
	a.	Erikson's claim that general responsiveness determines whether an attachment forms.
	b.	the claim that there is an innate predisposition to form attachments.
	c.	Freud's emphasis on feeding behavior cannot fully explain development of attachment.
	d.	learning theory explanations of attachment since infants become attached to the mother who reinforced them with food.

8.	Effects of early social deprivation in human infants
	a.	cannot be overcome.
	b.	can be overcome if infants are placed with affectionate and responsive caregivers.
	c.	can be overcome if the infants are exposed to multiple caregivers.
	d.	are usually not significant.

9.	With respect to the relationship between security of attachment during infancy and social competence during adulthood, research suggests that
	a.	quality of infant attachment does not predict adult social competence as well as peer relations during adolescence do.
	b.	quality of infant attachment has no relation to social competence during adulthood.
	c.	quality of infant attachment to parents is the most important predictor of adult social competence.
	d.	individuals who were securely attached as infants always have positive social relationships.

10.	Casey is securely attached to her mother and her father. When she enters preschool, she is MOST likely to
	a.	strenuously resist separating from her parents.
	b.	cling to her teacher in her parents' absence.
	c.	be popular with her peers.
	d.	be socially immature.

11.	Children who do not actually participate in play with others but watch others play are engaged in _____ play.
	a.	solitary	c.	parallel
	b.	unoccupied	d.	onlooker

12.	The capacity for pretend play emerges _____.
	a.	at birth	c.	around 1 year
	b.	around 6-7 months of age	d.	around 3 years

13.   Pretend play
      a.   can be used to assess children's level of intellectual functioning.
      b.   can provide children the opportunity to work through problems.
      c.   shows the same pattern in all children.
      d.   increases when children enter elementary school.

14.   Love that is high in passion, intimacy, and commitment characterizes what Sternberg calls _____ love.
      a.   consummate   c.   secure
      b.   companionate   d.   triangular

15.   Steve, a 32-year-old, is fiercely self-sufficient and refuses to accept help from others. He claims that he has no time for relationships, and when he does date, he feels that his partner wants more out of the relationship than he does. Steve's internal working model of attachment is BEST characterized as _____.
      a.   secure   c.   dismissing
      b.   preoccupied   d.   fearful

REVIEW INTERNAL WORKING MODELS

Review the various types of internal working models that occur when a positive or negative model of self is combined with a positive or negative model of other. In the table below, provide the name of the internal working model, the type of attachment history that typically leads to each type of internal working model, and a brief description of each model. Use Figure 14.7 on page 475 of the text to check your answers.

	Positive Model of Self	Negative Model of Self
Positive Model of Other	Name: Attachment History: Description:	Name: Attachment History: Description:
Negative Model of Other	Name: Attachment History: Description:	Name: Attachment History: Description:

CRITICAL THINKING QUESTIONS

By answering the following questions, you will strengthen your understanding of the material in this chapter. These questions require higher-level thinking skills such as integration and application of concepts. Sample answers are provided for three of the questions. These illustrate one possibility, but there are other answers you could provide that might be just as good. For the other questions, you can check yourself by referring to the text (a hint is provided), or by asking a peer or your instructor to review your answer.

1. What are the likely outcomes for children who, as infants, were insecurely attached to their caregiver? What factors influence the outcome for these children?
   [*Sample answer provided.*]

2. What aspects of children's development are fostered by engaging in pretend play?
   [*Sample answer provided.*]

3. What factors influence whether a child is popular or rejected in peer relationships?
   [*Sample answer provided.*]

4. What similarities exist between the attachments of infants-caregivers and the romantic relationships of adults?
   [*Hint: Read the section on "Attachment styles" in the Adult section.*]

5. What influences do peers and parents have on adolescents?
   [*Hint: Review the section on "Parent and peer influence" in the Adolescent section.*]

ANSWERS

Chapter Summary and Guided Review (fill in the blank)

1. proximity
2. imprinting
3. critical period
4. internal working
5. peers
6. primary
7. self-conscious
8. biologically
9. positive
10. negative
11. social referencing
12. emotion regulation
13. synchronized
14. undiscriminating
15. discriminating
16. proximity seeking
17. goal-corrected
18. separation anxiety
19. stranger anxiety
20. secure base
21. Strange Situation
22. secure
23. resistant
24. avoidant
25. disorganized-disoriented
26. contact comfort
27. resistant
28. avoidant
29. temperament
30. disinhibited attachment
31. responsive caregivers
32. internal working models
33. goal-corrected
34. gender segregated
35. social
36. pretend

37. social pretend
38. rules
39. concrete operations
40. emotional
41. sociometric
42. popular
43. rejected
44. neglected
45. controversial
46. average
47. self-disclosure
48. psychological
49. co-rumination
50. cliques
51. crowd
52. status
53. bonding
54. social convoy
55. socio-emotional selectivity
56. quality
57. positivity effect
58. filters
59. homogamy
60. triangular
61. passion
62. intimacy
63. commitment
64. consummate
65. companionate
66. secure
67. preoccupied
68. dismissing
69. fearful
70. equity
71. quality
72. confidant

Review of Key Terms
1. imprinting
2. resistant attachment
3. separation anxiety
4. clique
5. equity
6. chumship
7. crowd
8. contact comfort
9. avoidant attachment
10. peer
11. confidant
12. Strange Situation test
13. stranger anxiety
14. attachment theory
15. goal-corrected partnership
16. homogamy
17. synchronized routines
18. emotion regulation
19. secure base
20. companionate love
21. attachment
22. secure attachment
23. pretend play
24. sociometric techniques
25. social convoy
26. disorganized-disoriented attachment
27. socioemotional selectivity hypothesis
28. internal working model
29. social pretend play
30. self-conscious emotion
31. social referencing
32. ocytocin
33. disinhibited attachment
34. positivity effect
35. triangular theory of love
36. consummate love
37. co-rumination
38. bonding
39. reactive attachment disorder

Multiple-Choice Self-Test
1. C (p. 450)
2. A (p. 453)
3. C (p. 456)
4. D (p. 456-457)
5. B (p. 458)
6. D (p. 459)
7. C (p. 459)
8. B (p. 461)
9. A (p. 463)
10. C (p. 463)
11. D (p. 465)
12. C (p. 465-466)
13. B (p. 467)
14. A (p. 475)
15. C (p.475-476)

Critical Thinking Questions

1. *Infants with insecure attachments tend to have parents who are inconsistent with their caregiving or provide inappropriate amounts (too much or too little) of it. Characteristics of the infant also influence whether a secure or insecure attachment develops between parent and child. In situations where there is a poor fit between the infant's temperament and the parent's caregiving style, an insecure attachment may develop and have long-lasting effects. Children who had been insecurely attached as infants tend to be less curious and less likely to pursue their goals than children who had been securely attached. They also tend to be socially withdrawn and less likely to draw other children into play. This carries through to adolescence, with insecure children less adjusted in terms of both intellectual and social skills. These differences may relate to how children process information. Children who have formed insecure attachments develop internal working models that lead them to have negative expectations of interactions with others. In contrast, securely attached children tend to remember positive events and have more positive expectations of interactions.*

2. *During childhood, there is more to play than just having fun. Pretend play helps children understand and prepare for adult roles. Children who engage in lots of pretend play tend to score better on measures of cognitive development, language development, and creativity than children who don't engage in much pretend play. Pretend play helps children work through all sorts of possible scenarios so that when they are faced with a real problem, they have some experience to draw upon in formulating a response. Pretend play with others also forces children to see other perspectives, which helps their role-taking skills and the development of theory of mind. Because of this, children who engage in more pretend play often have skills that make them more popular with other children. Engaging in pretend play may also help children act out their emotions in safe situations and allow them to cope with stresses in their lives.*

3. *Children who are popular are well-liked by most members of their group and are rarely disliked. In contrast, children who are rejected are rarely liked and often disliked. To some extent, whether a child ends up popular or rejected depends on characteristics of the child that are difficult to change. For example, physically attractive children and those who are intelligent are more likely to be popular than children who are physically unattractive or are not very bright. Bright kids likely know how to successfully orchestrate a social interaction. Temperament and personality characteristics also contribute to popularity. Children with easygoing temperaments are likely to be more popular than children with difficult temperaments. Children who are argumentative and not very good at "reading" social signals (i.e., weak social cognition skills) are more likely to be rejected.*

CHAPTER FIFTEEN

THE FAMILY

OVERVIEW

We all live in some sort of family, whether it is our family of origin with our mother and/or father and siblings, or in a family with our spouse and possibly our own children. Or we might be a member of a gay or lesbian family or a single adult who thinks of friends as family. What effects do these family systems have on our development? This chapter focuses on this question, looking at both traditional and nontraditional types of families. At the beginning of the chapter, it is noted that traditional families of a working father and a stay-at-home mother are no longer typical. Cultural changes of the 20th century have led to many different family configurations.

Have you ever wondered what life is like for parents after their children are grown and leave home? Or perhaps you are curious about whether siblings, amid the rivalry and fighting, have any positive influences on one another? Do fathers interact any differently with their babies than do mothers? Are adolescents and their parents consistently battling it out with one another? These are the sorts of questions addressed in this chapter on the family. In reading the research about family systems across the lifespan, you may gain some insight into processes within your own family.

LEARNING OBJECTIVES

After reading and studying the material in this chapter, you should be able to answer the following questions.

15.1   UNDERSTANDING THE FAMILY
1.   How is the family viewed by the family systems theory?

2.   How do individual family systems change? How have families in general changed during the 20th century?

15.2   THE INFANT
3.   How is the father-infant relationship similar to and different from the mother-infant relationship?

15.3   THE CHILD
4.   What are two basic dimensions of parenting? What patterns of childrearing emerge from these dimensions? How do these parenting styles affect children's development? How does social class affect parenting style?

5.   What effects do parents have on their children, and what effects do children have on their parents? What is the transactional model of family influence?

6.   What features characterize sibling relationships across the lifespan? How do siblings contribute to development?

15.4   THE ADOLESCENT
7.   What are relationships like between adolescents and their parents?

15.5   THE ADULT
8.   How does marriage and parenthood affect adults? What changes occur in the family as the children mature and leave home?

9.   What sorts of roles do grandparents establish with their grandchildren?

10.   How do various family relationships (e.g., spouses, siblings, parent-child) change during adulthood?

15.6   DIVERSE FAMILY EXPERIENCES
11.   What sorts of diversity exist in today's families? What is the life satisfaction of people in these different types of families?

12.   How does divorce affect family relationships?

15.7   THE PROBLEM OF FAMILY VIOLENCE
13.   Why might family abuse occur? What can be done to reduce spouse abuse and child abuse?

CHAPTER SUMMARY AND GUIDED REVIEW

The following summary provides an overview of the main points contained in this chapter of the text. Fill in the blanks with terms that appropriately complete the sentence. Scattered throughout the summary are questions in parentheses. These are meant to encourage you to think actively as you read and connect this summary to the more detailed information provided in the text.

15.1   UNDERSTANDING THE FAMILY
The Family as a System within Systems

According to family systems theory, the family is a social system, meaning that it is a whole unit consisting of interrelated parts. The (1) _____ family consists of a mother, father, and at least one child. Parents engage in (2) _____ as they work together as a team to parent their children. In a(n) (3) _____ family household, parents and their children live with other relatives. Families exist within a larger social system, and the cultural context influences the experiences within families.

The Family as a Changing System

Family membership changes over time, and the relationships within families also develop and change over time. One family development theory uses the concept of a family (4)_____ to characterize the sequence of changes in family membership and relationships that occur over time.

A Changing System in a Changing World

The changing family exists within a changing world, and several social changes of the 20th century have significantly affected the family. Our society has a greater number of unmarried or (5)_____ adults, and more adults are delaying both marriage and childbearing than in the past. More women are participating in the labor force, and our society has seen a rise in the divorce rate and in the number of children living in poverty. There are more single-parent families and more (6) _____ families as divorced adults with children remarry. For a variety of reasons, adults today spend more years without children than in past generations, and increased longevity contributes to longer relationships with parents, grandparents, and even great-grandparents. These multigenerational (four or more) families are referred to as (7)_____ families. These family and societal changes mean that there are fewer caregivers for our aging adults.

15.2 THE INFANT
Mother-Infant and Father-Infant Relationships

Despite the stereotype of mothers as the primary caregivers for infants, fathers are as capable as mothers when it comes to caring for infants. Still, mothers do spend more time with children than do fathers, and much of their time involves direct (8)_____. Fathers' interactions with their children involves more (9)_____interactions. Boys and girls both benefit from having fathers who are involved in their development. (*What are some of the benefits to children of having involved fathers?*)

Mothers, Fathers, and Infants: The System at Work

In addition to these effects, parents have many (10) _____ effects on their children through their ability to influence their spouses. (*Can you provide several examples of this type of effect?*) Children benefit from a three-person system in which parents support each other, allowing each to be good parents.

15.3 THE CHILD
Parenting Styles

One dimension of parenting, called (11) _____, describes how supportive, affectionate, and sensitive parents are toward their child. A second dimension of parenting describes the degree of autonomy that parents allow their children, and is labeled (12)_____. Four basic patterns of childrearing emerge from crossing these two dimensions. Parents who are very restrictive, impose many rules without explaining their importance, and often use physical means to gain compliance to the rules are using a(n) (13)_____ style. With a(n) (14)_____ parenting style, children are allowed a fair amount of freedom, but rules are clearly stated, explained, and enforced. A lax style where few rules are imposed and children are encouraged to express their feelings and impulses is the (15)_____ approach. Finally, (16) _____ parenting occurs when parents are uninvolved in their children's upbringing. (*What are the characteristics of children raised with each of these styles? Which of these styles of parenting seems to have the "best" outcome in our society and which is associated with the worst outcomes?*)

Social Class, Economic Hardship, and Parenting

Parenting styles are related to socioeconomic status of the family. (*Can you describe differences in parenting or goals associated with social class?*) Differences might result because of stresses associated with economic problems or because of differences in skills useful or necessary to parents in blue-collar versus white-collar jobs. Cultural and ethnic variations also lead to differences in parenting styles.

Models of Influence in the Family
        According to a (17) _____ model of family influence, parents influence their child's behavior. The (18) _____ model turns this around and highlights how children can influence their parents. In addition, a child's age, competence level, and (19)_____ can all elicit a particular style of parenting and a compatible discipline method from the parent. Parents and children influence each other in an ongoing reciprocal manner according to the (20) _____ model of family influence

Sibling Relationships
        A second child in the family often creates feelings of competition, jealousy, and resentment between siblings, or (21) _____. Many sibling relationships are also characterized by (22) _____ or a combination of closeness and conflict. While sibling relationships can involve negative conflicts, siblings also have many positive effects on one another. For example, siblings provide (23) _____ support for one another. Older siblings often provide assistance or (24) _____ services for younger siblings and serve as teachers for new behaviors. Having another child in the family to interact with may also enhance siblings' (25) _____ skills.

15.4   THE ADOLESCENT
Ripples in the Parent-Child Relationship
        Some people believe that adolescence is a particularly stressful period for parent-child relationships. Most teenagers, however, view their relationship with their parents as positive and close. Conflicts between parents and their adolescents tend to increase over early adolescence but involve minor, not major, issues.

Achieving Autonomy
        A major task of adolescence is to attain (26) _____, or the ability to function independently. This creates some conflict with parents until adolescents and parents renegotiate the power and rules between them. While adolescents work to achieve autonomy, they also try to maintain a close attachment with their parents. (***How can parents help adolescents successfully achieve autonomy?***)

15.5   THE ADULT
Establishing the Marriage
        Most adults in our society marry and typically marry for love. Marriage is a major adjustment for both partners, and some deterioration in the relationship occurs during the first year. Married couples who end up unhappy often started out with more negativity and problems than couples who remain satisfied over time.
New Parenthood
        Many couples have children within a few years of getting married, which is another major life transition with both positive and negative changes. Marital satisfaction tends to (27)_____ from before to after the birth of a child, and this change is more

© 2012 Cengage Learning. All Rights Reserved. May not be scanned, copied or duplicated, or posted to a publicly accessible website, in whole or in part.

pronounced for women than men. Some babies are more difficult than others, which increases stress, and some adults are less equipped to deal with the stress of parenthood. A lack of resources, including spousal support, can also increase stress of parenthood.

The Childrearing Family

Having a second child is another stressful event for the family, and marital satisfaction typically remains somewhat depressed with the addition of more children to the family. Despite these declines, many couples are more satisfied than dissatisfied with their family situation.

The Empty Nest

As children reach maturity and leave their parents' home, the family system changes once again. "Empty nest" is used to describe the family structure after all children have left the home. Marital satisfaction tends to (28) _____ following the departure of children. (***Why do parents react this way to their children leaving home?***)

Grandparenthood

Many adults become grandparents in middle age and do not fit the stereotyped image of white-haired elderly grandparents. Researchers have identified three major styles of grandparenting. (29) _____ grandparents are largely symbolic figures who do not interact a great deal with grandchildren. (30) _____ grandparents frequently see their grandchildren and enjoy sharing activities with them. Grandparents who are (31)_____ assume a parent-like role and provide some degree of childcare for their grandchildren. Relationships between grandchildren and their (32) _____ grandmothers tend to be the closest.

Changing Family Relationships

As noted above, marital satisfaction appears to decline when children enter the family and increases when children leave the family. Women tend to be more affected by changes in the family structure than men. Many factors other than stage of family life cycle determine marital satisfaction. (***What are some of these factors?***)

Sibling relationships also change across the lifespan. Adult siblings typically keep in touch with each other, but the relationship is (33) _____than when siblings were young, and adult siblings rarely discuss intimate problems with each other. Nevertheless, siblings often report feeling close to one another, particularly as they get older. The sibling relationship can change in response to specific events, such as geographical moves, divorces, loss of a spouse, or illness.

Parents and children develop new relationships as the children become adults and leave home. The relationships are often more friend-like and (34) _____, with recognition that each is an individual and has roles other than parent or child. Middle-aged adults continue to feel close to their parents. The relationships among different generations tend to be (35) _____, which means that each contributes something to the relationship and gets something back in return. In most cases, there is no (36) _____ in which parents become dependent on their children and their middle-age children take on the caregiving role. Middle-aged adults may also experience (37) _____ because they face demands from both their children and their parents. This can lead to (38) _____ as their personal resources become stretched by providing care for aging parents who may have impairments.

15.6 DIVERSE FAMILY EXPERIENCES

Adult lifestyles in our culture have become quite diverse. Many adults delay marriage, remain single, or become single through divorce or death of a spouse.

Singles

There are an increasing number of adults who never marry. Living with a romantic partner without being married, or (39) _____, is more common than it used to be. Some couples use living together as a test of compatibility before marrying. However, couples who live together before marrying actually seem to be more dissatisfied with the marriage and more likely to (40) _____ than couples who marry without first living together.

Childless Married Couples

More couples are choosing not to have children than in the past, although for many couples, childlessness is not a choice but a result of infertility. Childless couples tend to have somewhat (41) _____ marital satisfaction than couples with children during the childrearing years. Following the childrearing years, couples with and without children are similar in their levels of marital satisfaction. As older adults, individuals who have lost their spouse and never had children may experience a lack of (42) _____.

Dual-Career Families

In many families, both mothers and fathers work outside the home. Events from home can affect work and vice versa, known as (43) _____. These effects can be positive as well as negative.

Gay and Lesbian Families

Overall, gay and lesbian couples are more similar to heterosexual couples than they are different. The division of labor between these couples tends to be more (44)_____ than that of married couples. Children raised by gay or lesbian children are no different from children raised by heterosexual parents and may be better off than children raised by single parents.

Divorcing Families

Divorce is a series of experiences, not a single event that has finite beginning and end points. It is unclear what processes cause divorce, but there are several factors that seem to place some couples at a greater risk for divorce than other couples. (***What are some factors that increase the likelihood of divorce?***) Families experiencing a divorce typically experience a (45)_____ during which there is much disruption. The stress of a divorce places individuals at greater risk for depression, physical problems, and even death. Adults experiencing divorce often have problems parenting. Custodial mothers tend to become less accepting and responsive, as well as less consistent in their discipline. While custodial mothers often use a more restrictive style of parenting, noncustodial fathers often become more (46)_____. Most of the problems between parents and children dissipate in the two years following a divorce, but the divorce continues to affect both children and adults. (***What factors influence family members' reaction to divorce?***)

Reconstituted Families

Most divorced parents remarry within five years after a divorce, creating
(47)_____ families. While boys seem to suffer more than girls when parents
divorce, they apparently benefit more than girls when their custodial mothers remarry. (*What are
some possible reasons for this finding?*)

15.7   THE PROBLEM OF FAMILY VIOLENCE

Unfortunately, some families experience violence in some form. Mistreating a child
physically or emotionally constitutes (48) _____. Children who are abused or
neglected broadly fall into the classification of (49) _____. In some households,
children may not be the target of abuse but may witness abuse of another family member, often
their mother.

Why Does Family Violence Occur?

Many child abusers were abused or neglected themselves as children. This reflects the
process of passing down parenting styles from generation to generation, known as
(50)_____. Abusive mothers are often the target of abuse from their spouse.
Abusers are often insecure individuals with (51)_____. They may also be
intolerant of normal behaviors of young children. Some children may have characteristics that
make them more likely targets of abuse than other children. In addition to parent and child
characteristics, the surrounding social climate and lack of social (52) _____ may
contribute to the likelihood of abuse in the family.

What Are the Effects of Family Violence?

Child abuse negatively affects its victims in a number of ways. These include physical,
social-emotional, psychological, and cognitive problems. Children who have been physically
abused often do not show normal signs of (53) _____ in response to other's
distress. (*Can you describe some other developmental consequences of abuse?*) By identifying
families that are high-risk candidates for family violence, it may be possible to provide the
support necessary to prevent abuse from occurring.

REVIEW OF KEY TERMS

*Below is a list of terms and concepts from this chapter. Use these to complete the following sentence definitions. You
might also want to try writing definitions in your own words and then checking your definitions with those in the text.*

acceptance-responsiveness
authoritarian parenting
authoritative parenting
autonomy
caregiver burden
child abuse
child effects model
child maltreatment
cohabitation
coparenting

demandingness-control
empty nest
extended family household
family life cycle
family systems theory
indirect effect
intergenerational transmission of parenting
linked lives
middle generation squeeze
neglectful parenting

nuclear family
parent effects model
permissive parenting
reconstituted family

sibling rivalry
spillover effects
transactional model

1. A family that consists of parent, stepparent, and at least one child from a previous marriage is called a _____.

2. A flexible parenting style in which parents set clear rules and provide explanations for rules but allow children some freedom and input is _____.

3. According to the _____, children influence their parents.

4. A _____ consists of a mother, father, and at least one child.

5. In a _____, nuclear families live in separate households but have close ties and frequent interaction with other relatives.

6. The feelings of competition, jealousy, and resentment that can develop between siblings are referred to as _____.

7. When single adults live with a romantic partner without being married, they are in an arrangement called _____.

8. A dimension of parenting that describes the degree of autonomy that parents allow their children is referred to as _____.

9. In a(n) _____, a family unit lives with other relatives.

10. A critical task of adolescence is achieving _____, in which adolescents must develop independence in various realms.

11. The _____ consists of the sequence of changes in family composition, roles, and relationships that occur from the time people marry to the time they die.

12. A restrictive parenting style in which parents impose many rules and use power tactics to ensure obedience to these rules is _____.

13. According to a _____, parents and children influence one another reciprocally.

14. After children are grown and leave home, parents may experience the _____ syndrome.

15. A dimension of parenting that describes how affectionate and responsive parents are toward their child is called _____.

16. Two parents who coordinate their parenting and function as a team are _____ their children.

17. A parenting style in which adults make relatively few demands, encourage children to express their feelings, and rarely exert control over their behavior is _____.

18. The effects that parents have on their children through their influence on their spouse's behavior are _____.

19. Abuse and/or neglect of a child's basic needs constitute _____.

20. Each individual's development is intertwined with that of other family members, a concept called _____.

21. A style of parenting in which parents are uninvolved in their children's upbringing is _____.

22. Passing parenting styles from one generation to another occurs with _____.

23. According to _____, the family is whole unit, with interrelated parts that influence each other.

24. According to a _____, parents are assumed to influence their children, but not vice versa.

25. Middle-aged adults who must care for a parent with health problems may experience _____ as they try to incorporate this with their other family responsibilities.

26. With _____, events at work can affect home life and events at home can influence work.

27. Harming a child physically, emotionally, or sexually constitutes _____.

MULTIPLE-CHOICE SELF-TEST

For each multiple-choice question, read all alternatives and then select the best answer.

1. The family life cycle
   a. refers to the sequence of changes in family membership and roles between marriage and death.
   b. refers to family units that consist of a parent, a stepparent, and at least one child.
   c. refers to the changes that have occurred in the family system during the 20th century.
   d. undergoes dramatic changes every 10 years.

2. A family unit consisting of a mother, father, and at least one child is called a _____ family.
   a. reconstituted
   b. extended
   c. nuclear
   d. intergenerational

3. Compared to mothers, fathers in general
   a. spend as much time with their children.
   b. spend less time with their children.
   c. treat boys and girls more similarly.
   d. serve as disciplinarian in the family.

4. Which type of parenting style places few demands on children and allows them to express their desires freely?
   a. Permissive
   b. Authoritative
   c. Authoritarian
   d. Neglectful

5. In which style of parenting do parents value obedience for its own sake and impose many rules that are typically not fully explained to children?
   a. Permissive
   b. Authoritative
   c. Authoritarian
   d. Neglectful

6. Children of parents who use a(n) _____ style of parenting are typically more self-reliant and achievement oriented than children raised with other styles of parenting
   a. permissive
   b. authoritative
   c. authoritarian
   d. neglectful

7. Feelings of rivalry or jealousy following the birth of a new sibling
   a. are strongest if parents maintain the same regular schedule they had for the first-born before the arrival of the new baby.
   b. can be minimized if the first-born had already established a good relationship with parents.
   c. can be minimized if the parents lavish the first child with attention.
   d. are always worse if the first-born is a boy.

8. With respect to adolescent-parent relationships, research indicates
   a. there is a huge gap between generations in their values and attitudes.
   b. adolescents generally report being unhappy with the relationship.
   c. boys are much more dissatisfied with the relationship than girls.
   d. adolescents are strongly influenced by their parents on important issues.

9. Which of the following is TRUE regarding marital satisfaction?
   a. Marital satisfaction is highest following the birth of a child.
   b. Because of the adjustments that must be made, marital satisfaction is lowest right after marriage
   c. Marital satisfaction declines following the birth of a child
   d. Marital satisfaction declines across middle and older adulthood

10. The relationship between adult siblings
    a. disintegrates once the siblings leave school.
    b. remains close although less intense than during childhood.
    c. involves a great deal of sharing and discussing feelings.
    d. continues to be as intense as during childhood.

11. Cohabiting couples who later marry
    a. are more dissatisfied with their marriages than couples who had not lived together before marrying.
    b. are more satisfied with their marriages than couples who had not lived together before marrying.
    c. are less likely to divorce than couples who had not lived together before marrying.
    d. are no different from couples who had not lived together before marrying.

12. Adults who never marry
    a. typically have some psychological problem.
    b. are lonely and maladjusted.
    c. are much happier and better adjusted than married adults.
    d. are somewhat less happy than married adults.

13. Evidence indicates that following a divorce,
    a. both boys and girls settle into a new lifestyle with few adjustment problems.
    b. boys take longer to adjust than girls and exhibit more behavior problems.
    c. girls take longer to adjust than boys and exhibit more depression.
    d. neither boys nor girls adjust to the new lifestyle within several years of the divorce.

14. Reconstituted families where children in a mother-headed family acquire a stepfather
    a. seem to benefit boys more than girls.
    b. seem to benefit girls more than boys.
    c. seem to benefit boys and girls equally.
    d. do not benefit any of the children, just the adults.

15. Child abuse is LESS likely in families where
    a. the parents had been abused themselves, giving them personal knowledge of the negative impact that abuse can have.
    b. there are multiple sources of stress.
    c. there is a strong support network available to parents.
    d. parents have difficulty "reading" their child's signals.

REVIEW CHILDREARING STYLES

Review the four basic patterns of childrearing that arise by crossing the acceptance and demandingness dimensions. In the table below, provide the name and a brief description of each of the four parenting patterns in the appropriate square. Check yourself by referring to Figure 15.2 on page 490 in the text.

	High Acceptance–Responsiveness	Low Acceptance–Responsiveness
High Demandingness-Control		
Low Demandingness-Control		

CRITICAL THINKING QUESTIONS

By answering the following questions, you will strengthen your understanding of the material in this chapter. These questions require higher-level thinking skills such as integration and application of concepts. Sample answers are provided for three of the questions. These illustrate one possibility, but there are other answers you could provide that might be just as good. For the other questions, you can check yourself by referring to the text (a hint is provided), or by asking a peer or your instructor to review your answer.

1. What type of parenting dimensions and parent control have the best outcome for children? What makes these parenting styles effective?
    [*Sample answer provided.*]

2. What are the effects of divorce from the perspective of parents and children?
    [*Sample answer provided.*]

3. What factors increase/decrease the likelihood of family violence?
    [*Sample answer provided.*]

4.   What affects can children have on their parents across the lifespan?
     [*Hint: There is a little information on this topic scattered throughout the chapter,
     including the sections on "Models of influence in the family" and "The childrearing
     family."*]

5.   What are potential advantages and disadvantages for individuals who marry, individuals
     who remain single, couples who have children, and those who do not have children?
     [*Hint: Review the section in the text on "Diverse family experiences."*]

ANSWERS

Chapter Summary and Guided Review (fill in the blank)

1. nuclear
2. coparenting
3. extended
4. life cycle
5. single
6. reconstituted
7. beanpole
8. caregiving
9. playful
10. indirect
11. acceptance-responsiveness
12. demandingness-control
13. authoritarian
14. authoritative
15. permissive
16. neglectful
17. parent effects
18. child effects
19. personality
20. transactional
21. sibling rivalry
22. ambivalence
23. emotional
24. caregiving
25. social
26. autonomy
27. decline
28. increase

29. remote
30. companionate
31. involved
32. maternal
33. less intense
34. mutual
35. equitable
36. role reversal
37. middle generation squeeze
38. caregiver burden
39. cohabitation
40. divorce
41. greater or higher
42. social support
43. spillover effects
44. egalitarian
45. crisis
46. permissive
47. reconstituted
48. child abuse
49. child maltreatment
50. intergenerational transmission of parenting
51. low self-esteem
52. support
53. empathy

Review of Key Terms

1. reconstituted family
2. authoritative parenting
3. child effects model
4. nuclear family

5. modified extended family
6. sibling rivalry
7. cohabitation
8. demandingness-control

9. extended family household
10. autonomy
11. family life cycle
12. authoritarian parenting
13. transactional model
14. empty nest
15. acceptance-responsiveness
16. coparenting
17. permissive parenting
18. indirect effects

19. child maltreatment
20. linked lives
21. neglectful parenting
22. intergenerational transmission of parenting
23. family systems theory
24. parent effects model
25. caregiver burden
26. spillover effects
27. child abuse

Multiple-Choice Self-Test

1. A (p. 485)	6. B (p. 491)	11. A (p. 505)
2. C (p. 484)	7. B (p. 494)	12. D (p. 505)
3. B (p. 488)	8. D (p. 496)	13. B (p. 507-508)
4. A (p. 490)	9. C (p. 498)	14. A (p. 509)
5. C (p. 490)	10. B (p. 502)	15. C (p. 510-511)

Critical Thinking Questions

1.   *Parents who are warm and responsive foster more positive qualities in their children than parents who are insensitive and rejecting. These positive qualities include secure attachments to parents, high self-esteem, and competence in academic and social settings. It is also important for parents to have some degree of control with respect to decision-making. Parents who set no rules (permissive parenting) have children who are impulsive, aggressive, low in self-control, and not very achievement oriented. On the other hand, parents who are overly controlling also tend to have children who exhibit some behavior difficulties. For example, authoritarian parents who set many rules without giving good explanations for why these rules are important and expect strict compliance to them, often have children who are moody, easily annoyed, and not very pleasant. The best child outcomes are seen when parents use authoritative styles of childrearing. Authoritative parents set rules but clearly explain why they are important, they are consistent in their enforcement of rules, and they allow their children to be involved in family decision-making. Children raised in authoritative homes tend to be pleasant, self-reliant, cooperative, and achievement oriented. These traits continue to be evident into adolescence.*

Children raised in authoritative homes have learned the value of limits and have learned to control their own behavior. Children whose parents are overly permissive never have to learn self-control at home, which follows them into other settings. Similarly, when parents are very restrictive and demanding, they do all the controlling and do not give children the opportunity to learn to control their own behavior.

Finally, the worst child outcomes result when parents are neglectful; they are simply not involved in their children's lives and signal to their children that they don't really care. These children tend to be resentful, hostile, and prone to getting into trouble as a way of lashing out at uncaring adults.

2.   *Divorce affects all members of the family, parents as well as children. For parents, there is a great deal of distress, as well as anger and perhaps some relief. The emotional turmoil puts them at greater risk of depression and physical health problems. Parenting skills tend to deteriorate during the divorce phase, which begins months, even years before the actual divorce and extends beyond the date of the official divorce decree. Both parents need to readjust their identities and take on different roles. Usually the mother becomes the custodial parent and has added responsibilities for childrearing. The father usually becomes the more distant parent and sees his children less often. Both parents may experience financial stress as they have to each manage separate households on single salaries rather than one household with (normally) two salaries.*

Children are similarly distressed by the divorce and the disruption in family life. They may experience anger, fear, and guilt. Their emotions make them more difficult, with increased behavior problems and emotionality (e.g., more crying, tantrums, and whininess). Children have to get used to going back and forth between two households

For both parents and children, divorce can have lifelong effects. While some of these effects can be negative, especially those occurring during the period of the actual divorce, other effects can be positive. If families were dysfunctional when the parents were married but can become more functional following the divorce, then both parents as individuals and children can benefit.

3.   *Researchers have identified several factors that predispose families to violence. For one, parents who abuse their children often grew up in families where they were abused or witnessed violence. Mothers who are abusive are often victims themselves of spousal abuse, so they may believe that abuse is a viable way of solving problems. Abusers are also more likely to have low self-esteem and deal with their insecurities by bullying others. Parents who are abusive may have unrealistic expectations of how children should behave at different ages. They may abuse their children for doing things that are developmentally normal. There is also some evidence that some children are more at risk for abuse than others because of personal characteristics, such as a difficult temperament. Finally, abuse is more likely to occur in families experiencing stress and weak social support. Stress can result from numerous factors, including poverty, loss or change of jobs, and changes in family structure (e.g., divorce or addition of stepchildren).*

CHAPTER SIXTEEN

DEVELOPMENTAL PSYCHOPATHOLOGY

OVERVIEW

This is a substantial chapter, covering a variety of psychological disorders. Some of these disorders are fairly unique to a particular age period, such as eating disorders during adolescence and dementia among older adults. Other disorders, though, are prevalent throughout the lifespan, most notably depression. Before getting into these specific disorders, the chapter discusses how experts distinguish abnormal from normal behavior, and which criteria are used to diagnose psychological disorders. Then, like other chapters, it covers the overall topic for each major period of the lifespan. For infancy, the focus is on autism. For childhood, the discussion distinguishes between externalizing and internalizing problems and then considers these problems in the context of the nature-nurture issue as well as continuity-discontinuity. The section on adolescence covers eating disorders and drug use, and the section on adults discusses dementia. Throughout all the sections, there is discussion of depression. For each disorder, characteristics, suspected causes, typical treatments, and likely outcomes are presented.

LEARNING OBJECTIVES

After reading and studying the material in this chapter, you should be able to answer the following questions.

16.1   WHAT MAKES DEVELOPMENT ABNORMAL?
1.   What criteria are used to define and diagnose psychological disorders?

2.   What is the perspective of the field of developmental psychopathology? What sorts of questions or issues do developmental psychopathologists study?

3.   How does the diathesis-stress model explain the causes of psychopathology?

16.2   THE INFANT
4.   What are the characteristics, suspected causes, treatment, and prognosis for individuals with autism and its related syndromes?

5.   In what ways do infants exhibit depression-like conditions? How is depression in infants similar to, or different from, depression in adults?

16.3   THE CHILD
6.   What characterizes internalizing and externalizing problems? What factors contribute to these problems and to what extent do childhood problems persist into adolescence and adulthood?

7.   How is depression during childhood similar to, or different from, depression during adulthood?

8.   How do interactions of nature and nurture contribute to psychological disorders? Do childhood problems persist into adolescence and adulthood? Explain.

16.4   THE ADOLESCENT
9.   Are psychological problems more prevalent during adolescence than other periods of the lifespan? Explain.

10.   What are the characteristics, suspected causes, and treatment of eating disorders such as anorexia nervosa?

11.   What is the course of depression and suicidal behavior during adolescence? What factors influence depression during adulthood?

16.5   THE ADULT
12.   What are the characteristics and causes of dementia?

CHAPTER SUMMARY AND GUIDED REVIEW

The following summary provides an overview of the main points contained in this chapter of the text. Fill in the blanks with terms that appropriately complete the sentence. Scattered throughout the summary are questions in parentheses. These are meant to encourage you to think actively as you read and connect this summary to the more detailed information provided in the text.

16.1   WHAT MAKES DEVELOPMENT ABNORMAL?
There are three general ways to define abnormal behavior. The first criteria looks at whether a person's behavior falls outside the normal range of behavior, thus constituting (1)_____. The second classification uses the extent to which a behavior interferes with personal and social adaptation, or (2) _____. The third classification is whether or not a behavior causes an individual (3) _____.

DSM Diagnostic Criteria
More specific diagnostic criteria have been described by the American Psychiatric Association in the *Diagnostic and Statistical Manual of Mental Disorders (DSM-IV)*. This manual specifies symptoms and behaviors associated with all psychological disorders. For example, DSM-IV defines (4) _____ as at least one episode of feeling profoundly depressed, sad, and hopeless, and/or losing interest in and the ability to derive pleasure from almost all activities. Some individuals may show bodily symptoms, or (5)_____ symptoms, rather than psychological symptoms.

Developmental Psychopathology
Developmental psychopathology is the study of the origins and course of abnormal behavior across the lifespan. Some developmental psychopathologists believe the DSM is too focused on problems as diseases and that instead, psychopathology should be viewed as another aspect of (6) _____. Others note that the expectations about how to act in a particular context, or the (7) _____, must be considered, along with societal expectations about what behaviors are appropriate at various ages, or (8) _____. The

(9) _____ model suggests that psychopathology results from the interaction of a predisposition to a disorder and the experience of (10) _____ events. (***Can you provide an example of this model?***)

16.2   THE INFANT
<u>Autism</u>

Autism is a disorder beginning in infancy that is characterized by deviant social development, deviant (11) _____ skills, and repetitive, stereotyped behavior. The language of autistic children may include (12) _____, where a child repeats or echoes sounds or words produced by someone else. Rather than being a single disorder, there is a group of disorders called (13) _____ disorders. One of these is (14) _____ syndrome, in which children have significant problems with social skills but have normal intelligence and verbal skills. Contrary to older stereotypes of autistic children as exceptionally bright, many (about 80%) are (15) _____. In particular, autistic individuals seem to have trouble understanding mental states and the role of mental states in behavior, showing a lack of a (16) _____. This may be caused by malfunctioning of the (17) _____ system that allows us to internally simulate what others are feeling and thinking. In addition, the (18) _____, or the ability to plan and control behavior, may be deficient. One recent hypothesis is that autism represents an exaggerated version of systemizing or analyzing, an idea that has become known as the (19)_____ hypothesis. Although no specific causes have yet been pinpointed, autism appears to have both genetic and environmental causes. Unfortunately, long-term prognosis for autistic children is generally (20) _____. The best outcomes occur when treatments begin early and most treatments focuses on intense (21) _____ training.

<u>Depression</u>

Infants are not capable of expressing the (22) _____ symptoms of depression, but can show behavioral symptoms. Infants who have lost an attachment figure are the ones most likely to show depressive symptoms. A condition called (23) _____ occurs when infants who are raised in a stressful situation fail to grow normally and become underweight for their age. If removed from the stressful situation, infants recover their weight very quickly.

16.3   THE CHILD

Although many children experience developmental problems, most do not develop the more serious psychological disorders.

<u>Externalizing and Internalizing Problems</u>

Children who have undercontrolled disorders, or (24) _____ problems, engage in behaviors that disturb other people and conflict with societal expectations. Children with overcontrolled disorders, or (25) _____ problems, focus their problems inward. There is a gender difference in expression of problems with externalizing problems more often observed in (26) _____ and internalizing disorders more often observed in (27) _____.

Developmental disorders typical arise from the influence of family interactions working along with genetic predisposition and environmental stress.

In some cases, childhood problems persist into adulthood, showing (28) _____ of development. But many children with disordered behavior do not have problems as adults, illustrating (29) _____ in development. At-risk children who overcome problems show resilience suggesting that there are (30) _____ that prevent them from developing disorders.

Depression

It is now recognized that children can become depressed. Children and adults do not display depression with the same behaviors, which can make diagnosis difficult. Further, many individuals with one disorder have other disorders as well, a condition referred to as (31) _____. Many clinically depressed children continue to experience some episodes of depression later in childhood, adolescence, or adulthood. Fortunately, many have been successfully treated with the process of (32) _____, which involves identifying and changing the distorted thinking that leads to maladaptive emotions and behaviors.

16.4   THE ADOLESCENT

Storm and Stress?

Adolescence is not really a period of storm and stress as G. Stanley Hall suggested. However, adolescents do seem to be more vulnerable to some forms of psychological disorders.

Eating Disorders

Eating disorders are more prevalent in adolescence than at other ages, and are much more common among girls than boys. Refusal to maintain weight that is at least 85% of one's expected weight is (33) _____. Bingeing and purging is associated with (34) _____. Some girls appear to have a genetic predisposition to develop an eating disorder, possibly because genes influence one's (35) _____. Further, girls who develop eating disorders often experience disturbed (36) _____ relationships and stress. (***What is the prognosis and treatment for adolescents with eating disorders?***)

Substance Abuse Disorders

In their quest to establish an identity, some adolescents will experiment with alcohol or illegal substances. Those who consume substances to the point where they experience adverse consequences meet the DSM-IV definition of (37) _____. More serious is (38) _____, which refers to continued use despite adverse consequences, along with increased tolerance, withdrawal symptoms if the use is stopped, and inability to quit. A majority of high school students report having tried alcohol and/or other substances and nearly 25% of high school seniors admit to binge drinking. According to a multifactor model called the (39) _____, each factor contributing to substance abuse builds on all the other contributing factors gaining strength as each is added to the mix.

Depression and Suicidal Behavior

Adolescents who are depressed display many of the same cognitive symptoms that depressed adults display, as well as other problem behaviors. Girls are more likely than boys to engage in (40) _____ by dwelling on their problems. The rate of

---

(41)_____ has increased, making this the third leading cause of death among adolescents. Suicidal thoughts are common during adolescence. Adolescents are more likely than adults to attempt suicide, but are less likely to "succeed" at killing themselves. As with other behaviors, suicidal behavior results from an interaction of genetic and environmental factors. (***What are some factors that contribute to suicidal behavior?***)

16.5   THE ADULT

Most adults must cope with some degree of stress in their lives. Young adults seem to experience more stress than older adults, leaving them at greater risk for mental health problems.

Depression

Contrary to a popular belief, elderly adults are not more depressed than younger adults. This may be because depression is often undiagnosed in the elderly. (***Why might this be the case?***) Women are more likely than men to be diagnosed with depression. (***Why are women more likely than men to be diagnosed with depression?***)

Aging and Dementia

Many people fear "losing their minds" as they get older. Dementia, sometimes called (42)_____, is not a normal part of aging. It refers to progressive deterioration of intellectual functioning and personality. The most common cause of dementia is caused by (43)_____ disease, which is progressive and irreversible deterioration of neurons, resulting in increasingly impaired mental functioning. A brain affected by this disease shows characteristic patterns of plaque from a build up of (44) _____ . Early signs of Alzheimer's include trouble learning and remembering verbal material. Over time, Alzheimer's patients lose their ability to function independently. Some forms of this disease appear to have a (45) _____ basis, and researchers have found potential links between Alzheimer's and genes on the 19th and 21st chromosomes. Some older adults seem to have greater (46) _____ to draw upon that helps them compensate for loss associated with brain disease. (***What is being done to treat Alzheimer's disease?***)

Another irreversible dementia is (47) _____ dementia, which results from cardiovascular problems such as strokes. Some forms of dementia are reversible. (***What factors might cause a reversible dementia?***) Some elderly adults may be experiencing (48)_____, which is mistaken for dementia because of the similar symptoms (***How can these two problems be distinguished from one another?***)

REVIEW OF KEY TERMS

Below is a list of terms and concepts from this chapter. Use these to complete the following sentence definitions. You might also want to try writing definitions in your own words and then checking your definitions with those in the text.

age norm	beta-amyloid
Alzheimer's disease	bulimia nervosa
anorexia nervosa	cascade model of substance use
Asperger's syndrome	cognitive behavioral therapy
autism	cognitive reserve
autism spectrum disorders (ASDs)	comorbidity

delirium
dementia
developmental psychopathology
diathesis-stress model
DSM-IV
echolalia
executive functions
externalizing problems
extreme male brain hypothesis

failure to thrive
internalizing problems
major depressive disorder
mirror neuron hypothesis
ruminative coping
social norm
somatic symptoms
vascular dementia

1. The existence of more than one disorder in an individual is _____.

2. Problems that are disruptive to the individual and include conditions such as anxiety disorders, phobias, and severe shyness are considered to be _____.

3. Alzheimer's patients develop senile plaques encrusted with _____, a toxic protein that damages neurons.

4. According to the _____ of autism, malfunctioning in specific brain systems cause the deficits in imitation, theory of mind, empathy, and language.

5. The field of _____ concerns the study of the origins and course of maladaptive behavior.

6. According to the _____ of autism, this disorder results from an exaggerated version of stereotypically masculine intelligence.

7. A group of disorders characterized by progressive deterioration of intellectual functioning and personality is collectively called _____.

8. The term _____ is used to describe infants who are neglected, abused, or otherwise stressed fail to grow normally, becoming underweight for their age.

9. The _____ proposes that psychopathology results from the interaction of a predisposition to a disorder and the experience of stressful events.

10. Managing stress by using _____ involves dwelling on problems and trying to analyze them.

11. A disorder called _____ involves progressive and irreversible deterioration of neurons resulting in increasingly impaired mental functioning.

12. Clinicians use a manual called _____ to diagnose psychological disorders.

13. Mental deterioration that results from cardiovascular problems such as strokes is diagnosed as _____.

14. Individuals who act in ways that disturb other people and conflict with societal expectations are exhibiting _____.

15. An expectation about how to behave that prevails in a culture or subculture is called a _____.

16. Refusal to maintain a weight that is at least 85% of the expected weight for one's height and age is diagnosed as _____.

17. Autistic children often exhibit _____, a form of language where a child echoes or repeats sounds or words made by someone else.

18. A disorder characterized by normal intelligence and verbal skills, but deficient social-cognitive and social skills, is _____.

19. A diagnosis of _____ is made when individuals feel profoundly depressed, sad, or hopeless, lose interest in activities, and/or are not able to derive pleasure from activities.

20. A model that considers multiple influences that combine in an ever-strengthening manner culminating in full-blown substance use is the _____.

21. A(n) _____ is a reversible condition characterized by periods of disorientation and confusion alternating with periods of coherence.

22. Repeated episodes of bingeing and purging are diagnosed as _____.

23. Bodily symptoms such as loss of appetite or changes in normal sleep patterns are called _____.

24. The disorder _____ begins in infancy or early childhood and is characterized by deviant social and language development, and repetitive, stereotyped behavior.

25. The prefrontal cortex of the brain controls the _____ that are involved in planning and organization functions.

26. A collection of pervasive developmental disorders called _____ involve social and communication problems.

27. A treatment approach that identifies and tries to change the maladaptive thinking that causes disturbed emotions and behaviors is _____.

28. Some individuals seem to have extra cognitive capacity called _____ that they can draw upon when aging and disease begin to affect brain functioning

MULTIPLE-CHOICE SELF-TEST

For each multiple-choice question, read all alternatives and then select the best answer.

1. According to developmental psychopathologists, psychopathology is a
    a. pattern of behavior that develops over time.
    b. medical condition that you either have or do not have.
    c. disease that can be treated with medicine.
    d. developmental disorder that lies solely within the person.

2. Social norms are defined as
    a. the ages when it is appropriate to act in a deviant manner.
    b. societal expectations about what behavior is appropriate at different ages.
    c. societal expectations about how to behave in different contexts.
    d. the average ages when people are most susceptible to various disorders.

3. According to the diathesis-stress model, psychopathology
    a. is caused by a major traumatic event.
    b. results from an interaction over time of a predisposition for a disorder and the experience of stress.
    c. occurs because individuals are genetically predisposed to develop certain disorders.
    d. arises from poor parenting.

4. A disorder beginning in infancy and characterized by deviant social development and communication skills is _____.
    a. anorexia   c. autism
    b. dementia   d. internalizing disorder

5. Which of the following is an example of echolalia?
    a. Using "you" to refer to one's self
    b. Hearing the echo of a phrase after someone has said something
    c. Substituting one phrase for another
    d. Repeating something that has just been said

6. Autistic children
    a. typically outgrow the disorder as they get older.
    b. have physical problems in addition to deficits in social and communication skills.
    c. are often mentally retarded.
    d. show marked improvement after they enter elementary school.

7.   Which of the following seems to be a promising explanation of the cause of autism?
      a.   Autistic children have cold, distant parents.
      b.   Autistic children have inherited a recessive set of genes for the disorder.
      c.   Autistic children are unable to verbalize their thoughts.
      d.   Autistic children have malfunctioning mirror neuron systems that lead to difficulty with empathy and theory of mind

8.   Children who act in ways that conflict with rules and other people are said to have _____.
      a.   an internalizing problem   c.   masked depression
      b.   an externalizing problem   d.   autism

9.   Problems that exist in early childhood
      a.   disappear when children enter elementary school.
      b.   are nonexistent by the time children leave school.
      c.   are more likely to disappear than persist, although some do persist.
      d.   typically are still present later in life.

10.   Which of the following is TRUE?
      a.   Most children who have problems grow up to have problems as adults.
      b.   Many adults who have problems also experienced problems as children.
      c.   Children are most likely to overcome undercontrolled problems.
      d.   There is very little change over time in the course of any psychological disorder.

11.   Depression
      a.   is displayed in similar ways across the lifespan.
      b.   is not present until children are old enough to verbally express their feelings.
      c.   is an undercontrolled disorder.
      d.   can be present throughout the lifespan but is expressed in different behaviors.

12.   Eating disorders such as anorexia and bulimia
      a.   are caused by the body's inability to properly metabolize food.
      b.   develop, in part, as a result of a genetic predisposition interacting with stress and social pressure.
      c.   are easily controlled with a properly managed diet.
      d.   are present during adolescence and then disappear.

13.   According to the cascade model of substance abuse,
      a.   environmental factors combine with genetic predisposition to create disordered behavior.
      b.   the disorder arises from the accumulation of multiple factors that interact with one another over time.
      c.   an environmental stressor triggers a genetic predisposition, leading to emergence of the disorder.
      d.   distorted thinking leads to negative emotions that are "self-treated" through substance abuse.

14. With respect to suicide,
    a.   adolescents are more likely to attempt suicide than adults but less likely to succeed.
    b.   adolescents successfully commit suicide at a higher rate than any other age group.
    c.   males and females are equally likely to end up killing themselves.
    d.   elderly adults commit suicide at a rate somewhat higher than adolescents and younger adults.

15. One difference between Alzheimer's disease and delirium is that
    a.   Alzheimer's disease affects mental functioning and delirium does not.
    b.   patients with Alzheimer's disease have periods of lucidity, while those with delirium do not.
    c.   Alzheimer's disease occurs only in old age, while delirium occurs only at younger ages.
    d.   Alzheimer's disease is irreversible, while delirium is reversible.

CRITICAL THINKING QUESTIONS

By answering the following questions, you will strengthen your understanding of the material in this chapter. These questions require higher-level thinking skills such as integration and application of concepts. Sample answers are provided for three of the questions. These illustrate one possibility, but there are other answers you could provide that might be just as good. For the other questions, you can check yourself by referring to the text (a hint is provided), or by asking a peer or your instructor to review your answer.

1. What gender differences are found across the lifespan in the diagnosis or course of mental disorders? What factors might account for these differences?
    [Sample answer provided.]

2. How does depression manifest itself across the lifespan?
    [Sample answer provided.]

3. Are individuals with an autism spectrum disorder (ASD) qualitatively or quantitatively different from individuals without ASD?
    [Sample answer provided.]

4. How would you explain the development of psychological disorders from the perspective of each of the major developmental theories (Freud and Erikson's psychoanalytic theories, Piaget's cognitive-developmental theory, Skinner and Bandura's learning theories, and Bronfenbrenner's ecological theory)?
    [Hint: Go back and consult earlier chapters, particularly Chapter 2, to gather information about the theorists that will help you explain or interpret psychological disorders.]

5. What are the current theories about the cause(s) of autism? What support is there for each theory?
    [Hint: Review the subsection on "Suspected causes" in the section on autism.]

ANSWERS

Chapter Summary and Guided Review (fill in the blank)

1. statistical deviance
2. maladaptiveness
3. personal distress
4. major depressive disorder
5. somatic
6. development
7. social norms
8. age norms
9. diathesis-stress
10. stressful
11. language and communication
12. echolalia
13. autistic spectrum
14. Asperger's
15. mentally retarded
16. theory of mind
17. mirror neuron
18. executive functions
19. extreme male brain
20. poor
21. behavioral
22. cognitive
23. failure to thrive
24. externalizing
25. internalizing
26. boys
27. girls
28. continuity
29. discontinuity
30. protective factors
31. comorbidity
32. cognitive behavioral therapy
33. anorexia nervosa
34. bulimia nervosa
35. personality
36. family
37. substance abuse
38. substance dependence
39. cascade model of substance use
40. ruminative coping
41. suicide
42. senility
43. Alzheimer's
44. beta-amyloid
45. genetic
46. cognitive reserve
47. vascular
48. delirium

Review of Key Terms

1. comorbidity
2. internalizing problems
3. beta-amyloid
4. mirror neuron hypothesis
5. developmental psychopathology
6. extreme male brain hypothesis
7. dementia
8. failure to thrive
9. diathesis-stress model
10. ruminative coping
11. Alzheimer's disease
12. DSM-IV
13. vascular dementia
14. externalizing problems
15. social norm
16. anorexia nervosa
17. echolalia
18. Asperger's syndrome
19. major depressive disorder
20. cascade model of substance use
21. delirium
22. bulimia nervosa
23. somatic symptoms
24. autism
25. executive functions
26. autism spectrum disorders
27. cognitive behavioral therapy
28. cognitive reserve

Multiple-Choice Self-Test

1. A (p. 519)
2. C (p. 520)
3. B (p. 521)
4. C (p. 523)
5. D (p. 523)
6. C (p. 524-526)

7. D (p. 524-525)	10. B (p. 529)	13. B (p. 536)
8. A (p. 528)	11. D (p. 531)	14. A (p. 537-538)
9. C (p. 529)	12. B (p. 534)	15. D (p. 543)

Critical Thinking Questions

1.   *Overall, males and females are equally likely to have psychological disorders, although there are some differences in the types of disorders that affect males and females. In general, boys are more likely to show externalizing problems that put them in conflict with others, such as conduct disorders or hyperactivity. Girls are more likely to have internalizing problems that cause inner conflict, such as depression or eating disorders.*

There may be genetic or biological reasons for these differences. For example, hormone levels differ for men and women and could contribute to different rates of depression. Think about the dramatic hormone changes following the birth of a baby that can lead to postpartum depression in women. Hormones cannot account for all the differences, though, between men and women. Socialization may also explain differences in depression. Women are socialized to internalize their problems, and it is socially acceptable for women to seek help for their problems. Men are socialized to externalize their problems and are not encouraged to seek help. Men and women may also learn to cope with their problems differently. Some evidence suggests that women ruminate about their problems more than men, which tends to prolong the problem, while men distract themselves from their problems, which tends to curtail the problem.

2.   *Depression can occur at any point throughout the lifespan. Infants who have lost a caregiver or who haven't formed a secure attachment can display behavioral and bodily symptoms of depression. These include loss of interest in activities and loss of appetite. If these persist, it can lead to failure to thrive, in which the infant doesn't grow normally, loses weight, and becomes underweight.*

Depression during childhood is uncommon but still possible. Children can show the same depressive symptoms as adolescents and adults. Among children who meet the criteria for depression, many also meet the criteria for other disorders as well, especially anxiety disorder, ADHD, and conduct disorder. Young children are likely to display the behavioral and bodily symptoms of depression and less likely to express the cognitive symptoms. Thus, they may lose interest in favorite activities, have trouble sleeping, and eat poorly, but may not verbalize their feelings.

Adolescents are more vulnerable to depression and express cognitive symptoms (e.g., hopelessness) as well as the behavioral and bodily symptoms, just as adults do. They often have other problems along with their depression, such as substance abuse (which may be their way of "medicating" their depression), eating disorders, anxiety, and antisocial behavior. The rate of attempted suicides escalates during adolescence, but the rate of committed suicides is higher among older adults.

Depression is one of the most common psychological problems of adulthood. More women than men are diagnosed with depression, and younger adults are more vulnerable than older adults. Depression in elderly adults is often overlooked because some of the symptoms of depression (e.g., fatigue, sleeping problems, memory problems) are mistaken for "symptoms" of old age. The underdiagnosis of depression during older adulthood may help explain why the suicide rate is higher among this age group.

3.	*There are numerous theories about what causes autism. According to some of these theories, autism represents a qualitative difference from "normal" or average. For example, according to the theory of mind hypothesis, individuals with autism are different from individuals without autism because they are not able to form a theory of mind, which limits their ability to understand mental states and how mental states affect behavior. And according to the executive dysfunction hypothesis, autism is a deficit in executive functions, which are the processes that allow us to plan and inhibit actions. In contrast, scientists such as Baron-Cohen argue that autism is just an extreme version of the male brain. Thus, it is a quantitative difference: people with autism just have more of what characterizes the male brain (e.g., analyzing things to figure out how they work and extracting rules). At this point, there doesn't seem to be a single, best explanation of autism. This might mean that autism can stem from multiple sources and might contain elements that are qualitatively distinct from others as well as elements that are quantitatively different from others.*

CHAPTER SEVENTEEN

THE FINAL CHALLENGE: DEATH AND DYING

OVERVIEW

This chapter covers some of the physical realities of death, such as biological definitions, factors that affect life expectancy, and leading causes of death at different ages. But the focus of the chapter is on psychological interpretations and reactions to death. How do people of different ages understand death? How do they grieve and cope with death? Two theories that are prominent in this chapter are Kübler-Ross's theory and the Parkes/Bowlby attachment model of bereavement. Kübler-Ross proposed that our reaction to death goes through a series of five stages. Although flawed, the theory has been instrumental in highlighting different emotional responses to death. Parkes and Bowlby proposed four overlapping responses to grief that are similar to the separation anxiety experienced by infants. Factors related to coping and ways to lessen the grief associated with death are also discussed.

The chapter closes by summarizing the major developmental themes running throughout the text. These themes help one understand the developmental changes occurring throughout the life span. You should be able to describe the major themes and apply or give examples of each one.

LEARNING OBJECTIVES

After reading and studying the material in this chapter, you should be able to answer the following questions.

17.1   MATTERS OF LIFE AND DEATH
1.   How is death defined? Why is the definition of death controversial? How does the social meaning of death vary across groups?

2.   What factors influence life expectancy? Is it possible to extend life expectancy?

3.   What is the main difference between programmed theories of aging and damage theories of aging? What is an example of each type of theory?

17.2   THE EXPERIENCE OF DEATH
4.   What are Kübler-Ross's stages of dying? How valid and useful is this theory?

5.   What is the Parkes/Bowlby attachment model of bereavement? Is there evidence to support this model?

17.3   THE INFANT
6.   What is the infant's understanding of separation and death?

17.4 THE CHILD

7. How do children's conceptions of death compare to a "mature" understanding of death? What factors might influence a child's understanding of death?

8. What is a dying child's understanding of death? How do dying children cope with the prospect of their own death? How do children grieve?

17.5 THE ADOLESCENT

9. What is the adolescent's understanding of death? Is an adolescent's reaction to death different from the reactions of a child or adult?

17.6 THE ADULT

10. How do family members react and cope with the loss of a spouse, a child, and a parent?

11. What factors contribute to effective and ineffective coping with grief?

17.7 TAKING THE STING OUT OF DEATH

12. What can be done for those who are dying and for those who are bereaved to better understand and face the reality of death?

13. What are the major themes of lifespan development that have been covered throughout the text?

CHAPTER SUMMARY AND GUIDED REVIEW

The following summary provides an overview of the main points contained in this chapter of the text. Fill in the blanks with terms that appropriately complete the sentence. Scattered throughout the summary are questions in parentheses. These are meant to encourage you to think actively as you read and connect this summary to the more detailed information provided in the text.

17.1 MATTHERS OF LIFE AND DEATH

What is death?

Biological death is hard to define because death is not a single event, but rather a
(1) _____. The "Harvard" definition of biological death is that of
(2) _____ death. This means an irreversible loss of functioning in the entire brain. To be judged dead by this definition, a person must be totally unresponsive to
(3) _____; fail to move for one hour and fail to breathe for three minutes after disconnection from life support systems; show no (4) _____ such as an eye blink; and show no electrical activity in the (5) _____ of the brain. (***Why is there debate over when someone is actually dead?***) Hastening someone's death when that person is terminally ill is referred to as (6) _____. This may be accomplished through active means—actually doing something to hasten death—or it may be through passive means—allowing someone to die naturally without intervening with extraordinary treatments. Between these two options is (7) _____, which provides the means to an individual who wishes to die. Ideally, individuals will have communicated their wishes regarding the end of their life through an advance directive, or (8) _____.

The meaning of death, and reactions to death, vary greatly across cultures and subcultures. (***What are some examples of cultural differences in the social meaning of death?***)

What Kills Us and When?

The average number of years that a person is expected to live, or one's (9) _____, is almost 78 years in the United States, although this number varies by gender and race/ethnicity. Life expectancy has increased over generations because fewer people are dying young and adults are living longer as a result of better health and medical technology. The leading causes of death in the United States change across the life span. Infants typically die of complications surrounding birth or from (10) _____. Children typically die from (11) _____. Adolescents and young adults are generally healthy, but susceptible to accidents and violent deaths (homicides and suicides). Middle-aged adults are more likely to die from (12) _____ diseases, such as cancer and heart disease.

Theories of Aging: Why Do We Age and Die?

Theories of aging fall into two main categories. One category focuses on the genetic control of aging; these are the (13) _____ theories of aging. The other category focuses on the cumulative effects of damage to cells and organs over time; these are the (14) _____.

An assumption of the first set of theories with their focus on genetics is that all species have a (15) _____ life span, or ceiling on the number of years that any member of that species can live. This figure varies across species, suggesting that (16) _____ genes may control how long we live. A premature aging disease called (17) _____ arises from a mutation in a single gene. Genes influence aging, possibly because of the (18) _____, which refers to the fact that human cells can only divide a certain number of times. Cell division may be restricted because the stretch of DNA at the end of chromosomes, called the (19) _____ does not replicate itself like the rest of the chromosome does. Children with the condition (20) _____ age prematurely and provide evidence of a genetic component to aging.

According to one damage theory, normal metabolic processes produce toxic by-products called (21) _____ that damage normal cells.

Many factors, both genetic and environmental, interact to produce aging and bring about death.

Some researchers are interested in finding ways to extend life, possibly raising the average age of death to 112 years. This may be possible by increasing the number of times that cells can divide. Or, it may be possible to inhibit the damage caused by free radicals with (22) _____ such as vitamins E and C. Another option that shows some success is significantly reducing unnecessary food intake through (23) _____. (***How might this technique work to extend life?***)

17.2   THE EXPERIENCE OF DEATH
Perspectives on Dying

Kübler-Ross proposed that people who are dying progress through a common sequence of five stages. In the first stage, (24) _____ and isolation, a person responds to the news that he or she is dying by refusing to believe that it is true, a common defense mechanism to keep anxiety-provoking thoughts out of conscious awareness. In the second stage, the dying person responds with (25) _____ or feelings of rage. In the third stage, the person tries to (26) _____ to gain more time and be given a second chance. When it becomes apparent that death is really going to occur, the dying person experiences (27) _____ and, if the person can work through the earlier responses to death, he or she may come to the final stage, which is (28) _____ of their death. Throughout all the stages, Kübler-Ross believed that people retained a sense of (29) _____ regarding their death.

A major problem with Kübler-Ross's characterization of death is that dying people really do not experience these reactions in a stage-like fashion. For example, some experts believe that dying patients alternate between denial and (30) _____, rather than moving systematically from one reaction to another. Another problem with Kübler-Ross's theory is that it does not account for how the course of an illness affects one's emotional responses. A third problem with Kübler-Ross's theory is that it ignores how an individual's (31) _____ affects their response to dying. (***Can you explain how this factor can impact one's experience of dying?***)

The Experience of Bereavement

A state of loss is referred to as (32) _____. The emotional response to loss is (33) _____, and (34) _____ is the culturally defined ways of displaying reactions to loss. Many people experience (35) _____ prior to the actual death of a loved one, unless the death is quite sudden. Parkes and Bowlby characterize grieving as a reaction to (36) _____ from a loved one that progresses through several overlapping phases. The first reaction is (37) _____, which occurs in the first hours and days following a death. The second phase is (38) _____, which is most intense about 5 to 14 days after the death, and is accompanied by restlessness and preoccupation with thoughts of the loved one. Anger and guilt are also common reactions during this phase. The third phase is disorganization and (39) _____ when the person realizes that the loved one is gone for always. Finally, in the fourth phase of   (40) _____, a person begins to move on with life by forming new relationships and getting involved in new activities. Actual responses to bereavement may be more   (41) _____ than the Parkes and Bowlby model suggests. According to the   (42) _____ model of coping with bereavement, individuals move back and forth from coping with the emotional loss, coping with everyday life, and taking breaks from coping in order to reenergize.

17.3   THE INFANT

Infants experience death of a loved one as that person's (43) _____ from their life, but do not understand death as the ending of life. Infants separated from their attachment figures show reactions that are similar to the reactions of bereaved adults, including (42) _____ and despair.

17.4   THE CHILD
Grasping the Concept of Death

Young children are curious about death and begin to show some understanding of death, but have not reached a "mature" understanding. A mature conception of death requires the following understandings:

- Death involves the end of all life processes—it is (44) _____;
- Death cannot be undone—it is (45) _____;
- Death happens to everyone—it is (46) _____; and
- Death is caused by internal or (47) _____ factors.

Preschool-aged children tend to think dead people retain some of their living capabilities and that death might be reversible. Between the ages of 5 and 7, children begin to realize that death is cessation of life, irreversible, and universal. It takes children a few more years, however, to fully understand that death is caused by biological factors. Children's understanding of death is affected by their level of (48) _____ development and by their life experiences. (*What life experiences affect understanding of death?*)

The Dying Child

Terminally ill children are typically aware that they are dying and experience a variety of emotions such as anger and depression. (*How do terminally ill children of different ages respond to their situation?*)

The Bereaved Child

Children who lose a loved one grieve, but express their grief differently than adults do. They may display a variety of problems, including problems with sleeping, eating, and other daily routines. Because children are very dependent on their parents and do not have adult-level coping strategies, they are particularly vulnerable to long-term problems following the loss of a parent.

17.5   THE ADOLESCENT

Adolescents have developed a mature understanding of death and may spend time contemplating death and its meaning. Adolescents grieve similarly to adults, but are influenced by general themes or concerns of the adolescent period.

17.6   THE ADULT
Death in the Family Context

Adults who lose a spouse often experience other changes as well and are at greater risk for illness and physical symptoms. But there is great diversity in how individuals respond to the loss of a spouse. Longitudinal research starting before the loss of a spouse shows that individuals who are well adjusted and have good coping resources <u>prior</u> to their spouse's death often display (49) _____ in response to the death. Some individuals actually experience less depression after their spouses' death, likely because they experienced (50) _____ prior to the death. In some cases, individuals experience (51) _____ grief due to the nature of their relationship with the deceased. In some cases, individuals show (52) _____ grief that is unusually prolonged and impairs their functioning.

The loss of a child seems particularly difficult to cope with, in part because we do not expect children to die before their parents. The child's (53) _____ does not really affect the intensity of a parent's grief. For an adult, the death of a parent may not be as disruptive as the loss of a spouse or child, because in some ways, it is expected.

Challenges to the Grief Work Perspective

According to the grief work perspective, bereaved people must confront their loss in order to cope adaptively. People tend to believe that there are several forms of complicated or (54) _____ grief. However, this view is challenged by cross-cultural research. What might be considered unhealthy grief in our society may be perfectly normal expression of grief in other societies. Many individuals maintain attachments to the deceased by reminiscing and otherwise expressing (55) _____ of connection.

Who Copes and Who Succumbs?

Some people cope more effectively with the loss of a loved one than others. Several factors affect how well a person copes with loss. Bowlby argues that early (56) _____ relationships impact on our later ability to cope with grief. (*Can you describe the relationship between early experience and later coping ability?*) An individual's coping style and (57) _____ also influence how well they cope with death, as does the closeness of the relationship between the bereaved person and the deceased. Finally, the (58) _____ of death also influences how a person responds to the loss. Grief at any age can be positively affected by the presence of (59) _____, and negatively affected by the presence of additional (60) _____.

Bereavement and Human Development

Bereavement is painful, but can also have positive effects on development. For instance, many bereaved individuals feel more confident and independent after recovering from their loss than prior to their loss.

17.7   TAKING THE STING OUT OF DEATH
For the Dying

Some people who are dying are cared for by a (61) _____, a program that supports the dying person. These services are part of a longer movement called (62) _____ care aimed at meeting a variety of needs faced by a dying person. (*What are the characteristics of these programs?*)

For the Bereaved

Although most bereaved individuals do not need professional intervention, therapy and support groups are available and can be beneficial to bereaved individuals.

Taking Our Leave

The major themes in human development can be summarized with the following points.

1. Nature and nurture truly interact in development. Biological and environmental factors together explain both universal trends in development and individual differences in development. The best developmental outcomes arise from the (63) _____ between a person and the person's unique environment.

2. <u>We are whole persons throughout the life span</u>. Physical, cognitive, personal, and social developments are intertwined during each period of the life span.

3. <u>Development proceeds in multiple directions</u>. Development becomes increasingly differentiated and integrated. It involves gains, losses, and changes that are simply different but are not gains or losses.

4. <u>There is both continuity and discontinuity in development</u>. This issue raises questions about whether change is stagelike (qualitative changes) or not (quantitative changes), and whether or not early experiences predict later traits (or carry over to adulthood).

5. <u>There is much (64)</u> _____ in development. Human beings have the capacity to change in response to their experiences.

6. <u>We are individuals, becoming even more diverse with age</u>. There is an incredible amount of diversity among humans, which makes it difficult to form generalizations about them. And as we age, human development becomes less and less predictable.

7. <u>We develop in a cultural and historical context</u>. Development is affected by broad cultural and historical contexts, as well as the individual's immediate environment.

8. <u>We are active in our own development</u>. We actively explore the world and create our own understandings of the world rather than being passively molded by the world around us. The person and environment reciprocally interact and influence one another.

9. <u>Development is a lifelong process</u>. Development in any one phase of life is best understood by viewing it as part of a lifelong process.

10. <u>Development is best viewed from multiple perspectives</u>. Development may be best understood by integrating multiple theories and adopting a contextual perspective that emphasizes variations in development.

REVIEW OF KEY TERMS

Below is a list of terms and concepts from this chapter. Use these to complete the following sentence definitions. You might also want to try writing definitions in your own words and then checking your definitions with those in the text.

anticipatory grief	grief
antioxidants	grief work perspective
assisted suicide	Hayflick limit
bereavement	hospice
caloric restriction	living will
centenarians	maximum life span
complicated grief	mourning
continuing bonds	palliative care
damage theories of aging	Parkes/Bowlby attachment model of
denial	bereavement
disenfranchised grief	progeria
dual process model of grief	programmed theories of aging
euthanasia	telomere
free radicals	total brain death

1. The _____ suggests that there is a limited number of times that a human cell can divide.

2. A defense mechanism where anxiety-producing thoughts are kept out of conscious awareness is _____.

3. The technique of _____, eating a highly nutritious but very restricted diet, may increase life span.

4. The act of killing or allowing a person who is terminally ill to die is _____.

5. The emotional response to loss is termed _____.

6. A _____ program supports dying persons and their families through a caring philosophy.

7. In general, _____ explain aging through systematic genetic mechanisms.

8. Substances that may increase longevity by inhibiting the activity of free radicals are _____.

9. An irreversible loss of functioning in the entire brain occurs with _____.

10. According to the _____, bereaved individuals must confront their loss and work through their painful emotions.

11. A _____ is a tiny piece of DNA on the end of chromosomes.

12. The ceiling on the number of years that anyone lives is the _____.

13. Culturally prescribed ways of displaying one's reaction to death are known as _____.

14. Toxic byproducts of normal metabolism, called _____, can damage normal cells.

15. According to _____, damage to cells and organs accumulates over time and eventually causes a person's death.

16. Someone who lives to be at least 100 years old is a _____.

17. A _____ is a document used to indicate whether someone wants extraordinary medical procedures used to extend life when he or she is hopelessly ill.

18. Grieving that begins before a death occurs in anticipation of what will happen is called _____.

19. A state of loss is referred to as _____.

20. Helping someone else bring about their own death is _____.

21. A genetic disorder that causes premature aging and early death is called _____.

22. The _____ describes loss of an attachment figure in terms of numbness, yearning, disorganization and despair, and reorganization.

23. According to the _____, bereaved individuals vacillate between coping with their emotions, coping with everyday tasks, and taking breaks from coping.

24. A bereaved person with _____ experiences an unusually prolonged or intense emotional response that impairs grief.

25. Care that focuses on a dying individual's personal needs rather than on curing them is known as _____.

26. Maintaining a connection with a deceased loved one through reminiscence, use of their possessions and so on is _____.

27. Grief that is not recognized or fully acknowledged by others is called _____.

MULTIPLE CHOICE SELF TEST

For each multiple choice question, read all alternatives and then select the best answer.

1. The Harvard definition of biological death is
   a. the point at which the heart stops beating
   b. irreversible loss of functioning in the cerebral cortex
   c. irreversible loss of functioning in the entire brain
   d. failure to breathe without life support systems

2. Cross-cultural research on death and dying indicates that
   a. cultures have evolved different social meanings of death
   b. all cultures have similar ways of coping with death
   c. people of some cultures do not experience grief
   d. there is universal agreement on the definition of death

3. The average length of time that a person can expect to live is termed
   a. life span
   b. life expectancy
   c. age norm
   d. maximum life span

4. The Hayflick limit is
   a. the number of times that a gene can "turn on" or "turn off" to bring about maturational changes
   b. the ceiling on the number of years that anyone lives
   c. the speed with which the body can repair damaged cells
   d. the limited number times that a human cell can divide

5. Theories that focus on the genetic control of aging are called _____ theories and those that focus on gradual deterioration of cells are called _____ theories
   a. genetic; environmental
   b. programmed; damage
   c. damage; programmed
   d. biological; psychological

6. According to Kübler-Ross's stages of dying, a person who expresses resentment and criticizes everyone is in the stage of
   a. denial and isolation
   b. anger
   c. bargaining
   d. depression

7. According to Kübler-Ross's stages of dying, a dying person who agrees to stop smoking and drinking in return for a little more time is in the stage of
   a. denial and isolation
   b. anger
   c. bargaining
   d. depression

8. One of the biggest problems with Kübler-Ross's stages of dying is that
   a. dying is not really stage-like
   b. patients go through the stages in order but at different rates
   c. they are focused on a person's cognitive understanding of death rather than the person's affective response
   d. they describe a person's response to death of a spouse or parent but not the response to one's own impending death

9. The emotional response to death is referred to as
   a. bereavement
   b. grief
   c. mourning
   d. depression

10. In the first few days following the death of a loved one, the bereaved person
    a. is usually unable to function
    b. experiences anticipatory grief
    c. experiences the worst despair of the mourning process
    d. is typically in a state of shock and numbness

11. Preschool-aged children are likely to believe that
    a. death is inevitable and will happen to everyone eventually
    b. dead people still experience sensations and perceptions, just not as intensely as live people
    c. people die because of changes in internal bodily functioning
    d. death is irreversible

12. Terminally ill children typically
    a. accept their impending death with equanimity
    b. have no idea that they are dying or what it means to die
    c. go through Kübler-Ross's stages of dying in sequential order
    d. experience a range of negative emotions and express a number of negative behaviors

13. Children's grief
    a. can be reduced by not talking about death and the deceased
    b. can be reduced if they have a number of other stressors to deal with at the same time
    c. can be reduced if appropriate social support systems are in place
    d. is always expressed openly through behavior such as crying

14. Grief over the loss of a child
    a. is greatest if the child is young
    b. does not differ in intensity as a function of the age of the child
    c. is less intense if the child dies from an accident beyond the parent's control
    d. is more intense for fathers than mothers since mothers in our culture are encouraged to express grief more openly than fathers

15. Research on grieving and bereft families indicates that
    a. there are common techniques that can successfully help the grief-stricken family forget about their loved one.
    b. the nature of the relationship to the deceased has no influence on the grief process.
    c. it is unhealthy to continue to think about and maintain an attachment to the deceased.
    d. families cope more successfully when they have social support and when they are able to participate in making decisions before, during, and after the death of a loved one.

CRITICAL THINKING QUESTIONS

By answering the following questions, you will strengthen your understanding of the material in this chapter. These questions require higher level thinking skills such as integration and application of concepts. Sample answers are provided for three of the questions. These illustrate one possibility, but there are other answers you could provide that might be just as good. For the other questions, you can check yourself by referring to the text (a hint is provided), or by asking a peer or your instructor to review your answer.

1. In general, what factors contribute to the process of aging and death?
   [*Sample answer provided.*]

2. Integrate the understanding of death with Piaget's stages of cognitive development and apply this to the practical situation of coping with the death of a pet or the death of a parent. For example, how would you help a child in the preoperational stage understand

and cope with death of a parent? How would you explain that the pet dog has died? How would your conversations with children in the concrete operational stage and adolescents or adults in the formal operational stage differ from the conversation that you have with the preoperational child?
[Sample answer provided.]

3. What factors influence how someone copes with the loss of a loved one?
   [Sample answer provided.]

4. How does the Parke/Bowlby model use attachment theory to characterize grieving? Is there any evidence for this view?
   [Hint: Review the section on "The Experience of Bereavement," starting on page 495 of the text.]

5. An important theme that runs throughout the text is "Nature and nurture both contribute to development." Explain what this means and provide evidence illustrating the influences of both nature and nurture.
   [Hint: Review the section on "Taking our Leave."]

ANSWERS

Chapter Summary and Guided Review (Fill-in the blank)

1. process	25. bargain
2. total brain	26. depression
3. stimuli	27. acceptance
4. reflexes	28. hope
5. cortex	29. acceptance
6. euthanasia	30. personality
7. assisted suicide	31. bereavement
8. living will	32. grief
9. life expectancy	33. mourning
10. congenital abnormalities	34. anticipatory grief
11. accidents	35. separation
12. chronic	36. numbness
13. programmed	37. yearning
14. damage	38. despair
15. maximum	39. reorganization
16. species-specific	40. individualized
17. progeria	41. dual process
18. Hayflick limit	42. disappearance
19. telomere	43. protest
20. free radicals	44. final
21. antioxidants	45. irreversible
22. caloric restriction	46. universal
23. denial	47. biological
24. anger	48. cognitive

49. resilience
50. caregiver burden
51. disenfranchised
52. complicated
53. age
54. pathological
55. continuing bonds
56. attachment

57. personality
58. cause
59. social support
60. stressors
61. hospice
62. palliative
63. goodness of fit
64. plasticity

Review of Key Terms

1. Hayflick limit
2. denial
3. caloric restriction
4. euthanasia
5. grief
6. hospice
7. programmed theories of aging
8. antioxidants
9. total brain death
10. grief work perspective
11. telomere
12. maximum life span
13. mourning
14. free radicals
15. damage theories of aging
16. centenarians
17. living will
18. anticipatory grief
19. bereavement
20. assisted suicide
21. progeria
22. Parkes/Bowlby attachment model of bereavement
23. dual process model of bereavement
24. complicated grief
25. palliative care
26. continuing bonds
27. disenfranchised grief

Multiple Choice Self Test

1. C (p. 548)
2. A (p. 550-551)
3. B (p. 551)
4. D (p. 554)
5. B (p. 553-554)

6. B (p. 557)
7. C (p. 557)
8. A (p. 558)
9. B (p. 558)
10. D (p. 558-559)

11. B (p. 561)
12. D (p. 563)
13. C (p. 564)
14. B (p. 567-568)
15. D (p. 570-571)

Critical Thinking Questions

1. *Aging and death result from a combination of genetic and environmental factors. Research with twins shows that genes contribute to life expectancy—identical twins show similar patterns of aging. Laboratory research indicates that human cells are limited in the number of times that they can replicate, suggesting that there might be a genetically programmed clock for aging and death. Other research suggests that damage to the cells from environmental toxins and free radicals produced by normal metabolic processes accumulates over time and eventually kills us. Unfortunately, we do not have much control over genetic factors and we all breathe and metabolize food and live in environments with some degree of pollution, pesticides, etc. At this point, the only method that has been shown to extend the life span (of animals in the laboratory) is dietary restriction: eating a highly nutritious, but very limited diet. It has yet to be demonstrated that this method works with humans.*

2.   *According to Piaget, children interpret the world differently depending on their stage of cognitive development. Infants in the sensorimotor stage would have little understanding of death. Towards the end of the sensorimotor stage, when they acquire object permanence, they would be able to recognize that someone who had been present is currently missing, but they would not be able to really understand what this means. Children in the preoperational stage would not be able to think logically about death, but would instead, try to understand death in terms of their limited cognitive abilities. Just as they struggle with the concept of reversibility on conservation tasks, they may illogically believe that death can be reversed. They may apply transductive reasoning and argue that two things are connected when in fact they are not. For example, they may believe that they caused their goldfish to die because they slammed the door to the room with the fishtank.*

     Children's understanding of death becomes much more advanced when they move into the concrete operations stage. They can now reason logically and understand that death is not reversible and is final. They no longer attribute life-like characteristics to dead people (e.g., they know they can't feel the cold and don't get hungry). They may still struggle with understanding the biological causality of death, however, because this requires some understanding of abstract concepts. Children in the concrete operational stage still have trouble thinking about abstract or hypothetical ideas—ideas that are not concrete and haven't been personally experienced. Once they achieve formal operational thought, however, they can imagine all sorts of possibilities, including how the death of a loved person will affect multiple areas of their life and how it will impact on others as well.

3.   *How well you cope with the loss of a loved one will depend on several factors. One obvious factor is the relation or attachment to the person prior to death. For example, coping with the loss of a child would be very difficult for a parent because parents don't normally anticipate that their children will die before them. Coping with the death of a parent who is old might be easier for a grown child than coping with the death of a parent while still young. Personal resources are also important. Some people are more resilient than others and have better coping strategies. They think of life issues in a way that is more productive in terms of getting on with their own lives. Other people have a life perspective that might be more counterproductive and make it difficult to move on after the death of a loved one. Social support is another important factor in determining how well people cope with loss. People with strong social support are generally better able to cope. On the other hand, people with less social support or people with additional stressors cope less well.*

Chapter Seventeen